# Seamless
# Subtleties

**By Michael Raymond**

Seamless Subtleties

© 2014 Michael Raymond

ISBN-13: 978069234708-9

# Table of Contents

Note to the Reader:

If we were fish swimming in the ocean and questioned what was responsible for the sustenance and creation of our lives, and it was the ocean itself, how easy would it be for a conscious fish to realize this? We may look at every rock, and every other fish for answers but we may very well be swimming in the answer. We may then elevate the idea of an imagined God of all fish and say that image is responsible. All along we may be swimming in what's responsible but may never be aware of that. The grandeur of the ocean may very well be the grand thing we were looking for. All along what surrounded us was always in and of us, and we were always in and of it as well.

As human beings, we are part of, and one with what is the most magnificent thing there could be. We have all these powers available to us. We have incredible and unimaginable strengths we should accept. Yet, there are those who deny this, and they suppose there is always something or someone else we should be in respect of.

We look outside of us in physical forms to find what is always better. We look outside of us in spiritual imaginations for what is the creator. We elevate images of what is out there and use it to replace the embrace of ourselves. Our bodies are the wire to the electricity and the ocean to the gravity. We are of the most splendorous and the most powerful. To honor an image outside of us downplays our greatness. It's nothing other than a manipulation by those who are afraid to honor the value in their self.

Our bodies are a conduit for an amazing energy that is responsible for the whole cosmos. Love yourself and all you are. Let the glory of life fill you every single second.

# I  Little Ole Me

It seems early in life a whole bunch of wrong information was thrown at me with one song and dance after the next. I then spent the rest of my years trying to make sense of it all. As I unraveled all the lies that were once handed to me as fact, I came upon new situations as an adult that also left room for doubt. Once again lies were pontificated that left me with the same incongruence that I felt as a child. Throughout my life people have strongly imposed their will and pretended to know when oftentimes they truly didn't have a clue.

Within what appears simple and basic oftentimes rests the most complex ideas possible. This has been shown to us throughout history. The people who slowed down the most were able to experience more deeply. They were truly the most perceptive of all.

Isaac Newton, who watched an apple fall like billions before him, saw what no one did when he discovered the formula for gravity. Even after he wrote it all out, it took more than a hundred and fifty years for a true understanding of what he accomplished to be realized.

Leonardo da Vinci saw a bird fly like billions before him and knew that those same physics could be replicated to make flying possible for us to use as well. It took a long time for what was pure genius to be honored. The Wright Brothers embraced the concept four hundred years later when only a few in the world thought it was possible. Their relentless trial and error allowed adjustments to be made with great specificity to finally perfect flying.

Benjamin Franklin saw a bolt of lightning like no one else did, and it spurred experimentation and research toward the development of the first battery. Thomas Edison saw hundreds of things like no other because he had an unwavering ability to stay with feelings and mysteries longer than others. He lit the world with his invention of the light bulb.

The habits of great people didn't lend themselves to skimming over the surface of things. It wasn't in moving as quickly as possible that proved superior in the end, it was moving slower and deeper that revealed in the simplest of things the most insightful, complex realizations human beings ever achieved.

My first recollection of life came in the Bronx on Pearsall Avenue. We lived on the ground floor of a two story house. My dad was chasing my mom around the kitchen table and I feared for her safety. I was mentally urging her to get away but he threw the table out of the way and she ran into the bedroom, but unfortunately she didn't lock the door in time. Crying, hitting, and screams could be heard through the door and it scared me to realize that this was my dad hitting my mom. My sister was the one who shrugged her shoulders when I looked up at her with a look of question. I couldn't believe that the two people who were supposed to represent love to me wanted to kill each other.

Unfortunately, the early days of my life were tumultuous. Incredible fear consumed me with these very first thoughts and many after that. That was the first time I remember being aware of my thoughts. Welcome to awareness. Welcome to life with all its hardships wrapped up in people who were trapped in their heads. I remember how I suddenly stopped being in a child's daze when it happened. I was only one and a half, but I remember it like it was yesterday.

When something happens that's incomplete it tends to hang in there with me until it's dealt with. The sequence or age it took place during is secondary to what that event truly meant. My family treated me as if I was a piece of furniture that couldn't feel, see or hear. They thought I was too young to be in touch with it all, but I found I had an ability to recall a great deal of what happened when I was extremely young. I think I was feeling a lot more than they were. I sure know I would have been a lot different if my first moments of life were of love rather than of incredible fear. What meant anything if all that was supposed to feel like love was hate?

I sure was a lot better off the minute before all this consciousness than I was the minute after it. My confidence was shattered. I was confused why these things called thoughts controlled those fighting around me. I was supposed to be too young to know better but I mounted up, at the very early age of one and a half, onto the bucking horse world of thought consciousness. I now stayed there, instead of enjoying the natural daze of a child, for fear of my own life. Although I was now aware of my thoughts, I still realized the people around me were far too over-attached to theirs.

Was I the next one who was going to be beaten until I was screaming and crying? I didn't know for sure. I was so scared of that happening to me that even when words did start to come, I didn't communicate them until I could figure out how to avoid such a horror. I didn't speak for the next three years, except in my head. I figured if I remained low-key and didn't talk for a while, I could figure out everything to make it more secure when I did. Security never came and it's a wonder I ever talked at all.

Nobody would expect anything of me if I couldn't even talk. I wouldn't have to explain what I knew and what I didn't. Sometimes I feel like that today because what I see around me is so dreadful, the silent watcher is the only one who can disassociate from it.

I noticed when my parents spoke to anyone else there was a very strong chance malfunctioning communications could occur if the words chosen were not tailored correctly. Even if the parties in the conversation knew the intended feelings, the wrong words could produce a very dangerous result. They weren't highly educated people so a lack of vocabulary could affect the outcome in communication. Feelings that would have dictated opposite results if expressed more clearly, were badly communicated or never properly expressed at all. There wasn't awareness outside of the chosen words. It became the new feeling just because of the horrible choice of words selected and the previous references they contained. Communications were constantly going awry while I was the quiet observer, and they still do.

I didn't like the weight of words as a kid and I don't like them now. I feel there's more agreement and compassion before the spoken word. People stand on a cliff surrounded by the air of judgment hanging on every word waiting to jump off. I think in the very use of language we compromise some of the best parts of being human. We lessen spiritualism, the feeling of oneness with nature, and a sense of oneness with others. We change caring, sensitivities, empathy, touch, love, and our shared existence in mystery by needing to talk. We make the utterances become the total meaning and act as if we know so much.

Words spoken internally can have the same inherent problem as words expressed externally. Words are used as the catchall for every feeling. There are so many feelings not easily expressed and oftentimes they are lost trying to put them into the only words that come close. The exchange of inexact words then becomes a bantering of egos, where one person is trying to sound better or act more "right" than the other.

Fifty years later I don't participate in word battles when people are expecting me to. I'm not going to get trapped in the rhetoric. As a child, I hated speaking and probably wouldn't have if the world didn't keep forcing me to. I watched people get so hung up on their own thoughts, and need to be right, that word wars prevailed to the point of dissension.

Both my parents were too stubborn, immature, and strong willed. Both had an overpowering need to be right that ended up prevailing over any love or compassion that should have taken precedent. Both were victims of the brain/word monster and certainly not in witness of it. It was a microcosm of the world. Bad communication and an attachment to words and thoughts robbed love and human compassion. The damning, judging, and intolerance became the master which even love had to serve all the way up to the point where no more love remained.

In retrospect, there weren't any valid reasons why violence had to be defaulted to in front of a one and a half year old child. Sometimes no amount of understanding could ever matter more than the callous, hurtful, effects that people create. It happened at such a vulnerable emotional point when all I had was naivety and trust. My state of being was jolted. Years later even after I understood every cause and effect, the result is still something very different than these traumas never happening.

In my silence I was scared every day. How could I sit here and say the trauma was reversed once it was understood? There is no way to reverse what it did then, and what it did afterwards. I suffered from other things because of the ways I was affected, but I also observed so much at such an early age and from such a different perspective, that the insights gained will stay with me the rest of my life. I recognized the dysfunction of being trapped in the reflexes of the brain.

My father and mother were impervious to the effect they were having on me. They were trapped in thoughts that allowed them to engage in destructive acts. My father of course is to blame here. When is a man physically beating a woman the proper answer to any problem? These thought propelled actions surrounded me throughout my childhood from both my parents. They were emotionally charged people whose thoughts tended to overtake them. They were the servants of the thought once the thought happened. They obsessed over it to the point where they were incapable of anything else. They were not the observers of their thoughts, they were prisoners of them. It made for an insecure, fearful childhood. Yet, it forced me to be more aware of my thoughts rather than becoming them because I knew their direction couldn't be right.

The habits of the adults around me were dictated by reflex reactions to whatever thought popped into their head. It could get violent at the drop of a hat. Horrible results dominated my surroundings growing up. There was a child then, and now there's an adult, and I still don't know why people can't love each other without being the victim of the next random thought.

Spiritually, a newborn may be more connected than at any time throughout its life. Yet, ironically, the manifested world has a baby being very small, and that gives the impression that everything bigger is what's right. It also implies that it's not only what's right physically, but it's what is superior spiritually as well. If full grown adults, were engaged in movement away from spiritual connectivity, then maybe they should actually become considerably shorter. If we shrunk when we gravitated away from our truest selves, our beautiful little babies with all that magnificence shining through them could be assisted just a tad. They wouldn't feel that their experiences through ages one, two, and three were so wrong. They wouldn't feel that embodiment limitations represented their total value.

An imposing presence poses the illusion of better and more complete even when it may be coming from spiritually robbed people. There would be greater truth imposed early on if adults experienced the grandeur and pure beauty of a baby's presence instead of having the delusion of superiority simply because of size. I see so many adults look at younger people as if they don't count yet. I know we can't help the size we are born, but adults can consider that a newborn may very well be even more connected metaphysically than they are, even while new physical challenges consume an infant a great deal of the time.

In seeing with the eyes of a child, adults can be a little more respectful of the purity of source, even though it comes in a small package. Life experiences tarnish so much of our love of self, love of life and love of others. A young person is a precious gift being shown to us. Without seeing through the eyes of a child we diminish what in the long run may be our greatest truths. Everything and everyone appears to be better and more valuable due to their size and imposing presence.

If our deepest connection to our source was represented in size, and those more closely connected spiritually were larger, then we would be assisted by our five senses. The physically imposing impressions we got from those most enlightened would point to what was true beyond the five senses. We would have one less illusion directing the image of strength to what didn't deserve it. Instead, if you believed that we were closest to our spiritual essence when we were born, our experiences would have the opposite appearing true, and this misperception would go on many years into every person's foundation in this world.

The human species may never be able to truly connect to its source because of this indoctrination. We may forever be lost in deception giving our strength to what appears bigger, more beautiful, or more powerful. Only a small percentage can go beyond the concrete dominance of everything. There may be *you* in that percentage. You may be someone who can reverse the effects of your foundation and further experience the power and the truth from what are extrasensory perceptions.

We need our imagination to assist us with misperceptions so that we could more appropriately depict worth from what is truly more valuable in living. Imagination could help us more throughout our life by not losing our self to what is physically bigger, louder sounding, or acting superior. Many systems seek to command meaning for us when we arrive in this thing called the human body. Family habits, educational trends, religious dogmas, and societal pressures force us away from ethereality. Body, brain, thoughts, and words lack recognition to our greater inherent strength, yet they still tend to command the order of the day.

I remember while growing up I felt that everything big was not so comforting. My parents conflicted and my father left. My relatives were no longer visited with. Everything I thought was important was treated as if it all meant nothing. Everything I believed to be the most solid things were made meaningless. I was made to feel wrong for caring about them. In a desperate attempt to connect to something that wouldn't change I found trust in little things and made them bigger. All the big things seemed to fail, so I focused on smaller things that gave me satisfaction that couldn't easily be taken away.

It's cute to make playing with dirt engaging, but I never forgot how secure I felt knowing it couldn't turn on me and it was real. It seems trite, it seems cute, but it saved me then and it still saves me today to find joy in what is less subject to change. Today, fifty years later I paint, because the color is the color, the canvas is the canvas, and the mark made is not to be taken away. I do it when things around me feel so wrong and so misdirected. Some things that seemed trite, or cute at the time, were the unconscious foundations for how my life was affected for a long time after that. Believing that age is more a dictator than messages understood is a mistake.

I found joy in the magic behind something, rather than the something itself. The something itself was sometimes so painful that looking beyond it was the only way. The joy and magic in and of myself made me happy without needing anything or anyone. In the end, I guess that's the biggest get of all. Small, true, and stable things did mean a lot, but the unseen behind everything meant even more.

Soon after the fight my parents had, we moved from Pearsall Avenue in the Bronx, to Fleetwood in Yonkers. Fleetwood is located on the Bronx/Yonkers border. I thought my dad was going to rejoin us there for good but that didn't last too long. I went into a shock because everything and everyone kept changing and nothing seemed right. It was happening when I went from age two to four and when most kids would start to talk, I chose not to. I remember making that decision. I remember my mom bending down to me and asking, "Why won't you talk Michael, don't you want to talk?" I just looked at her in quiet fear, and she hugged me while tears came out of her face. She moved away, wiped her tears, and said, "Don't worry Michael, you'll talk when you feel like it, it's OK."

I sure got tired of all the doctor visits telling my mom my vocal chords were fine. They told her that I could talk, but I just didn't feel like it. She suffered a lot in her life, but had a lot of love for me. It wasn't always expressed in the way I needed it, but it was there nonetheless.

In retrospect, it was amazing that everyone seemed so unaware of the reasons I didn't talk. They told her that I would speak when I was ready, but those visits took all the responsibility and guilt off everyone around me. Now they didn't have to look at themselves as the cause for scaring me out of my mind. I stuck to my code of silence. It was hard-coated and nothing was going to bring me out of it. For so many years and for so long I resisted communication because I feared the way people were and the way they communicated. I would listen when they thought I wasn't. I would press my ear up against the door or the wall to hear the way people spoke. It just didn't seem like the way they communicated was ever considerate enough for me to want to be part of it.

Words serve preconceived ideas and categories. We are the person behind the movie camera. The body is the movie camera, and the scenes we experience are the lines of the script. Analogies used to find the essence of us behind words and behind the camera are misleading.

I remember once I had to test what an electric socket was so I put a screw driver in one of the holes. It flung me about ten feet across the room. I don't know if my mom and sister were more surprised that I did it, or that I still didn't utter a word after that. After they saw that I was alright, we settled down to have some dinner. My sister said if I didn't talk after that I wasn't ever going to talk. My mom got so mad at her for saying that, she yelled, "Don't you ever, ever, say that again." My sister left the table crying. It was rough with just the three of us. We felt robbed of something. All three of us felt robbed of something, we just showed it in different ways.

My dad came back for a spell and I started talking but there was nothing but tension between him and my mom, so I stopped again. Soon afterwards he got thrown out again and this time in even more violence. The police came, and I didn't see my dad for years. I was in a deep shock. Everyone was so much in their own hurt that they ignored mine. They treated me like I was too young to know what was going on. In their minds I didn't matter, and no signal coming from me made a difference. It was not exactly nurturing. I felt like everyone wished I wasn't there.

A few years later I started pre-K, but it was very late in the school year. My family just had other things going on and that was not a priority. I wasn't ready for school, but this didn't stop my mom. She went to the school across the street from where we lived and met with the director. I waited outside the office and listened by the door. She used her persuasiveness in conversation and a small amount of money to overcome objections about it being too late in the school year. The director and my mother both came out with smiles, so we all proceeded to go to a class in progress.

The teacher, a heavy set strict looking old lady, was a bit taken back by the intrusion and change to her class size, but my mother explained that I really didn't talk so I wouldn't be much of a problem. The teacher and Director were startled. The teacher eased the tension by saying that not talking was good because most kids in her class talked too much.

This school was real close so it worked out well, for my mom anyway. She was going to beautician school to get some skills for a job. Mom wasn't employed when she was raising two kids and married to my dad, but Dad's money wasn't consistent anymore so she had to work.

She was very grateful to the pre-K teacher. The teacher was an old-timer with a focus on the rules. I was in my own world, very much in my own world, and strictly an observer of people and life. I was still getting over the shock of all the tension and turmoil, as well as the pain of my dad not being home any more. She left me off there that same day and I remember the instructions were for me to be good, to listen, and to talk if the teacher asked me something.

The last instruction surprised me. Mom tried to sneak it in. A complete stranger now was more important than everyone else up to that point. People who brought me into this world can't even get a sound out of me and I'm now supposed to talk to some stranger because she belonged to a system. She was special because she had a title called "Teacher". I walked in the class with the teacher and sat in the back of the room. She told everyone my name and then she went back to a lesson in progress.

They were just finishing up with instruction on letters when some questions and answers ensued. She called on a few people and then called on me. I didn't even know her five minutes and was now supposed to talk to her. She obviously didn't read the book on me. I peered through her like a clear rubber raft as she asked the question again. I didn't budge and I was surprised she put me on the spot. I mean you got to be kidding me. You mean the system was more important than my own family. Was that the new message? Was everybody crazy or was it just me? No way was I going to talk. She moved on to the next person a little frazzled even after she was told I don't talk. I ignored her. We finished up with the alphabet lesson and had to get ready to go to recess.

We all lined up at the door to go across the street and play in the park. There must have been about a dozen of us. I lived across the street and played in the park many times. I remember wondering why I needed them to play in the same park where I played by myself without them. I thought it was silly that my hard working mom had to pay for a school when all they did was have me go to the same park where I went all the time without them. Between that, and the pressure the teacher put on me to talk, I was done before I began.

We all were asked to line up at the front door to get ready to leave. This heavy set teacher moved slowly getting her things ready. Her face was so stone-like and rigid that if she ever smiled I'm sure it would have cracked into pieces. She was an old-timer with old ways. She was a hard-nosed teacher who looked like she was teaching far too long. She made sure three different times the line was perfect at the door with the taller kids up front waiting to leave to go to the park. Nobody could talk. Twice she had to tell people not to talk. There wasn't any cause for the rules except to have rules.

I was kind of tall, almost ready for the next grade, so I was right up front. The teacher forgot her purse and had to get a few things so she left us standing there. One of the boys looked at me and whispered, "C'mon open the door. You can reach the lock on top". Another little girl kid said, "Yea, you can do it, just turn that top one that way", and she motioned around to her left. So, sure enough I did. I had little allegiance to the old bag who thought who the hell she was. I figured the worst that could happen was I could get out of the whole thing. Well, as soon as I opened the door all the children came rushing through, ran across the street, and headed toward the park cheering. The teacher went ballistic. The look on this fat old lady's face chasing after us was an absolute heart attack. Her hands were waving in the air frantically while she was running and screaming for us to come back. She was in such a panic. It was as if the world was ending.

She gathered us all up and brought us back instead of just letting us play anyway. I then knew she wasn't going to let it go and it was all going to come back to me. She made everyone go back to the school, sit down, and asked who opened the door. Nobody budged. Most of the kids knew it was me, but nobody budged. She said everyone was going to have extra work and no play if we didn't tell her. Nobody said a word. I felt bad that everyone else would suffer for what I did. She asked again who did it and I stood up and raised my hand. She made me sit in the corner facing the wall and told me my mother is going to be called to come get me.

I was destined not to follow the norm. I really didn't roll well with systems and the set ways of doing things. My mom got an earful when she arrived as she was very upset that she was forced to leave beautician school to come get me. I got expelled from pre-K without ever uttering a word.   So my mom gave me an earful while dragging me home and gave me a beating the second we got home. She didn't know what to do with me while she was out trying to get employed. It was a real problem. So, yea, I had to get a beating. What would I do without that?

After the beating she grabbed me by the hand and walked me toward the front door. I thought for a moment that I was getting thrown out. She did that to my father, and since I was a boy too I thought I could be next, but it wasn't that. Mom had a brainstorm.   She walked me out to the other side of the front door and handed me a milk crate. I looked at her inquisitively. She said the milk crate goes near the door, you step up on it and now you can reach the lock. She asked if I could get on the milk crate without any help. After I did she showed me how to open the door. She gave me the key and asked me to try to open the door. I obviously was now a veteran of locks and opened it without a problem. Mom made a joke about how I already showed that I knew how to open a door. I looked at her fearing she might hit me again. She said you can stay in all day, but if you go out bring the key, and don't forget how to open the door. I nodded up and down. That was a lot for me. I'm not even five yet, but I got a key to get in and a milk crate to reach the lock.

Actually, I was just grateful she wasn't throwing me out. Thoughts of locks, doors, milk crates, and leaving with a key was all fine, if I wasn't getting hit and I was able to be home. Mom was thrilled I got the idea. Wow, I was on my way toward independence in the world and all without ever having to say a word. Kind of wish it was still like that in a way.

My sister was two years older than me so she started school first and my mother had to go to work, and to beautician school, so there wasn't much money for a baby-sitter. I stayed home by myself and promised her I wouldn't answer the door. I mostly stayed in my room and just laid on my bed thinking about things. I looked out the window and observed people's behavior when they passed. Sometimes my cousin would come over and baby-sit. Baby-sitting meant I did the same exact thing, but she was in the other room on the phone with her friends. Sometimes her friends came over even though my mom frowned on that. My cousin cut school sometimes to baby-sit. It helped that she was there because it put my mom at ease. I was alone a lot even when people were around. Nobody really played with me or engaged me that much. They all had too much going on.

My sister didn't get home until three o'clock, so I was on my own until then. My mother would usually be home around dinner time. Sometimes my sister would get me something to eat. That was a lot to ask of a six and a half year old but she did it. My sister suffered with all this stuff and had two years before me to suffer with it even more. She was never that nice because of it. She took it out on me a lot. That's not what I needed. Fifty years later she's still the same. She still mistreats me with a mean streak that comes out of nowhere. She says and does things behind my back that undermines me. The little kid in her that had to hurt something or someone because she was hurt never changed.

As a four and a half to five year old kid I ventured out by myself sometimes. I stayed near the playground and watched people and their reactions to the games they were playing. I watched people do everything from playing ball, betting cards, or even rolling dice for money. I even watched the old men play chess. My dad had a chessboard so it made me feel good to watch even though I didn't understand it. I focused more on how people were with each other than the games themselves.

In the days following my expulsion from pre-K, I occasionally would see a kid from that class. They would come to the park where I stayed. When they saw me by myself they would come over and replay that moment of how I opened the door, and how the teacher reacted. They got a kick out of it and laughed. They wondered why I didn't talk even when they were speaking with me privately, but I smiled with them when they recalled my escapade. I was so pensive for a kid that age. People would talk to me and I would be thinking and experiencing things so deeply that talking would be the furthest thing from my mind.

I liked the ones that didn't press the non-talking issue. I would stay away from the ones that tried to get me to talk. Hey, if you can't take who I am, then split, I'm independent you know. I got a key and a milk-crate. My two hours in pre-K was about as much school as I wanted at that point. I didn't miss it. We just put school off until we moved to a new neighborhood.

I certainly didn't like the way the people around me were conducting themselves. The very first group of people I was introduced to in my life was my family, and they obviously had terrible issues. My two hours with the pre-K group didn't fly either. I really wondered if I could just be me without having to belong to any group. Could I just always have keys and a milk crate and be left alone? All was OK. Even though I wasn't quite five, I had the key to the apartment, and all I had to do was stand on the milk crate to reach the lock and nobody was home inside.

Yet, one day the unimaginable happened, the milk crate was gone. The woman next door saw me waiting near the door and was so appalled I was alone that she offered to take me in to her apartment for a few hours. When I went in I saw she had the milk crate. I wondered why she took it and I just looked at her inquisitively without speaking, of course. She kept asking me stuff, but I didn't talk so she was getting a little peeved about that. I certainly didn't trust her after seeing she took my independence away.

She told me that I could play with her children until my mother got home. That didn't work out. Her kids were crazy wild and I wanted no part of them. Every time her back was turned they were doing something they shouldn't, and then she would put me on the spot to confess what happened. I never talked so she was out of luck with me as her new snitch too. She gave my mother an earful when she got home about leaving me on my own at such a young age. My mom said, "If you didn't take the damned milk crate, everything would have been fine. Maybe you should just mind your own business". Mom just didn't know what to do any more. She had to figure out how to earn a living, she couldn't leave me alone and she couldn't afford to pay anyone to take care of me. For someone who didn't talk I sure was causing a lot of problems.

I really didn't like the collective way of doing anything and felt that words and talking did less to communicate than silence. I felt very unique and really enjoyed the ability to call my own shots and be secluded when I wanted. Nothing has ever really changed. The body got older but there are certain things about me that will always be the same. No experiences were smaller just because I was. Everything was meaning a lot.

## II  Why are we here?

We moved from that Fleetwood, Yonkers apartment back to the Bronx again.  Mom got her beautician's license, and got a job in Co-op City in the Bronx doing hair.  She was psyched.  It was the happiest I ever saw her.  I was going to go to school there.  Mom had it all worked out.  It was a new life, a new place, new job, and a new school for me and my sister.  I remember my first day of kindergarten.

The teacher told us where the blocks were, the wooden cars for the boys, and the dolls for the girls.  She told us when lunchtime was and said if it was nice outside we could all go out.  She told us that when it was rest-time we had to put our heads down on the desk and our thumbs had to be up.  The thumbs being up showed we weren't sleeping.  Sleeping wasn't allowed, but resting was.  She then asked if anyone had any questions.

I remember how excited I was thinking that since she asked if anybody had any questions, she must be the one who can answer some of the big questions I had.  I had a question I wanted to ask.  OK, I built up enough nerve to talk so I raised my hand and so did a few other children.  She called on two people before me.  They asked questions about where we met in the morning before school and whether it was possible to be asleep and still have your thumb up. I was thinking so many things while the other questions and answers went by.  She didn't know that speaking for me was a big deal.  I mostly did a lot of thinking.  I didn't talk at all until I was four and a half and I didn't speak much between four and a half and five either.

I thought about certain things for many years and this was my opportunity to finally ask the one question that was most important to me throughout that time.  I waited to ask someone outside of my family because my family seemed to have some major issues.  I needed to get an answer from someone who wouldn't look at me in preconceived ways.  I needed to ask someone who was put in a position where they represented knowledge and respect to me.  I asked my kindergarten teacher who was in charge of thirty-five children.  I remember thinking to myself how this one person is responsible for all these children so she must have deserved some respect for her integrity and know-how.  She did have a helper but she was the bigwig.

I repeated the question in my head many times to make sure my words and sounds were right. She finally got to me, and after verifying who I was, she asked me what my question was. She said she wasn't answering any more questions about the possibility of sleeping while your thumb was up. I told her that wasn't my question, because I understood that. She said, "OK, what's your question?" I thought since my question was different than theirs that it would be preferred, so I spoke right up and asked my first question ever, "Why are we here?", I proudly asked. She looked up my name and verified what class I should be in and said, "It shows you're in K-1, do you think you should be in K-2?" I said, "No, no, not why are we here in this class, why are we alive?" She almost dropped dead. She was so stunned. I felt like everything in the world just came to a halt.

She looked out of the top of her eyes as if she had glasses on peering at me through this look like she was in some kind of surreal moment. She was amazed that those words came out of me. There was a silence for about ten seconds that had ten million feelings exchanged. She said she was teaching kindergarten twenty years and nobody ever asked that question before. I didn't know whether to feel good or bad but I felt like she was biding time to figure out a way to dodge the whole thing. I felt disappointment before she even uttered a word. I knew the words wouldn't do what the non-words just expressed. The non-words were amazing, and for a little while, it took away the separation from everyone in the room. We were one until the words finally spoken took it all away.

She said I needed to ask my parents that question. She then stood quiet again looking at me with this look that gave me and everyone considerable pause. To me, it seemed every child in the class was frozen with the weight of how the question was being handled. She then said it again. She said, "Yes, you need to ask a religious instructor or your parents that question." She tried to go to the next subject and asked if there were any more questions, but all the other kids who had their hand up before no longer did. I guess it was a hard question to follow. She moved on but she did so with this haze over her that made me wonder if I was in trouble or something. She verified my name, wrote something down, and the rest of the day I wondered what it was.

She made herself feel better by telling us we can all go play, so we all did. She repeated where the blocks, trucks, and dolls were and told us to play quietly and nicely. We then all left our seats to go have fun. I was pensive and had no desire to play. I was still thinking about what just happened. I didn't really play much per se'. I didn't have any toys at home and I was more in a space of observance than actually doing. I was sure confused why the very rudiments of our life were not the very rudiments of my education. I was shocked that knowing where the toys were was more important than my question. I was feeling sad that what I thought was the most important question, that I waited so long to ask, was deflected back to where it couldn't be asked. There was no dad around, mom was busy, and I didn't know what a religious instructor or religion was yet.

I was kind of caving in with a private sadness while going near the general play area when a cute little girl with curly blond hair came over to me and told me her name. Since most names were new to me, I made her repeat it. She so sweetly said, "Mindy is my name, and I liked your question a lot because I had the same question, but was afraid to ask it." I was blown away to get any recognition. This was my first positive interaction with a girl. It probably would have saved me a lifetime of challenges if I proposed to Mindy right then and there. Just when I was thinking of connecting further, some big boy stepped between us instead and told her where the girls play. He then protected his truck with his life, put his arm around me and asked me if I wanted to play. I really didn't want to. I really wanted to talk to Mindy, but I went away with him while looking back at her, and looked to see what the big fascination was with the trucks.

I started to play with the truck lover a bit but it just wasn't my cup of tea. I moved away and went over to some books on the side of the classroom. I really enjoyed looking at them but the teacher told me abruptly to leave them alone because we weren't up to looking at those yet. Again, I was made to feel wrong. I couldn't imagine what level I had to be at to simply glance at books but obviously squashing my curiosity had to take place so I could be diminished even further.

I couldn't easily be with the girl, I didn't like hanging out with the guy, and the books were off limits, so alone I was and alone I stayed until we reconvened back at our desks and went through the day. Now it was time for the famous heads down thumbs up. In that space I wondered why I felt so very different than what everyone else wanted me to be. There was so much energy around trying to make me feel different than what I really felt.

At the end of the day the teacher took me aside from everyone else who were lined up waiting for the bell. When it sounded they were released to their parents. My mom was sectioned off and was talked to about how strange I was. The teacher didn't want me to ask those questions anymore and she wanted my mom to handle it. My mom took me aside and told me that she couldn't afford to have me thrown out of this school too because she had to go to work and she couldn't leave me all alone again. She told me, in school, I should just stay quiet and listen without asking too many questions. She looked sternly at me and said, "Can't you just stay quiet?"

There was this pause as time stood still and I looked up at her with big eyes wondering what she just said. I thought it was a perplexing thing to ask since I didn't talk the first four and a half years of my life and barely talked during the next year following that. Now when I finally did speak a little, I was told keep quiet. She looked back at me and said, "I know, you never talk and now when you do, I'm telling you to be quiet." She hugged me and said "Oh my son, please just find a way to fit in with everyone else so the teacher doesn't get upset, OK?" She got my head nod and she hugged me again. I looked up at her to see if I was still OK and she said, "C'mon, let's go home, I got something good for dinner, I made money on my first day of work."

I was very quiet and perplexed from the first day of kindergarten and the way my first question was handled. I was greatly surprised about the systems adults valued the highest. To me, they were immersed in what I thought was wrong. To me, if the most basic questions couldn't be handled without giving me grief, then school wasn't worth its salt. I stayed quiet the rest of the year because Mom had so many challenges I never wanted to give her another one. Welcome to the world of communication and education.

Why talk? What would it have been? They killed me on the first great question I had, so now what was I going to say? Why support a communication about power abuse? That's what it is. It's taking what's right and turning it into what's wrong because someone else has the power to do that.

How would it have been if it was all handled differently? Wouldn't it have been a better result if I was treated with respect for asking such a great question? Maybe if I was complimented for being smart enough to ask it, and I was reinforced for the question, everyone would have felt better about sharing the common mystery. The teacher would have removed all imagined separation between her and the students with our acknowledgement of common mystery. It also would have created this amazing bond with everyone in the room. Instead, she had to be the elevated one who knew so much better than everyone else by deferring it out. Now any other kid who had a question remotely resembling that one wouldn't ask it either. They also had to feel this dissension between what was natural and what they had to be.

It would have also boosted my confidence and the confidences of all the others feeling the same question. If the common truth of wonder and mystery was shared between me and that teacher, it would have been shared with everyone in the classroom. It would have changed all our lives for the better because the idea of not knowing our origins would have been made acceptable. Going forward, searching and allowing for mystery, when investigating many things, would have always enabled greater insights into everything after that. The constant need to move away from what's mysterious by grasping at wrong answers first, ends up being the habit instilled, and this is what causes the most damage. The foundation is established for fear and angst to be associated with anything unknown. It's what undermines patience, consideration, deeper thoughts, and discovery.

I had to be reminded that there was one parent I never saw whom I couldn't ask the question to, and the other parent who just wanted me to be unobtrusive. I had to be treated like a bother instead and now be referred to someone else who would also view me as a bother. So I had nothing but disappointment, and staying quiet again became my best answer. Education laid down its foundation and that is what it was always going to mean to me.

I am giving love to the young man in me and the young person in you who asked a million questions and got answers to other questions in return. I am feeling great for the times I forged past feeling so alone, so down on myself, so forlorn, so empty, and so afraid to be unaccepted for something said or something done.

Give me the wonder back from the newborn's face. Give me the naivety of the questions from that very young person begging for truth and mystery. Give me the ocean of strength that washes over every second when we allow for what we can't know, instead of losing everything by grasping onto what we pretend to know. Give me that sparkle in the eyes of a newborn and let me not feel wrong for just letting it be. Give me life before the imagined strength derived from veiled weaknesses and before we served the all-consuming egos. Give me that eternal sparkle of hope before the wrong answers and misdirected controls squashed it. Can I revel in divinity without feeling so alone? Let me renew my zest for life and living. Let me remember the sparkle in my eyes that experienced wonder. What would it feel like to regain that? What would it feel like to reverse every action that demeaned me? Can I give myself back that love and always feel the inherent greatness in me?

Whose message is more important than our own message to our self? Whose opinions somehow crept in and somehow became elevated because of one vulnerable state or another? Was it a parent or guardian? Was it a teacher, a priest, a rabbi? Was it an employer? Was it all of these? Was it a husband or a wife? Did money become the dictator of opinion? Were any of these things truly bigger than you? Nothing is bigger than you are. Everything that is shown to us clamors for its own value rather than pointing to our own. There isn't anything bigger than you or more important than you because you are already of the biggest thing there is. People act as if they're bigger when they are not. Beliefs in one thing or another take on a collective acceptance that they are bigger than us and they most certainly are not.

What should be valued more than what allows us to be in the first place? We make the mistake of identifying who we are with what has happened to us. We also equate our worth to a measurement of things achieved or not that we erroneously regard as more valuable than us. Schooling, relationship, jobs, money, and material possessions impose beliefs that make us feel that unless we are good at these things, we aren't good at all. Closely identifying with cultural goals, only meant to accommodate us, can make us feel inadequate.

Mental narratives about our perceived "successes" and "failures" are like a battering ram hitting us. It's the up and down, right and wrong, bad and good within the values of a culturally imposed belief system. We created money to assist us in trade and then determined that nothing is worth our time unless it can be equated to a value within the money medium. Our very own value is trapped in two illusions quantifying a worth, the value of the things out there, and our self-determination equating to the accumulation of those things.

It's all in an attempt to value the priceless and define the indefinable. The image or expectation we impose on our self, that does not materialize, leaves no room for life's real happiness. Our very self is endangered because we're invested in the results of what we equated our own value to. A failed image acts as a raincloud, and that raincloud can only be dispersed by awareness.

One of the earliest things taught to us are numbers. We started with "zero" and then proceeded to the value of "one". "Nothing", is put forth as what we don't see and "nothing" is less than "one". What we don't see means nothing of any significance worth considering. Then there is the number "one". There were notches found in stone dated more than 25,000 years ago representing a form of counting. The number "one" is the first significant whole value after what has no value. In Sanskrit, considered the oldest language, the symbol of "0" meant empty. This is very basic. Yet, if we equated "one" as ourselves, and what came before us as "0", it would be surmised that what we can't see within us, counts as nothing of any significance.

In that logic we have subtly determined that there isn't a rarefied essence worth valuing accompanying the "one" body we appear as. The body is the only life there is and an essence besides that during life, before life and after life is "0" since it isn't "1". No consideration would ever be given to anything that didn't appear in substantive form with this approach. It would be what wasn't a "one" and wouldn't have any value. So math in a seamless and subtle way removes our ability to value our incorporeal essence. Numbers and how we use them affect our view of reality.

In reality, zero isn't an empty "no value". It is the all value. It's an amazing container for all values. For symbol purposes, it isn't the apparent "no value" that appears in the middle of the circle, it is the endless value that is represented by the arc that makes the circle. The arc goes around and around forever. The infinity in that approach is closer to the infinity of our source and more representative of the all value of "zero", and the unseen infinite value in and of our self.

Numbers are universal and can affect the way people think. The origin of numbers seems to have begun with the counting on fingers, which explains the base-ten system. Of course before anyone could put up a finger to count "one", there had to be the life before that. Again, there had to be the life before and after the finger was lifted and there is an immeasurable essence before, during, and after every representation of so-called value. We are greater than any value that can be represented. Let this remind us what will always be more important than all numbers, all measures, all gains, and all perceived advantages.

All that exists ultimately came from what would appear as nothing or very small to the human eye. Human beings come into this world from very tiny things which can't be seen with the naked eye. The tallest apple tree in the world came from a tiny little seed that appeared as almost "nothing" yet created thousands upon thousands of apples over hundreds of years.

There are habits in our education that condition us to treat the unseen as insignificant. There are habits that are instilled in us early on in life that dishonor the greatest essence of us because we conclude that if something isn't seen, it is insignificant in relation to what is seen. We can't help but to then apply that error to our self as well.

How do we learn to honor our feelings, intuitions, and higher wisdom, when discounting all of it was at the cornerstone of our foundations? Our unseen and intangible essence becomes meaningless, undeveloped, unrecognized, squashed, and simply not considered because our rudimentary education told us that if it can't be seen, it has no value. Unfortunately, the point is driven home when all else around us has been poisoned with the same origin. We then walk in two directions the rest of our lives without feeling the unified grandeur of our being. When most of what's around us confirms this duplicity, it becomes even more elusive to connect to our truest essence.

Look at your hand. If you took the tiniest shaving of skin and cut it in half over and over to get to a piece so small you would need high-powered equipment to see it, and further split that down into smaller fragments getting to a neutron, then with the help of a little uranium and a few tweaks a massive explosion beyond that of your wildest imagination could be created. This is what happens when you get as close to nothing as you can get. You get something unimaginable. Yet, we still didn't get to "nothing", did we? When is "nothing" truly that definition we imagine it to be? Even in what is considered a "true vacuum" exists the tiniest discernible particles that come in and out of such a "vacuum" so as to negate the definition of even a vacuum as a true example of "nothing". The idea that there is ever truly "nothing" is actually not real.

There really isn't anything that we should blow off as "nothing", because chances are, there is always at least something, not being considered when we do that. We miss vital causes for massive results by eliminating a person, place, thing, experience or feeling as "nothing". The acceptance of the idea that "nothing" exists, outside of a numerical reference, erroneously allows for misrepresentation in situations containing tiny details. Later, the smallest detail brushed off as inconsequential, ends up subtly and seamlessly revealing itself to overtake the full definition of the event.

There are two people sitting on a stoop, both without a penny. One is musically talented and finds a guitar in the garbage the other is looking to jump off a bridge. Is having no money the same here? "Nothing" may be the money value applied, but when total value is equated to that, we are disrespecting the value of a human being. In this respect, we erroneously treat events and people as "nothing" and the great intangibles are oftentimes disregarded in every person.

The approaches used to create massive communication problems with mankind throughout history have failed without any one individual ever wanting such results. Things are happening in us, and in the world, that nobody really wants but they are happening anyway. If it's in the results, it's a space worth reconsidering. How would a person realize if an invisible cause was actually creating horrible effects? It certainly wouldn't be by being quick to deem something as nothing. Yet, what else would cause results contrary to our desires if not for causes that weren't easily seen? How else would this be explained if not for the dismissing of what in reality was at the heart of huge effects? Ingredients, that in origin either appeared in disguise, or appeared as "nothing", had to have been part of the problem.

Wind can't be seen, in and of itself, but you certainly can see its effect. The same air that looks like nothing, if moved with great speed, can wipe out a country. We don't ignore the wind because we can't see it. We measure the cause by the result even though the wind is invisible. We can easily say the air is nothing, yet, in reality, it's a great analogy to remind us that the greatest something there is, is always what appears as nothing. It's in that so-called "nothing" that everything is rooted.

All prioritizing should treat our common and shared life above all else. Comparison and measurement is what has taken our common connectedness and turned it into what divides us. Every day we see ridiculous fighting where people lower themselves to primitive habits without a second thought toward our immeasurable common humanity. In every area of life our greatest common virtues are dishonored. Division exists with millionaires hurting others because they somehow feel they still don't have enough. It exists to divide peoples all over the world where money, things, and categorical references take priority over compassion.

Common humanity has to have value. We must work harder to acknowledge a value besides what is tangible. This disgusting oversight has seamlessly imbedded itself in the habits of everything we do nowadays. Zeroing out our very spirituality cannot be lessened because of the rigidity of a number that pulls you in. What better way to hide the biggest matter of all than to treat what is unseen as insignificant, or to treat what appears smaller as less?

Education is conducted as if we don't have a thought in our heads until they give it to us. I would think the greatest amount of learning we could get would be to share our individual feelings with each other. If everybody in a classroom was able to really share their experiences, and what they meant to them, that would help everyone so much more. The synergy from thirty-five people truly sharing their insights, creativity, and challenges would be far greater than any single point from any one person no matter how intelligent they were. Wouldn't listening to others also help identify things in ourselves more pertinent to the current moment?

Clearing out what truly matters certainly would make some of the mandatory learning go a lot easier, but mandatory education without it is stifling individuality. A little difference in the way we handle things would create very positive results.

It wouldn't have made me feel so alone and inadequate if I knew someone else was going through similar problems. Isn't this an important part of learning and loving ourselves? Wouldn't that bring everyone closer together? Instead we have to strive to be better than the other person. We have to excel at studying things that have little to no benefit to us ultimately. It's as if we are being told that what we really care about doesn't matter, and what we are told "matters" is not what we care about. What does that do for your egos and self confidence? What does that do for our self-image when we have to hide all we really care about and amplify what we don't? How does this all get internalized when we have to put on a show for what's expected and we change who we truly are? This is the foundation of alienation in our self and our alienation with others. When we change who we are for the show, for the groups out there, and for all who support them, what do we become? Why doesn't this matter?

The things that make up what the brain does are projected outward and become what is at the heart of every group. The brain-machine by its very nature seeks attachment. The rules for using it keep you trapped in it without any ability to breathe in new ideas. Groups are like that as well. When attempting to use something besides the workings of the human brain people get insecure. This is how they act when questioning their adherence to groups. The workings of our brain and the workings of groups mimic each other. Each feeling is forced into a category.

All that is definable, measurable, quantifiable, tangible, comparable, and exclusive to a logic always pointing back to itself, is what insulates groups. We become dependent on the products of the human brain, which are words and thoughts, because we feel lost without them. Words and thoughts are the group we belong to that was generated by the brain. Groups also make it so we are dependent on them for our basic needs so we feel lost without them. Allegiance to the group is like food in that it keeps them alive. Words and thoughts are like food for our brain. Losing our self to the definition of something else is perpetuated in groups, and so is losing our self to words. Any experience that is independent of the functionality of our brain, or the functionality of a group, is usually accompanied with great resistance.

Without our first group, which is our family, we wouldn't have been created, and without the early ongoing attachment to it, we would have died. It is instilled at birth to put our allegiance to the group first and put aside any differences. Every person considers themselves very unique. Nobody would ever consider their identity to be merely the product of every group they were ever associated with. Yet with all these feelings of uniqueness and individuality, that are seemingly separate and distinct from all groups, there must be the realization that we are still, at least in large part, very much the effect of every group that we have ever been attached to.

It's happening all over the world. We are teaching our children the way to stop seeing. This sounds like a horrible statement, and quite ridiculous as well. Aren't we doing everything for our children? Parents I know would give everything they have for their children. In fact, outside of naturally abusive parents with deep mental problems, few parents in the world wouldn't give everything they could to their children. They would probably give them a meal while they were starving themselves. They would give them money when they had very little themselves. They would give them education even if they lacked to provide for it. They would give them clothing and literally the shirt off their back to help their children. How can I say that we are all helping our children to be blind? How can I say that we are trying to stop them from seeing?

Society praises the knower, or at least the one who acts like they know, and not the one in mystery. Even if the one who "knows" is putting across wrong information when the answers are temporarily unknown, it is embraced over being in mystery. All the "experts" relieve themselves of delving into complex issues such as the secrets of life, afterlife, or disembodiment, with quick summations. Religious instruction and group pressure introduced to us by our family is backwards and destructive. Every religious group needs to be looked at with new eyes and with a re-thinking of the real messages being given. The messages being given to us in all religions are that we need them, but the fact is that there isn't any need for them at all. There is only a need to allow the embrace of the indecipherable in ourselves.

The world is following leaders for the sake of their leadership rather than for the sake of truth. We are joining groups because the music is good during the occasion even though the messages are creating horrible results. We are becoming part of what has been known and accepted in one light of beauty, and in that we are accepting ideas about other things which are not beautiful. I know people who have gone to a certain temple because they boasted about having one of the best female cantors around, so they went there because they enjoyed hearing her sing. Yet, deep down inside, beliefs absorbed from the religious messages put forth in songs were seldom looked at too deeply. So, messages were imposed on people because they went along with things socially. This superficial stance veiled what was impinging itself on everyone's psyche while they were there.

We have fallen for the ingredients, the music, the togetherness, the apparent alleviation of mystery, the tradition, the illusion of security, but in doing so we have disregarded the effect. We have digested seeds of separation, alienation, judgments, damnation, and most importantly, we have absorbed the message that the greatest part of us is not within our power. In the glorification of another, it's digested that what we share with everyone else, is not really of us. Another force is selecting, choosing, and extending at its discretion who is privy to the occasion of this gift and who isn't.

Therefore our common bond is destroyed because we decided it wasn't common. There was something more powerful, and it was the choice of that something to either be selected for it, or not. So there became an implied message that the medium of religion bridged this selection for favoritism toward the group honoring the decision maker. This was used to control people for power, money, control, ego, to alleviate their own fear of the unknown, and to move away from their own discomfort of mystery.

When the time is taken to allow for mystery, fear is dispelled. The allowance of mystery dispels the illusion that strength only comes from knowing. Not knowing, and not assuming, is the most powerful of all positions. To believe otherwise would be a tragic mistake. Admitting the wonder of life is the position of Da Vinci, Newton, and Einstein. It is wisdom, and it is a common bond for all humanity. There is a greater wisdom in admitting the "not knowing" than the "knowing".

Family, education, religion, and employment tend to speed past insightful questions, and not accept mystery. It's in the habits of the majority everywhere to not have an appreciation for what takes longer. The work needed for truth is greatly avoided.

We find out (oftentimes when it's too late) that many people from our childhood, and throughout our adult life, who proposed to know, truly don't. Many people should go a lot slower, and propose a lot less, rather than go fast and truly not know what they're talking about. Maybe the ones who go the slowest are the wisest ultimately.

When Leonardo da Vinci or the Wright brothers looked up in the sky at birds for hours, days and weeks, would you have been the one to tell them they were crazy? Would you have been the one to delve even more deeply into what they were studying? Would judgments, labels, and quick mental summaries been the way you would have handled this unusual behavior?

It's a shame to realize the laws of the cosmos, and the connectivity of all things, only to have everyone dismiss it with their attachment to the next group that separates them. This deprivation of human authenticity is perpetuated through the charade of each group clamoring to etch out a more powerful and comprehensive definition for itself. In their masquerades, they have become larger than everyone. Definitions of self and life origins are instilled through the education group, the religious group, and "the outside world and how it views me" group.

Our greatest strengths and infinite splendor are controlled and named by the religious group. We are taught that our spiritual selves are not in us, of us, and part of the totality us. We are made to feel small in relation to it because something or someone else is responsible for anything impalpable. We take our very essence and give the embrace of it away to something in charge of the embrace.

Great accomplishments came from people who had the ability to immerse themselves in contemplation and quandary longer than others. This is the complete opposite of appearing confident and knowing in the face of looming questions. The great minds of the past should stand as an example of what was the better behavior. Being more receptive to what's not known should stand as the model to what brings people to higher wisdom, greater insights, and seeing greater ways of experiencing life.

Instead, moving quickly from one thing to the next is more of the pattern instilled. Education, religion, cultural patterns, societal norms and family habits seem to be accepting one thing that isn't proven to get to the next thing that isn't proven. The impression forced upon us has us believing that the gift is only in the appearance of "knowing", when the greatest gifts come in the package of being able to accept truly not knowing.

Poor Leonardo da Vinci, who was ridiculed for much of his youth for being born of a mother without a legal father, and struggled under the domain of powerful kings, only to become one of the greatest inventors and visionaries who ever lived. Poor Einstein, who was thrown out of grammar school because he was considered too slow and disruptive for his class, only to go on to establish scientific breakthroughs that credited him with being one of the greatest geniuses that ever lived. Poor Helen Keller, who changed the world for every deaf-mute person then and forever, but as a child was discarded as crazy. Poor Thomas Alva Edison, whose friends and family were so fed up with his obsessive personality that he was ridiculed and scorned. He went on to patent more than a thousand inventions that changed the world with the most impactful advances of the modern age. Poor Socrates, who lived in rags, ate from handouts, and was thought to be a rebellious and insane man. All the while he was laying the foundation of philosophy down that would stand as a stronghold for the next 2,500 years.

Poor Van Gogh, who was penniless and unappreciated most of his life, while mentally struggling with reconciling the pangs of creativity with everyday existence, only to be known today as one of the greatest artists who ever lived. Poor Beethoven, who was deaf and mistreated because of it, only to reveal feelings for the sounds of music, and the creation of new music, more than everyone around him. He is known today as one of the greatest composers who ever lived. Poor Walt Whitman whose book, "Leaves of Grass" was treated as hogwash, only to later be considered one of the greatest works of poetry ever written. Poor Orville and Wilbur Wright, who were laughed at while they broke bones falling down mountains, attempting to fly using wings, only to take that same failure and turn our skies into a means of transportation with planes taking us everywhere. So poor were all these people, but never so rich as to not need the approval of others.

Never so rich are you to not need the approval of others while exploring the new directions that you take. It's oftentimes much more to say you know much less. It's not some negative depiction of self to say you aren't sure. The need to clutch a truth filled with holes shouldn't be chosen in order to portray a veil of strength. It becomes a fortress with a crumbling foundation to later have to defend what's false.

Sometimes when we are protecting against weaknesses in our logic, we attack, to head off needing to defend. The belief of the best defense being an offense, takes over. Yet, the truth doesn't go away. It will swell, and the more we try to push it under the surface, the more it will force its way up. The buoyancy of truth appears in many ways and eventually there is nowhere to run. It will arise in ways when least expected. It finds you. It finds everyone.

Why am I here? It was the first question I ever asked in school. It was a good question. The answer should have been, "We don't know Michael. Nobody knows for sure. I don't know, your parents won't know, and nobody you will ever ask for the rest of your life will be able to say for sure. It's a great question young man. I'm very surprised how insightful you are at such an early age to ask such a question. In my twenty years of teaching kindergarten, it's the only time any child has ever asked me that question. I'm going to tell your mom how smart you are for asking one of the questions that nobody really knows. I congratulate you Michael." Wow, what a difference that would have created.

I am re-experiencing every thwarted expression of wonder and every unanswered question. I am empowering the child in me who was told to ask someone else, or instructed to just believe because the "more powerful", "more knowledgeable" said so.

Cheers I say! Cheers for expressing these differences and plowing through all the naysayers and all the discord. Congratulations on being you in the face of all who tried to make you small, and congratulations on not wearing definitions they tried to lay on you because of their own fears, that their own lack of will, and their own loss of character. Cheers to you my friend. You know what you didn't fall prey to and you know what it took to be true to the greatest essence of you.

# III   WHAT HAPPENED TO OUR WORLD?

The mediums of communication confuse how we should connect to our life force and to other people. There are subtle effects in the way we are brought up that increase this sabotaging of human relations. Living is difficult. People are difficult. Feeling like we're always trying for something that is more than what we achieved is difficult. Why are there disconnected feelings between where we are and where we want to be, regardless of all outcomes? There are hidden traps that are never really addressed that seep into our psyche.

The greatest communication that could ever take place would have to include touching upon the greatness in you, otherwise, it's simply not the greatest communication. What part of the miracle of us being here doesn't indicate to you that the miracle includes you? The miracle of a space that is flowing through us is magical but every miraculous feeling seems to get discounted away. Each miracle that connects us to our essence is given to something else or someone else.

We are given the impression that we have so much less value inside of us because the value outside of us is held so highly. Things become more important than people. Cars, houses, money, and possessions become more important than our very lives. Other people become more important than us. Movie stars, divas, models, and beautiful people become more important than we are. We rob ourselves of all the beauty and love we are of. Children ask what's important, and we tell them what's important is only found in things outside of them. There isn't anything about their explosive vibration and the amazing power inside of them that's ever expounded on.

We brush over our life as if an annoyance to get to somewhere else. Every moment is made passé. We name it and make it another thing to glance over. Why is appreciating the deeper messages brushed off? So many things are kept to ourselves because most don't really want to talk about it. Most don't like to delve too many layers down. They skim across the superficial top in fear of muddy waters instead of being more still, and seeing beneath the surface of the waters where the most amazing wonders await.

Our greatness is elusive because "words" themselves work in a way that undermine our highest wisdom. What could we do if the qualities that language possessed hurt us in subtle ways? We could only bring awareness to disguised tendencies and we could have an ongoing system that stopped that awareness from being derailed. Without this habit, the greatness in you would be portrayed in a version that would not fairly and fully represent you consistently.

Words spoken internally to our self, as well as externally to others, need to have a way to disarm their effect. Isolate what words do, in and of themselves, otherwise the greatness in you is confined to a very limiting instrument. It's a tricky concept to use an instrument to point out what's broken in the same instrument, but once the subtlety of word traps are realized a new state of mind arises, and that state of mind is truly powerful.

It's hard to imagine a thought without putting words to it. For many thousands of years human beings existed without words. Our encounters, and feelings about our experiences, were freer before we bound our feelings and emotions to the dogmatism of pre-defined symbols. To better see this, there has to be a place to go to that more clearly lets us separate from the trap.

Many would say that language is one of the greatest inventions ever created. Writing, reading, and technology allow us to share information and translate data worldwide. It separates us from lower functioning living beings. It enables the transmittal and growth of information generation after generation. There's no doubt that words and language are crucial for a civilized human existence. Literacy is a key element in evaluating the development of countries worldwide. Yet, language may very well be the worst invention ever created because it isn't presented with ways to direct us out of it.

Any machine that binds you to it in unnoticeable ways makes it a very dangerous machine. If the exit out of it was lined only with ways to take you back, and you continued without ever realizing it, then that would make it a very powerful parasite. If the medium of language and words, were in and of themselves detractors from the greatest messages, would we ever know it? We are never without them. The moment we are born the nonstop chatter begins and doesn't end until we die. We are made to feel that unless we are in the thought-focused, word-focused railway, we are less. We would feel more unified with our asomatous origins if not for the hidden traps. The worst trap would be one that has an elusive escape and feels like we are in a circle. It detours our path out of it by the very instrument we use to escape. What's needed is beyond words and thoughts, because words and thoughts, ironically, interfere with our enlightenment.

Words carry with them much more than what they portray as they attempt to define everything. They carry with them a way of thinking and a way of looking at life. They are confined to a certain direction. Experiences beyond language are not allowed for because our insecurities with things not specifically defined force us back to words that break it all down, categorize it, compare it, and ultimately change it.

It's important how we view the words "mind" and "brain" because when they are experienced as separate, that differentiation can then allow for a place beyond brain-based thought functioning. I am making this distinction here in this book even though these two words haven't always been used in distinctly different ways. The separation between "mind" and "brain" needs to be very clear-cut. One should never be used for the other. Words are a product of the brain and if there isn't a place to go beyond brain, then there is a dependency on words and therefore a dependency on thoughts. There has to be a place left to view the trap of words. The thing that oversees the brain is "mind" so mixing them together takes away enlightenment. The thing that oversees consciousness is also "mind". This is why this distinction between "mind" and "consciousness" is also crucial.

A re-evaluation of certain words can unlock spiritual powers. It seems like it doesn't matter that much, but when we label the place we go to beyond traps, and that very label has a trap intertwined with it, all experiences desired beyond that are stifled. If the word "mind" is intertwined with the word "consciousness" that will also trick us out of enlightenment. Consciousness is associated with the functioning of the brain. The implication that there is knowingness in consciousness is what reconnects the idea of it back to brain. The idea of "mind" can now be where the view of it all can come from. This critical way of re-defining these certain words, which normally would box us in, now allows for a viewpoint that is not attaching itself back to the brain and its functioning. Anything that the brain reincorporates back to itself doesn't allow for the viewing of it. It's a very dangerous machine, but this is one of the ways to disarm it.

"Being" before "knowing" is the place of wisdom. It's the place before using the cognition on the next thought or word implying a thought. It's "mind beingness" and it's our life before every play is acted out. Even the word named "mind" is trying to be affected by the brain and its categories of reference. Brain keeps trying to be bigger than the idea of "mind". It's a tricky hurdle. Thinking of the word "mind" has brain acting superior. Being the word "mind" without putting it back into brain-analysis allows for it.

Some mornings we need a cup of coffee to make a cup of coffee and then need our glasses to find our glasses. This disarming method is easier, because we already have what we need. It's already us. We only need to better allow it to be through the awareness of what keeps trying to stop it. Our words should no longer dictate our approach, but until we are more at home with our essence, the spoken or thought of word machine will keep tricking us back into its functionality.

"Mind" is that place where "brain" is a gravitational pull trying to pull us back into it. Much like the earth, we are of a gravitational pull, but not just the gravitational pull itself. The gravitational pull has to exist for life but it doesn't have to define us. Food is necessary for our life, but to only be one with that exigency would prevent all the magnificence available to us besides that. Brain food should not be what defines the splendor, grandeur, and higher wisdom of "mind".

The mind is the super-highway to our otherworldly powers. We naturally have super powers not of our five senses. Mind is overseeing the brain and certainly shouldn't be subservient to the machine-like workings of it. Mind your brain in a way that you're aware of its functioning. Let "mind" be the ultimate seer. The challenge is that "mind" is something the brain really doesn't welcome. The brain wants to be the exclusive one. The brain doesn't like to share the spotlight with the idea of mind. The brain is the attention hog

The brain never seems to be at peace! We are either moving our body, which our brain manages, sitting and relaxing, and then our thought stream is busy, talking with people, and then our thought and word stream is working, or sleeping, where our brain runs amuck with thoughts and various dreams that populate our state. It seems as though unless there is this continual stream of thoughts flowing through our brain, it is simply not happy. Even when we desperately want it to take a vacation it still haunts us.

Meditation attempts to slow it all down and bring presence, but anyone who has ever meditated feels momentum forcing them away from it. They also see that it's difficult to apply the greater state of peace achieved during meditation throughout everyday life. The brain is alive, and like all things alive it seeks out what it thrives on best. What the human brain needs like food is what I found to be nine functions it anxiously waits to apply to any event or experience that passes its way. Words are the brain-products that are used to facilitate these applications. The workings of the brain-machine needs to apply one or more of its nine features and it will hate it when you try not to use them. It will also forcefully redirect you when you try to reveal these strict applications that make up its limited functionality.

It's as if our brain was a separate animal that had to be pleased, and it's jealous and angry when we embellish what's beyond it. It discredits attempts that don't rely on its functionality. The brain demands how we view things much like a fellow employee who won't have it any other way but theirs. They won't even share information because they fear that if they don't have that control their job would be in jeopardy. Anything that shows how that person is not needed elicits a strong response, and anything that doesn't empower the brain encounters a very strong pull back to itself.

There are nine categories that shape our thinking, and nine corresponding words I will use to describe those nine functionalities of our brain. Clearly defining what these nine usages are, will leave us no place else left to go but to an experience beyond them. Beware of the extreme energy field that wants to pull everything into one or more of these nine categories. Without awareness of it, you become the pull, and the categorical references it uses to trick you back into its domain. Word usages demand attention to themselves even more so when you arrive at the place beyond them. The brain gets very sneaky as it seamlessly tries to rationalize its functioning by taking your wisdom beyond it, and baiting you back into using one of the nine categories it uses through one justifier or another. Watch it happen without becoming it. Stay in the place above it, in wisdom, in the watchful place, as a seer, in the splendor of "mind" beyond the pull of words and the categories they represent.

I use the acronym "SEER TRAPS" to remember the nine characteristics that words embrace. This awareness, of what words are truly limited to, more greatly allows us to recognize and embellish experiences beyond their limitations. Words keep us trapped in the brain, but seeing their exclusivity will enable our higher mind and our metaphysical powers to be better realized. Below are the nine descriptive word applications we force our experiences into:

<u>S</u>ituation
<u>E</u>xistence
<u>E</u>stablished Amount
<u>R</u>ank
<u>T</u>ime
<u>R</u>elation
<u>A</u>ctivity
<u>P</u>lace
<u>S</u>ubstance

Above are the traps that are used as the catchall describers that wait to be applied to sum up every experience in life. Awareness of what this brain-machine does, frees us up to all that it doesn't wrap around. Let's expound a little on each of these viewpoints that all our experiences are collapsed into with such enormous force:

The nine brain-machine functions are remembered using the acronym "SEER TRAPS" and begins with the feature using the description of thought in the word named "<u>S</u>ituation". "S" is for "Situation" and in using this descriptive word, the machine-like brain function is referencing an event. It's also applied when we are either immersed in or mentally leaving a current happening in a way to narrate the events of the past, present, or future. This is the first of nine brain functions addressed. A viewpoint about a situation, which occurs in the past, present, or future, tends to be the assessment most strongly demanded upon by the brain. There is a tendency to believe we are either the results of a past situation, the effect of a present situation, or about to be the effect of a situation we're getting into in the near or distant future.

In fact, we aren't any of these. We are of an essence far greater than any situation or its results could ever be. Yet, as long as the "situation" defines us, the brain and its usage can become what you believe completely defines you. Yes, I know our situation is important. We have to take care of this, and then of course we have to take care of that, but if life is just being what our situation is, was, or will be, then we are missing what experiencing life truly is. We are beyond what is every so-called "situation".

The second letter of our "SEER TRAPS" brain awareness acronym is the letter "E". "E" stands for "Existence", which is the state something or someone is in. Water could be running in a stream or frozen ice. People can be in different states of existence also. People can be sick, unhappy, paralyzed, gleeful, or dead. The mental narrative, which acts as an assessment of our "existence", strongly pulls us back into our brain. We tell ourselves and others this story which we decide is our existence.

The second "E" in "SEER TRAPS" is "Established Quantity". The "Established quantity" is the number assigned to the amount of people, places or things. This characteristic, feature, or facet of the brain instrument being applied establishes a value system where people and things are defined within that system. This applies to all systems around the world. The different places it happens, the various number systems used, and the language used directs human beings in similar ways. The human brain is applying these nine descriptive tools and establishing a definitive way to label things. This specific application is leaned on as one of the great categorical traps of the human brain. Somehow something is always not enough or too much because of the idea of "Established Quantity".

Even when we attempt to reveal and prevent its strong tendencies to define things only within "quantity" itself, it weaves its way back in by attaching itself to you with a very strong pull. The pull is reiterating how any movement away from it, won't yield you as much of a respect to the almighty "Established Quantity" of something. So we stay trapped in this function of brain called "Established Quantity" because within its value system, we feel unproductive unless we stay under the umbrella of its pull. Thus we are judging the departure and freedom of it by applying it, and because of this it's one of the hardest features of the human brain to break free of.

The first "R" in "SEER TRAPS" is "Rank". "Rank" is the grade given within a system of valuing. Something or someone is higher or lower because of a rank. It's a category, and with it comes some of the worst disasters in the history of the human species. "Rank" creates a blind faith approach to what has to be served. "Rank" has destroyed millions of people because those with the highest "Rank" had a power that was unchallenged. Insanity, atrocities, abuse, torture, and freewheeling power hungry people have destroyed masses because of illogical submission to their label under the "Rank" feature of the human brain.

The "T" in "SEER TRAPS" is "Time", and "Time" is referring to clock-time. I am not referring to a medium of time as a continuum or dimension, such as space/time, but as a unit of measurement that is consciously, and oftentimes unconsciously, coming into play structurally and specifically. It's referring to the second, minute, hour, day, week, month and year. It is a created function of a uniform reference to what ends up being the movement of things within a timeframe. We refer to it constantly and never seem to be at peace because something is supposed to take place that hasn't in a given period of time. It is the imagined period, in a number of days, weeks, months and years, we think we will live, and it's an approach we apply to everything because of that mental framework.

"Time" is damaging because it hangs over us as the constant reminder that something could be accomplished that is better than what has been accomplished. It compares, degrades, diminishes, and measures things in a way that acts against us. When we were young we felt like we weren't good until we got older, and then got older and wished we were young again. Time tells us something is not right with every area of our life until we run out of time.

The first "R" in the acronym "SEER TRAPS" is "Rank" but the second "R" in "SEER TRAPS" is "Relation", and "Relation" is a position referenced where one person, place or thing is compared to another person, place, or thing. So although "Rank" can be a relation, "Relation" doesn't have to be a "Rank". The reason why "Rank" is separated as a function of brain when it is a type of "Relation" is because within this "Relation", classifications pervade society and take on a meaning and domination that the brain isolates. "Rank" is one of the nine brain tools and is more than just a type of "Relation". Rank is what makes up the hierarchy and power prevalent in every group and therefore has a strong effect on us.

It might be "Relation" that is at the very reason why we are here in the first place. We may be life realizing itself through its relationship with everything else. We may be love actualized through a crystallizing process that would have to include a spectrum of opposites for it to be realized. "Relation" lets us know what up is and what down is, what happy is and what sad is, and the image of "Relation" is what is consciously and unconsciously being created constantly to determine what we believe is going on. We break up to make up and vice versa. Ultimately, we are defining who we are because of how we are viewing our "Relation" to what we decided matters. "Relation" is asking the thief to guard the safe because the parameters with which we decide "Relation" are flawed. Cornering ourselves into the parameters of the idea of relation, ignores higher wisdom and the grander experience beyond all so-called "Relation".

The "A" in "SEER TRAPS" stands for the brain tool "**A**ctivity", and is the interaction of one thing with another. This tricky part of "Activity" is it can be seen or unseen. On a molecular level something is always moving.

The "P" in "SEER TRAPS" is for "**P**lace", or the position and location. Even if it's only in our mind, it acts as a placeholder for what we then apply other brain tools to. It's the location where an object or person is either in action or resting. The ocean or a rock being in a place is not negated by the fact that one appears to be moving and one doesn't. "Place" is constantly changing whether it is seen or not. We like to freeze the idea of something in our mind because it lends itself to greater security. The floor certainly looks like it has been in the same place for a long time in my home, but nonetheless, it is constantly moving. Thinking of it as moving is less secure than not. Freezing the idea of a "Place" something is in makes everything we do after that a lot easier.

The second "S" in "SEER TRAPS" is for "**S**ubstance", and it is part of what makes up a larger whole. It's an ingredient or sub-particle to the stance of another. When we speak of something that is not part of something else we fall short. Speaking of oneness or the totality without it belonging to something else forces the brain into not subdividing and that is something that it's not comfortable with. This is why the totality, viewed as one whole, without looking for something or someone else that is responsible, becomes almost impossible on the level of brain.

Brain is a power tool. If you need it, go get it, turn it on, use it, and then put it back. If you forget it's still with you, and don't forget to shut it off, it can and will use the better part of you. It will take the image of you, and throw it in each of these nine trappings, making your very idea of yourself one that is categorized and discounted to the point of feeling meaningless. This is what our brain-machine will do if we let it go on automatic without controlling it or seeing it from a more aware state.

We take great comfort from our thoughts as they console every fear, mistake, guilt, or lazy path taken. Many things show us that we are of an essence far greater, but we default back to our thoughts and internal talk. It seems to take a lot of horrible things in life to force us out of our comfort zone. Our habits shelter us from the undefined awakening. Unless some structure shattering experiences force questioning, the need to look beyond thoughts and words may not be elicited in us.

The best way to keep a delusion in place is to have what analyzes it acting as a delusion as well. One delusion is kept in place by another. That circle could keep going throughout eternity. It's a circle in a circle. The circles, within the thoughts of our brain, are kept there by a language that doesn't allow experiences outside of what it describes. Never forget "SEER TRAPS" and you'll find yourself one with the energy of life.

The unseen depth of us is still prevalent even when we journey away from it, and just because we may have subtly learned to devalue it, doesn't mean it's not being portrayed in other ways. Total reality includes the unseen, so not including it doesn't mean there isn't part of the unseen reality seeping through what is seen. It could be that the structural existence we occupy enjoys a game of denying our spiritual side. Our brain is having trouble with anything it doesn't naturally thrive on. Spiritual embellishment does not float its boat.

Much like our dreams when we are asleep, situations come in the form of analogies attempting to reveal intangible messages. Unfortunately, more often than not we lose our self in the situation and ignore the intangible meaning referenced. Different events, situations, dramas, and conflicts appear to us in ways that help reveal the total truth.

We handle the overwhelming task of our demanding physical body by forcefully dismissing the intangible. Being born and growing up becomes all about what is substantive and recognizable by others. It is far more "secure" to recognize what is a shared tangible reference with others, as well as an easily definable way to represent our self. There's a generally accepted momentum in human habits to gravitate to what is perceptible to the five senses. So, even when we're ready to go beyond the physical, we're conditioned consciously and unconsciously to reaffirm the misperception that we are only what's incarnated. What is measurable and easily shared is chosen over the unseen because the human brain has trouble wrapping around it. Again, it would be like a fish trying to wrap around the ocean.

On a conscious level we oftentimes forget we're not just a tangible body, but it still shows up. We do everything to prove it with concrete answers alone. Since this is partially unconscious, we don't feel quite right, but we don't exactly know why. Since we do balance two dimensions, and since we do have to live in this body, maybe there's a way to see greater application when allowing the embrace of our intangible self. It would make more sense to go that direction if the benefit to us was understood better and made more mainstream. Here are fourteen reasons why we should value our intangible essence:

1.  Greater knowledge of the past and future
2.  Mental Telepathy-An ability to send thoughts to others
3.  More awareness of the thoughts of others nearby
4.  Being able to read the minds of people far away
5.  Heightened awareness of the present moment
6.  Heightened awareness of subtle or hidden things
7.  A more powerful attitude
8.  A more powerful and enduring body
9.  Intuition in spontaneous situations
10. Higher wisdom
11. Faster ability to cut to the heart of a complicated problem
12. A more vibrant aura and charisma
13. An ability to heal yourself and help heal others
14. Control, and a greater knowledge of when to apply the power of extrasensory perceptions (ESP)

Experiencing spiritual essence beyond our five senses will help us be more creative, and more connected to who we are. When we develop the spiritual side of us, amazing strengths are realized. We can gain a greater knowledge and understanding of not only the past, but the future. This is a great asset to have in everyday life. We sense the happening before the event. We can gain insights from these feelings, and sense when to shy away or approach situations, depending on intuitions beyond our five senses.

We can gain greater depth, alertness, awareness, and an eclectic viewpoint of life and the cosmos when we elicit this quality of being.

Spiritual connectedness allows us to gain greater access to our unconscious functioning. As a result we can be less blindsided by the effects of mental tendencies not consciously acknowledged. We can also command a charisma and attract more positive experiences. All these qualities help us become more of what we want in life. Wisdom, of not only our self, but of others is achieved. When we do need to go into a brain dependent situation we find ourselves using it in a more optimum state. We become more efficient in all aspects of life. We use the brain tool rather than it using us without our awareness. Greater connection to our totality would also allow greater flexibility in every situation and a greater mastery over how we experience life.

Other strengths are gained by tapping into these human qualities that await us. We can experience telepathy, whereby thought transmission becomes a very real experience. This power can be used to gain better communication with everyone near and far. Another power gained from embracing these strengths is that we become better healers of our bodies, and because of that we alleviate damage from mental and physical habits. So there are real payoffs when we embrace and give credence to what can't be seen. It's something we should accept rather than give away as if we don't deserve it.

At the end of reading this, one may get what is being said in experience, but lose it when the need for tangibility rears its ugly head. An approach that incorporates the unseen has always been met with many predispositions and great resistance. Fourteen human qualities shouldn't be put on a shelf or dismissed when these very real transmittable enhancements could improve the quality of our life.

We truly can't be honest if we stay bent on believing that we haven't experienced the unseen. We have experienced it in many ways. Sometimes we'll be thinking about another the same time they are thinking about us, and then they call you telling you they felt that. Telepathy can occur through great distances the same way it does with someone right next to you. Unseen powers are always with us, and we have experienced it by feeling another person's presence while having it confirmed that they were feeling our presence as well.

Our body emanates a magnetic field that sends out signals that are so powerful that experiences can happen from the waves themselves. Is this something you haven't noticed? Have you ever thought about something and out of the clear blue sky the person next to you knew what you were thinking about? How much do we have to experience before we accept the fact that in every situation what's unseen is just as important, if not more important, than what's visible? There's a fabric connecting all things, so what's far away is more conquerable than imagined. We see the gravitational pull of planets from great distances taking place and this invisible fabric that unifies everything explains why. We are not excluded from this fabric.

If all our happiness was in the measurable then it wouldn't be part of the very problem that haunts everyone. The devil is in the details and the details are ignored because they seem like they're insignificant. There are imposters that start the masquerade. The little tiny feelings absorbed as if they have no significance are commanding the whole experience.

There's a discomfort communicating with others and within ourselves about the glimpses we get from extrasensory perceptions. We squash the experience, the usage, and the development of these powers because of this discomfort. This is a horrible shame. We are forever frustrated by the incongruence that comes from the duplicity within. What we feel, versus what can be expressed and actualized, hovers around us our whole lives as an identity untapped. We squeeze spiritual powers felt within us into categories that in many ways remove them from us. Through the very process by which we try to more deeply embrace life's meanings, we actually push them further away.

It's not always so obvious why we run into problems, but when we avoid who we ultimately are, which of course includes who we are spiritually, natural energies will eventually reflect this procrastination. We end up attracting or creating events which will reveal suppressed unseen feelings in a more obvious way. It's as if we are trying to hide intangible effects by forcing them away from us when all along natural pressures exist to force them back.

We cannot be the "words" that determine the value and integration of our existence. Again, that's like asking the thief to guard the safe. If you wanted to come from the highest possible wisdom, would you use a tool with an application that didn't allow for it? If we wanted to go beyond the functioning of the human brain, would we then rely upon the very same human brain to do it? How would a higher mind and higher wisdom be realized if we were only duplicating the thief's action to do it?

The hidden trappings are fueled by the language we use. Words are taking away the highest wisdom, the grandest experiences, and the most powerful insights. What would be the greatest trap of all if not words themselves? What would be a way to insure that a delusion was always believed? A second delusion, that was part of the communication about the first delusion, would certainly keep the trap door closed on us. So, every communication that could ever take place would have illusions inherent in words.

There is a way to avoid the continual tendency of the brain to claim itself with each passing word. Run every word, sentence, idea and thought through the "SEER TRAPS" filter. This filter captures the specific functions of words. It reveals the contortions the brain goes through to squeeze every experience into these categories. Brain's systems are dismantled when the spell of thoughts and words are revealed. The brain is attempting complete control of every experience and we are stopping it, and permitting the existence beyond it to be reveled in.

It's a tedious task to keep applying a filter, but applying it connects you to your source. If it's one of the "SEER TRAPS", then it's using a brain function, and that's OK, but without the awareness of it the ability to ever go beyond it will be thwarted. A person would have to take each piece of information and decide whether they have stepped beyond the human brain in that experience or stayed trapped in it. In the beginning it's cumbersome and the brain tries to dissuade it, but after a while it becomes habit and you will laugh at the way it was previously robbing you.

The mere idea of a word as the all embracing security blanket is a farce. Words are only symbols. They aren't the thing we are describing by the enclosure of the mere word. We call something a desk. OK, what is a desk? Well this one is made of wood. OK, what is wood? On a molecular level we barely have a clue what wood atoms are, so how can we know what a desk is?

On a molecular level the desk is more than 90% air and is made up of atoms in motion. Are we in mystery yet? We should be in mystery always. Yet, we are so comfortable with the symbol that we act as if there isn't anything more to be aware of. The all consuming, all securing, all comfortable category of what we can place that thing into consumes its meaning to us. Any experience which comes from words and thoughts communicated internally or externally keep us trapped in our brain. The brain is the machine that creates words. It's a very self-serving machine.

Like all tools, words are best suited for only particular purposes and not all purposes. Instead, there is an unconscious entrapment kept in place by our brain where we treat words as if it they were king. We then sign on to serve them and in turn we change everything to suit them. Rather than using words and thoughts as merely tools, every feeling and experience that doesn't fit into words tends to be discarded or discounted away. We rob ourselves of our greatest essence through the dogmatism of pre-defined symbols called words.

There is an internal assumption that if words don't wrap it up, it isn't worth wrapping up. There is a moving value waiting to be applied to how well something could be wrapped up with words. Words are a product of the brain, and it's determined to keep its shelf space reserved by constantly claiming what it needs it to be thought of as useful by making everything serve its products.

Words bring a sigh of relief. There an anchoring to what otherwise is erroneously perceived as too free-floating and unconnected to be strong. We decide strength comes from what can be defined. Definable is what words do and nothing else. All directions since birth, which rely on words, infer that strength is in our relationship to what is definable and weakness is associated with what is indefinable. This isn't just a little bit misdirected. This is probably the single worst error a human being could ever make. It is the complete opposite of what is the deeper truth.

Once words are uttered the categorical reference is the only thing that the word is actually able to wraparound and all else is not allowed for. We then have trouble stepping out of the umbrella of the reference. This is what we have done our whole lives. A prisoner of words cannot be our fate. They are not working for us. They're an illusion. The system I created for looking at words can allow our spiritual space to flourish without anything undermining it. The see-er sees "SEER TRAPS".

We call something a dollar bill. The dollar bill is supposed to be backed by gold, but it isn't. It's supposed to be a representation of what we economically can do as a country, but it's not. What is a dollar bill if it's not backed by gold and if it's not our total assets divided by all outstanding monies? Is it a symbol? Does anyone truly understand what it is outside of that? Outside of what everyone accepts, or how it compares to any other country's symbol, is it anything? We compare what really isn't anything, to someone else's idea of what really isn't anything in their country's currency. We are in a world of many accepted comparisons, and oftentimes, outside of those comparisons, no inherent value actually exists.

This is hard to believe, and it shatters our foundation a bit, but nonetheless it is true. The dollar bill is a symbol, and it certainly is not a symbol for what we do know. It is a symbol for what we don't know. We are using symbols for many things we don't know, and comparing them to other symbols of things we don't know.

Words are like that. Outside of what everyone seems to accept, they really aren't anything. They only try to facilitate communication like the dollar facilitates trade; yet, in and of themselves they are nothing more than that. Words are symbols for what we don't know, and not for what we do. So if they hold no inherent value then why would we elevate them above what's intangible? Why would we elevate them above spirit, presence, the pulse of life, the formlessness, or the common mystery of everything and everyone? Isn't that the only true "value"?

I would like to have a whole relationship with someone from another country where words aren't possible because we both speak a different language to begin with. I think there would be a greater chance of being truer to our deepest essence that way. More is communicated in silence between people than could ever be communicated using utterances and symbols that act in its place. Our current course without the "SEER TRAPS" application has us using a boat with a hole in it to ride life's waves.

If you got ice cream from an ice cream machine, it wouldn't make the next batch of ice cream better to put the newly produced ice cream back into the machine. Most machines' products are not improved by putting the product it produced back in as an ingredient. It doesn't make it better. That's easy, right? Not so easy. We don't seem to acknowledge this simplicity when it comes to one very fundamental machine called the human brain. We put the word product back in it and the mix ends up destined for skewed outcomes.

The relationship of the final product in an ice cream machine is independent from its production once it is made. The product would not be affecting the ingredients or the machine in the future. This is not the case with the human brain. Once thoughts and words are created they affect the brain-machine and how it performs its processes in the future.

The ingredients the brain uses are experiences, information, references, thoughts and words.

Feelings go to thoughts, and thoughts are made up of words. The words used were previously produced in a prism where the final product was reused. It goes back into the machine as if it was the updated ingredient. So in going back to the ice cream machine's efficiency we see that it's never affected by its final product, and can apply different ingredients every time without having its functioning change with the last product it made. We are not doing that. We have been stuck under the cloud of language for thousands of years. We say we have evolved but I looked at some cultures from thousands of years ago, and outside of a few modern inventions, our ability to coexist is no more developed today than some of them were. In fact, in some cases I see we are even more primitive.

The brain's functioning is affected by different ingredients it uses because they contain the last product that was made. In turn, it becomes dependent on the characteristics of its previous product, which is a thought, as well as the product called "word". All the while what is lost in the use of words is not obvious because of this interdependent relationship in the way we communicate internally and externally. We rely on this circle at the cost of the invisible ingredients in us.

The unmanifested was there before the output, yet the output doesn't allow for its recognition. The new product includes the word description of the previous product, which also didn't allow for it. This is the circular dependency in the relationship between product and machine functioning. Ultimately, our proximity to our truest nature is what determines the greatest strength. We are consciously and unconsciously suppressing our unseen glory by cornering it into these pre-defined paths.

We diminish our power by limiting our definition of self by how we stand in relation to what we created. Our creation of things should not be our master. The most subtle self-created master is language. We treat language as a master rather than an accommodation. Language keeps a stronghold on evolution toward greater wisdom. There is also a tendency to affix feelings to word categories and afterwards that attachment becomes larger than the feeling before it. So, any changes to the previous feeling that was fixated to a category become much harder to change. The perception is that the new assignment of the feeling to this category is larger than the original feeling, and therefore more dominant than any changes needed afterwards to that feeling.

All that was felt before the word was spoken, gets discounted immediately after the word is spoken. There are infinite experiences that take you beyond the human brain. The grandeur of mindfulness then gets replaced by the machine workings of the human brain. We take the sea of spiritual beauty and what doesn't fit into the glass of the human brain is lost. These tendencies keep enlightenment at a distance as if it were an unreachable star constantly taunting us.

The greatest enlightened beings that ever lived shared messages using a medium that inhibited the truest expression of what they were seeking to express. They attempted to share what was huge using what was very small. They tried giving you the world without a way to truly see it. They felt the glory and magnificence flowing through them and they gave you the beach by handing you a grain of sand. They attempted to share the power and splendor of our life force using a medium called language that inherently would always fail to do so. It's the ultimate conundrum and the most disguised saboteur of all time.

Familiar things are being used to describe things that are not familiar and the truth is convoluted as a result. A word describes the nature, the quantity, the quality, and its relationship to other things. They describe the place or location where the object is, and whether it is moving or it is still. They address an object, or person's ability to either move, or not in the future; like a car that is resting in the driveway. We say it's resting because it has an ability to do something other than that. The chair is in the living room rather than resting in the living room. Each word is used to almost instantaneously group it with other things similar to it, or contrast it with something that it isn't. It either is, or isn't. Up isn't down, and down isn't up. It's so basic, but it isn't basic at all when we decide there is no other out for our experiences other than what words describe.

When a situation occurs that nobody would believe because it goes beyond what form-based properties would normally allow for, words attempting to embody it won't take you there. When you saw a baby being born, a perfect sunset, a rainbow, a moment with another where love was shared; can it really be fully described? When you feel spirituality, life's energy, instincts, intuition, and gut feelings that don't have any logical connection to anything else, is this dishonored because words can't embrace it?

If you ever almost died, saw your life pass in front of you, and witnessed the temporariness of your existence through some field of permanence, can any words fully embody that? Were you ever moved by something other than what you initiated, and felt that force running through you as if you were a wire for some grander current? Could words explain that completely without losing one iota of its real experience? As long as we don't specifically point out the misdirection that words are framing, our greatest journeys will elude us.

It is never mentioned to us in our education what we lack as part of our sole dependency on words. Throughout our existence it is never mentioned that language is erroneously forcing how we view life exclusively into words. It is never mentioned how this is to our own detriment. These tendencies are not allowing for what's outside of what words. We may be missing the greatest part of living if we end it there. We created it (language), it didn't create us. But like so many things we create, we tend to become its servant rather than its master. We lose meaning to what was initiated as an accommodation in its origin and gravitate toward serving it instead.

Word symbols act as a separate structure that connects the idea of "me" to them. This then gives me a fake security which acts as a stronghold I'm conditioned to desire. I then mentally connect to it whenever I'm in doubt. Doubt is really in us, of us, and around us every second. We aren't bigger denying mystery. We aren't bigger attaching to something else. We are as big as we can be admitting the mystery we are rooted in. Language acts as an umbrella of protection and security. We believe we know who we are by what's determinable rather than by what's indeterminable.

The magnificence of our spirituality is run through the religious washing machine with all its detergents and as a result we are left with the experience which completely categorizes it, names it, defines it, and in effect washes it out and removes it. It would be like trying to write down in words the feeling you have after making love. Could any words really do it justice? Why even bother? I enable this amazing experience to wash over me instead of trying to understand it. It's as if every cell in my body thanks me while I'm in the experience, and if I try to put it into words, I'll remove it. Why would I do that?

I am encouraging the child in me that feels a truth that is different than what everyone else is accepting. I empower you to overcome those against you regardless of the imposing images portrayed in this movie called "Testing the strength of your will". Go beyond knowledge and let wisdom be you.

Wisdom vs. Knowledge:

Knowledge, pretending to be intelligence, is loud
Wisdom is silent
Knowledge makes right and wrong which separates people and things
Wisdom connects and brings closer
Knowledge elevates and distances
Wisdom is the infinite allowance of itself
Knowledge is supported with structures
Wisdom is the wings to fly
Knowledge binds you to rigid forms
Wisdom is the caring that needs no knowledge
Knowledge is an excuse not to care
Wisdom sees what matters above all knowledge, wisdom sees love
Knowledge gives people the excuse to proactively hurt another
Wisdom doesn't judge and damn
Knowledge takes what is mysterious and pretends it's not
Wisdom revels in the mystery and pretends nothing
Knowledge is used to manipulate, creating rigid values and judgments
Wisdom places love, life and oneness before and after everything
Knowledge decides what something has to be and then decides what it can't be because of that decision
Wisdom watches the bickering, lies, word games, and ego battles and is not part of the debate
Wisdom stands on a mountain of integrity, and nothing is higher
Wisdom sees the trap and doesn't get lost in it
Wisdom puts a smile on your face while emanating from the very light of being
Wisdom realizes that without love, which is the source of everything, all conclusions are only temporary

## IV When All I Needed Was a Ball

It was 1965 and I started getting familiar with the new neighborhood we moved to in the Bronx, New York, but the frequent moving didn't make it easier. Every time I got comfortable with a place, we moved again. I always felt like I was playing life with a short hand, not only because of my broken home, but the lack of familiarity with so many people and things that came with moving had me always being the new kid in town. I was five years old, but I was on my own most of the time. There was loneliness for me because my parents weren't together. I seldom saw my father, and his absence put financial pressure on my mother to work.

My mom and sister were not that nice to me about my love for my dad. I missed him and identified with him as a man. They bashed him, and every time they did, I died inside. They really didn't know how to connect to a young boy, so they didn't. When I did see my dad, I loved him more than anything or anyone. Even though he terrified me as a young child, I felt he was someone that I connected with in many other ways. That kindred feeling I had with him didn't change when he wasn't around. I thought about the things he said a whole lot. I would replay conversations and remember every gesture until I saw him again, and replay that time until the next time. He acted a lot differently when my mom wasn't around. They brought out the ire in each other.

Nothing my mom ever did could come close to replacing my father and his wisdom. Dad and I thought alike, looked alike, spoke alike, and even had many of the same habits. She tried real hard to show her love but a boy's dad is not something that could be replaced by anyone. It's a real shame that parents get so wrapped up in their deal they forget how they felt when they were little. In all sincerity, could anyone ever replace a parent?

Although the marriage contract is with a man and a woman, I feel the marriage contract is only needed because of children. What happened to the contract parents were supposed to have with their children? Isn't that why the vows read "Until death do us part"? It wouldn't be "Until death do us part" if it was only implied to be with the both of them exclusively. People move on to new relationships, but when children are involved, respect and honor between each parent should always prevail. Wasn't that also why it is "For better or worse"? When worse appears, unmarried people readily break up, but when children are involved, finding a way to help the other person becomes even more important because children have to be considered. Even if there is a break-up, the vows of the contract were "Until death do they part", and not until divorce do they part. This is because honor is for always and children are supposed to feel that honor in their families and in turn with themselves.

My mom showed no honor and no respect for my father and what he meant to me. In turn, I had to overcome the feeling of dishonor. Growing up without my dad hurt me more than anyone could see. I was always a little sad and that sadness always stayed with me. Understanding it didn't seem to wash it away. When I got real sad at home and wondered why I couldn't have a dad like the other boys, I would leave the apartment and go looking for people to play with or talk to. Mom was real good with giving me my freedom. She was always more loose with me growing up than she was with my sister. I was always grateful for the freedom. Most of the time she was working anyway, but even when she wasn't, I always had a lot of freedom.

We lived in an apartment on the corner of Eastchester Road and Mace Avenue a good five or six years before moving again. The bad Bronx reputation was way off. I grew up in the Bronx, moved five times there, and they were all solid neighborhoods with good people. When I wanted to go out, I did. If it was real late or near dinner time Mom would want me nearby, but it was more that she could get done with what she needed to do rather than there was something to fear.

I liked the Mace Avenue apartment, because she could see outside the window and watch me across the street. After dinner, even sometimes when it was late, I could go across the street to the brick wall behind the supermarket that faced the window in front of my apartment building. The lights kept it pretty well lit past dark. Sometimes I would just sit there hoping someone would come by. It meant so much to me to somehow not feel so all alone and something saved me from that. It bridged the gap for me. All I needed was a ball.

I would do cartwheels to come up with twenty-nine cents so I could get that coveted pink rubber ball. With that ball my whole world opened up. Every kid, even the older ones, would gather around me like bees to honey once I got that ball. We could play flies are up, stickball, King-Queen, handball, catch, or fast pitching in.

When nobody else was around and it was just me, I would just start hitting the ball against the wall and practice my slice for King-Queen. When it was just me and my friend, we would put a stick in the crack in the sidewalk and take turns trying to hit the stick with that ball. We would create something from nothing with two guys and that ball. All of a sudden a stupid stick became the biggest focus, but hitting it was not as easy as it looked. You could easily try twenty times without hitting It, but once you got into the zone, you could sometimes hit it four or five times in a row. It was as if you could see a line from your hand to the stick. In all the games we played, basketball, baseball, stickball or whatever we made up, sometimes you would just lock in and show signs of greatness. We did it all for fun, but imagining you were a real star or had star potential during those times when you just couldn't miss, was always a great feeling.

Funny, when I had that magical pink ball, it was as though a vibe went out in the whole neighborhood. It was amazing. They could smell it. Mike got a ball. The word would go around. It was as if people knew I got a ball from blocks away. All I would do is just start hitting that ball against the wall and friends, acquaintances, new people in the neighborhood, and even adults would show up and play or watch. In no time there would be three to six people there and we would each be in a concrete square in front of the brick wall playing King-Queen in a line. The one who got the next guy out would move up a spot. The leader in the first box would stay there until someone got him out. He served the ball after a player missed a shot. The player who missed a shot would go to the end of the line.

When Colaccio showed up he would own that first spot for a long time. He had a cutter that was almost impossible to hit. It would hit the wall and squiggle off of it hugging the ground just below what a hand could get under. Kids of all ages, and sometimes even adults, would join in. All separations broke down as we tried to hit Colaccio's almost unhittable cutter. He was the king alright, but we all had a blast.

I was so happy during those games. There wasn't anything better in the whole world. It was spontaneous and carefree. I went from a deep sadness and feeling of loss to a wonderful comradeship. There was fun-filled competitiveness that seemed to bring a joy to everyone playing. I would forget about everything except what I was doing, and for those moments I couldn't be happier.

Sometimes we would play stickball in the same spot instead of the long way down the street, but that would be over very quickly. One of the big guys Ricardo or Colaccio would come by and with one swing of the broom handle we would watch my beautiful new rubber ball sail majestically over my apartment building. I would get mad for as long as I could get away with it, which was right about the time when a look came from one of the big guys to shut my mouth quick or else. I usually got the hint and forgot to be angry about my ball. How angry could I get with someone a foot taller than me and thirty pounds heavier anyway? It was such a thrill to be hanging out with the older guys. These kids were two, three and four years older than me, but all separations disappeared when I had that ball.

Sometimes the ball would bounce off the top of the building and end up, well, just about anywhere. We would look a long time for it together and sometimes we would be happily surprised that some storeowner down the block was holding it. Stories of who got hit or what window it missed came from the storeowner who would smirk and give us some grief as he handed it back. Sometimes a homeowner would be beefing about how it hit them in the head, but they always gave it back asking us to be more careful. They were kids once too and that's how they treated it. So, even the looking was part of the ritual that was shared near my home, when the king of the neighborhood, me, was the one with the bran new ball.

When we couldn't find it, sometimes one of the big kids would throw me a ball the next day or offer to buy me one, but twenty-nine cents was not easy to come by back then. Sometimes I would work five or six hours a day for two or three days. I would go around the neighborhood collecting two-cent returnable bottles until I returned fifteen of them, and that was just enough for another ball. He never charged me tax.

After school we took some chalk, drew a square on the brick side of P.S. 97 that faced the concrete playground, marched off 60 ft. for the pitcher, grabbed a stick that was usually an unscrewed broom handle someone's mom was looking for, and fast pitching-in stickball was created. Boy, we could do just about anything with that ball. We would play all day, five or six different kind of games with that one ball. We used that rubber ball for everything including football, where all the same rules applied, but we used that ball instead, and stoop-ball, where the steps from someone's porch became action-packed entertainment by the points achieved hitting the steps in a particular way. With that ball everything was possible.

There weren't any computers, cell phones, or electronic games. Television only had channels two, four, five, seven, nine and eleven. Channel 13 wasn't even out yet. There were a few shows at certain times we cared about, but everything else kids didn't care so much about watching. I never remember having to compete with TV to hang out with a friend. Television was never a priority over anyone. We enjoyed it, but people always came first. It wasn't even a second thought.

When baseball was on TV I would watch it for a while. Even then there was something beyond face value. I tried to figure out why some teams that apparently seemed to have superior talent man for man, would lose to lesser talented teams which possessed intangible strengths. It seemed to me the intangibles in baseball, like so many things in life, always meant more than the tangibles. The tangibles were just a little easier to talk about.

I would leave home during the game when it got long, and go outside to usually find a bunch of guys sitting on a stoop somewhere listening to the same game on radio. When enough guys gathered, it wasn't long before someone would say, "C'mon let's play it instead. Wouldn't everyone rather be playing instead of just sitting around and listening to it?" Nobody ever argued with that logic and away we would go gather up bats, gloves and balls to make it happen. The extent of our electronic world was minimal, and if I told you we were ten times better off, I guess you wouldn't believe me. Well, not unless you were my age. Then you would know exactly what we loved and exactly what's missing today. I know there are ways to get it back but I think we would first have to get everyone involved to acknowledge there's something missing in the first place.

It seemed children had face-to-face communication down better than adults did. Maybe we were less rushed. We talked more and seemed to build deeper friendships because we shared things in person more. We looked into each other's eyes a little more deeply and we shared things a little longer. There was less dominance of an imaginary ticking clock telling you how fast you were supposed to say something. There weren't any interruptions from anything else, like cell phones, when you spoke either. People who interrupted others while they were speaking were frowned upon. When someone had the floor it meant something. After the mistake was made to disrupt another, a price was paid for the error.

People wouldn't listen to you for a time if you did it. That was the penalty. You would be ignored if you didn't respect another's communication. Some people who kept doing it, weren't listened to at all, and became the one everyone avoided. This is done somewhat today as well, but it's not given the priority it was given then.

Timing in conversation was crucial, and when your timing was off you were the low man on the totem pole until you waited a while and tried again. Some space had to pass first, and waiting was something you now had to do. People started saying something, and once they started they had the floor. After they spoke, people thought about it for a while. There seemed to be one more level where it was verified what was understood before the next exchange took place. After all that happened replies came, and the replies meant a whole lot. The replies weren't empty and weren't just a reflex action. There was less word-banter and more real communication. The communication went a little slower, but it was right. There was no hurry to risk getting it wrong for the sake of speed.

No cell phone, no gadgets, no text message, no computer speed changed the sentiment you exchanged. This condescending attitude showing that what you said was never good enough didn't exist. The next moment wasn't always more important than the current one, and this superior attitude that some tech toy is better than your communication did not pervade existence.

A friend was a friend and you told each other things that nobody else should know. A secret was a secret and no accelerated mass produced communication was going to change that. People seemed a little more down to earth, more real, more straight forward, more caring, more compassionate and more giving. They wouldn't slam a door in your face while their attention was given to something they were holding. There wasn't this inconsiderate approach to all human beings because we had to serve some tech control, or thought of one, that took you out of the moment.

Nothing was a priority over the exchange of one human being to another human being. It was in so many ways what people would call today as not so advanced, and not so productive, but in reality I think it was more productive because the human concern was part of the equation. It was closer in many ways to what life should be like because human compassion was more greatly valued. Ultimately, what really should have a priority over what is the very essence of being human?

We didn't have any money. Mom worked crazy hours just to make ends meet. I would feel bad to ever ask her for anything, so I seldom did. Sometimes I would help the guy in the wheelchair who lived on my floor. Richie was his name. Richie would wheel himself out of his apartment and sit by the window at the end of the hallway. He looked so sad. I wished I could make him walk. People would come up and down the stairs and see him there. He would muster up a greeting, but still always looked sad and angry, so people kept their distance. It struck me that he didn't do anything wrong to be in a wheelchair, and if I was in a wheelchair I would be pretty sad and angry too.

I started talking to him one day, even though my mom told me to keep my distance. I liked him. I didn't have an older man to talk to and I needed that. I talked to him a bunch until I mustered up enough nerve to ask him how it happened. Richie told me it was a car accident. It hurt him to relive it. He told me how it happened and now he was stuck in that chair for the rest of his life. There wasn't any hope of changing it. He just sat there wanting that moment back that he could never get back. He cried and wheeled himself back to his apartment telling me he would talk to me another time. I looked at all the people who had an attitude toward him a little differently including my mom.

I saw him the next day. He was very grateful that I spoke to him and he came right out and said it. He explained to me how most people shied away from talking to him and he complimented me on not being afraid even though I was a little kid. He was the first guy in a wheelchair I ever saw. It made sense that company would be what he wanted. I once said to him that if he wasn't in a wheelchair it wouldn't be any different when we were speaking because I was sitting and talking with him, and so was he. I said, "See, sometimes there's no difference." He came out of his pain and looked at me and asked me to come closer. He hugged me and wiped a tear from his eye. He said I made him happy and told me to go play with my friends because he wanted to be alone to think about what I said.

One day he asked me to do a few things for him and I did. I got him cigarettes and a few other things. Yea, a nine year old kid could buy cigarettes back then. He was happy and he paid me. I would have done it for nothing but he always paid me. Now, I found a way to get the pink rubber ball without having to work so hard. It was great. Sometimes I would go shopping for him across the street at the supermarket. He would give me two bucks for doing that for him and I was king. I would go the candy store and get a vanilla malted or an egg cream, a pack of baseball cards, and of course, a new ball.

It was an incredible thrill to earn money and be able to get what I wanted. I would do it completely alone without any fear or anyone on my back. My mom was usually at work or busy with something, and my dad wasn't around until Saturday so I was on my own a lot. I would come up with all sorts of ways to get that twenty-nine cents but that was the best one. I got it because I cared about someone who looked scary to everyone else but me. I learned a lot talking to that man. Richie was a good man who caught a bad break. He gave me a little more confidence about myself. I sure needed that.

When my mother found out I was helping Richie she put a stop to the whole thing. She felt like he would feel entitled to other things involving her because he helped me. So many guys tried to get things from her over the years that she thought everyone was working an angle. I think he must have made a pass at her, or at least she pretended he did. She was attractive but maybe she was just weary of anything good that ever came my way. She didn't trust it and made me feel wrong about the whole thing.

The next day when I saw Richie he told me my mom didn't want him talking to me anymore. I apologized on her behalf. We both felt bad. She not only talked to Ritchie, but also got the superintendant of the building to stop him from sitting in the hallway at the window claiming he posed a threat to me every time I went up and down the stairs. Well, that killed my first real job. This wasn't the first time my mom kabashed what was good in my life and it certainly wouldn't be the last. She did things out of love that oftentimes ended up so much more damaging to me than if she just left it alone.

I remember one day I brought home a friend of mine from school who was black. I didn't even think about it one way or the other. We had a great time in school, at his house, and now we had a great time playing at my home also. I never told my mom about any of it because I didn't want it to change. We got along so well, but everything good always seemed to always be taken away.

A neighbor told my mom that I had a black person over after school, so she made me walk all the way over to his house and tell him that he wasn't allowed to come to my home any more. I remember every step of that walk and it was more than a mile away. I just didn't understand how human beings could be so cruel. All the way there I was wondering how I could possibly do such a horrible thing. How was I going to say it?

When I got to his house his mom answered the door. She saw the look on my face and that told it all. She said, "Your mom sent you, right?" I said, "Yea." She said, "It was about Washington coming over, right?" I nodded yes. She asked knowingly, "She was mad, right?" I said, "I'm sorry, my mom doesn't want Washington coming over any more, but, it's not how I feel." She said despicably, "O.K. I'll tell him", and she slammed the door on me. I cried a river all the way home. I never looked at my mom the same way ever again. I saw the ugliness in her that discriminated and I hated it. I saw Washington the next day and apologized. He said it happened to him once before. I told him that I thought it was wrong and he thanked me for feeling that way.

I had another black friend who I only saw in school. Tom was his name, and he found out about the incident and approached me with Washington by his side. I also had to tell him I didn't feel as my mother did but he wasn't as nice. He said you could have stood up against it. You didn't have to follow it. I thought about it, went home, got into a big argument with my mother about it and then got a beating for challenging her on it. That was the corporeal world. The mental world was very different. I believed what I believed.

I grew up when there was a lot of race riots and problems about busing and desegregation. One message I incorporated throughout my whole childhood was that I was not going to join any action against any other kind of people who seemed to appear different. My best friend soon after that was a kid who came from another country, who looked different and talked different. He was from the Dominican Republic. His skin was lighter than most from there so my mom let me play with him. He was one of my best friends for years. I'm still in touch with him more than forty years later. I remember thinking if he was simply one of the people from the Dominican Republic that had darker skin, I wouldn't have been able to have him as a friend. I also remember thinking how stupid and mean adults were for drawing lines of hate.

I later confirmed with others that my mom wasn't the only one doing it. All the kids agreed they didn't care much about what color people were, but their parents were real adamant about keeping distance from them, and because of that they had to listen or get hit. Some admitted they hid it from their parents and kept it away from home. It was alright to be friends in school but they couldn't be friends away from school. I felt I was in that camp, but I tempered communication in school a bit as well because I certainly didn't need any more headaches in my life.

Well, since mom killed my first job when she goofed up my connection with Richie, the guy in the wheelchair, I had to come up with another plan to make money. I went all over the neighborhood asking other people if I could help them out one way or the other. Some older people needed things done and I would do it for them and get paid for it. They were never as reliable or as generous as my friend in the wheelchair, so I still had to find other ways.

The supermarket across the street from me oftentimes had carts that weren't returned by customers. They would end up all around the neighborhood so I would return them. I would also bring back the ones scattered all over the parking lot. The manager would throw me a few bucks now and then, but he didn't want to get in trouble for paying a minor to work for him. When he got in trouble for paying me he acted as if he never wanted the help, and he complained to my mom that I was haunting him. Once again I had to find another way. I caught a tongue lashing for bringing attention to the family.

She never wanted to hear anything from anyone about anything so I always did my best to stay out of trouble. Heck, I was just trying to make some money. She didn't get as mad this time and it did dawn on her that I needed money sometimes and wasn't asking her for it. She was blown away that I took it upon myself to make money in all these different ways. She certainly didn't have extra to give me those days.

Getting the money to get that pink rubber ball was very important to me. Even the candy store owner, Vinny, knew what it meant to me when he sold it to me. He cared about me and knew I was on cloud nine when he took my twenty-nine cents for that beautiful, pink, perfectly inflated rubber dream ball. He would always say, "Have a great time, and try not to lose it so quickly this time." He would hold it up while selling it to me and remind me to be careful. Vinny also counseled me against being so generous with people who weren't considerate with it. He truly cared more about me preserving what I had worked so hard for, than making another profit on that twenty-nine cent ball. It was a little thing but it meant a whole lot back then.

I would sit in that candy store a good long time on many occasions over the years growing up. I missed my father all the time and felt much different than the rest of the guys. There were still waters resting in me that looked at life from a wiser stance because of so much turmoil around me so early on in life. During ages six, seven, eight, nine and ten you could find me in that wonderful little store, which seemed huge to me, with all the toys, games, gadgets, baseball cards, and candy. The wonderful man behind the counter represented consistency for me when there wasn't any. I quietly leaned on him without him realizing it.

When I returned enough bottles, found pay day on some job I dug up, or when Mom or Dad threw me a few bucks, that candy store was my haven. I loved going in there to eat a hamburger on a big roll with a vanilla malted. Vinny would always come over and spend time with me when I wanted him to, and always knew not to when I was too upset. My mom took up with some unsavory characters back then that made my life miserable.

Vinny was very perceptive, but never let on that he was. He looked at me and wondered how I could be so alone all the time. Maybe I enjoyed that candy store more than most because it was more than just a bunch of things and a friendly face to me. It was my escape from everything that had tension associated with it. I had too much stress surrounding me far too soon in my life and this was therapy for me in a way.

I thought I was alone with my private feelings about how much it helped me to lose myself in there, but it seemed like the Vinny knew I felt this way. He was a kind, middle-aged man, balding with gray hair and warm blue eyes. He would hear the scuttlebutt in the neighborhood, and found out enough about my situation to know it meant a whole lot to me to find peace in his wonderful little store just around the block from where I lived. Everyone talked and cared about the next person, so he heard there were troubles in my home even though he never exactly said it. He would certainly look out for me if anyone ever approached me in that store.

Here I was this little kid, sitting by myself eating a hamburger, and loving the big Bronx bread roll it was on while washing it down with my drink/desert, which was a big metal tin filled with vanilla malted. That tin would fill three and half coke glasses and I would savor every sip like it was a dream come true. He would put extra vanilla syrup in it just for me. People would come in and buy the newspaper, have coffee and a roll, have an egg cream or malted, and they would look at me and then look around the rest of the store to see what adult was with me. They thought it curious that there was this nine year old kid sitting there like he was fifty having a meal all by himself. Vinny always told them, "It's OK, he knows me, he's with me." He had me covered and he had my mom covered too. I guess she could have gotten in some trouble for always leaving a kid alone. Those days were different though. They were very different.

To tell you the truth, I never thought it was bad that I was on my own. I just thought it was unjustifiably lonely because I missed a parent, and that loneliness felt like I was playing five-card-stud with only four cards. Somehow I tried to win and get a better hand than everyone else anyway by being smarter. I just hid the fact that I believed I had only four cards.

I wasn't lonely when I was in that store though. Vinny was a cool guy. He walked with a kind integrity that emanated strength. It wasn't anything you would ever challenge. When he filled that metal container with vanilla malted he knew it was a joy for me to be there with him as more than just as a seller of goods. He knew I savored the moment so much because I lacked other things in my life. He knew that some of it was making up for a whole bunch more hurt than any kid my age should have had to deal with. He made it real pleasurable for me to be there. He had a type of kindness that meant more than he could ever know.

Sometimes I would just go there and look at all the new gadgets and games. He had all the things I loved. He had magnets, puzzles, Scrabble, and Monopoly. He would never bother me while I took a long time looking. Most of the time I didn't buy anything, but he let me look anyway. It gave me a hope to try to get something in the future when my current moment was sometimes so sad that any thoughts away from it were desperately welcomed.

I remember when I started collecting coins and would get two quarters together so he could give me a roll of pennies that I could scan for good ones. I would go through them one by one looking for key dates and mint marks, and then I would categorize them into decades and label them in packages. He always knew what I was doing and he never scanned them first. He would give them to me as he got them from the bank and always told me that he hoped I found some good ones. As I left the store he always wished me good luck. He was just genuinely kind.

One time he gave me change for a candy bar I bought and in the change was a penny worth one hundred twenty-five dollars. It was a 1909 VDB. I later told him about it and he was shocked, but he never stopped giving me the un-scanned roll, and never regretted letting the hundred twenty-five dollar penny slip by him. He even joked about it one day after I told him I landed a big one. "Should I be looking at these more closely?" he asked. Then he looked at me and said "No, I'll let you always be the one to find the good ones, OK?". He shook my hand and gave me another roll.

I remember when my mom took up with a man who was a complete jerk and it made things even worse than they were before, so I did something stupid. I was feeling so sad I just wanted to get over on something because everything seemed to be getting over on me. I took a candy bar from the front counter when he had his back turned and left. I felt so guilty it was eating me up alive. I went back a few days later, after I returned enough bottles, and left money on the counter for what two candy bars cost. I started walking away, but before I could leave the store he asked me what the money was for, and I told him the truth. Vinny got as mad at me as I ever saw him and gave me half the money back, and made me promise never to do it again.

At that very moment I felt like he did exactly what my dad would have done if he was around. I was disciplined for it and I deserved it. I felt like someone cared about me, truly cared, because he gave me back the extra money I put there. He didn't take the extra amount I gave him, and he made his point firmly but didn't want to take advantage of my guilt about it. Someone walked in during that moment who wanted to know what was up, but he said it was between him and me. He could have embarrassed me further by sharing it with another person, who undoubtedly would have told another, but he never disappointed me and he never let me down even during my worst times.

Everyone in the neighborhood had a smile for Vinny the candy store man. I recently frequented places in my adult life that I went to over the last twenty years and they don't give a hoot about me, my family or anyone. It's always this undercurrent of their money pressures, greed, and fears of thievery commanding the moment. I feel like the unspoken words are "Give me the money and let me see what I made on you". I find that compassion, caring, consideration, and building a relationship means so much less now.

I miss it so much I can't even tell you. It has no words that can describe it. It's simply lost in most parts and it's an endangered part of human exchange in others. Young folks today don't even know what you're talking about when you reference it. They only know they wish it all felt better, but they don't know exactly what would make it better because they don't have the same reference older people do and what it was like previously. They feel like something is lacking but without the reference, they could only feel bad inside for wanting something that doesn't seem to exist currently. I'm only grateful I enjoyed it while it still existed. I certainly would like to apologize to anyone under thirty years old on behalf of what the adults did. We didn't prevent trends which deteriorate human compassion. Technology created a coldhearted world and that's what we left you. You won't ever know the way it truly should be, and you certainly won't ever know the way it truly was.

I noticed I was a tad insecure without this ball growing up those years. I felt like I had to make up for being new to the neighborhood, or having one parent, or being half Italian and half Jewish, or being too this or too that. When I had to horn in on other people's action with their ball I was a little shy about that.

The first devastation of my dad getting thrown out stayed with me and I felt shorthanded after that. It hurt even more than it should have that we moved so much because my friends became the focus when my dad was no longer around, and then my friends would be gone soon after I got a little comfortable with them. My sister was mean and my mother was either working, getting mistreated by some man, or talking to her friends. She was either on the phone or sitting at the kitchen table with company. She was either out on a date, in with a date, or too tired to deal with anything.

When I went out to play and found someone else with a ball, they always seemed a little bit stingier with their ball than I was with mine. I was just so happy to have people hanging around me, so I wasn't too anal about my ball when I got it. Some kids took advantage of that with the careless way they treated my precious dream ball. I remember one kid wanted to show everyone how high he could throw it and simply took the ball, threw it on top of the school roof, and left. He was too big to fight, but me, Angelo, and Carlos sure wanted to. We were all set to play for a good long while and we didn't see the sense in such an inconsiderate act.

We could have taken him if all three of us ganged up on him but that was against street code. It was one-on-one or nothing. It was also against street code for a teenager to pick on a kid so when the news of that went around this showoff would get his. We would just wait for the right big guy to tell and he would avenge our precious ball and belittle this bully for showing off. There was a street law and there wasn't any running from it. It would find anyone who violated it sooner or later. We knew this guy was a fool and we were all confident that this was not the end of it. Things had a way of coming back to the offender and it did so worse than on an even basis because the person who initiated the harm made two errors. He violated a person's space and he committed a crime, so one-for-one was not a strong enough penalty. Forget "An eye for an eye". It was more like your hand for a finger. If you started it, there was a price for starting it and that went far above and beyond the damage besides that. You would be labeled and that label never left you. You would be nicknamed because of it and that name stayed with you forever.

If it was truth, and that truth was verified, you were stuck with the blame. It wasn't long before every store owner, every parent, every kid and every old-timer knew about it. People were closer so when something happened it spread. It became the news of the street. You could walk into the local candy store and old men would be talking about it over coffee.

It was so amazing how what you did became more important than any world event. World events were second to what that bully did to Angelo and me. They could have a hand in the bully's retribution, but not in the Vietnam War. There was nowhere to run with street code. You shot straight or the wrath of the whole neighborhood would follow you until you did. I liked it more than I ever knew at the time. I wish it was more like that now. The routine that has incorporated a lack of compassion and connection to each other has almost made people feel too intrusive to give even the slightest hoot about anyone else.

Funny how kids I hung around with when I was young later became something amazing. My best friend became a top surgeon written up in medical journals making all sorts of discoveries, and my second best friend became a very successful lawyer winning some landmark cases. In fifth grade the three of us swept all the awards during graduation. We were three peas in a pod. The graduation song was "The Impossible Dream", and dream we did. At that very moment nothing was impossible. We had the world on a string. We all went out after graduation to celebrate at the local pizzeria on Eastchester Road. We felt recognized for being smart kids, and it was probably the first time we got a pat on the back for it from anyone besides our parents.

Looking back on it, I wonder what it would have been like if we all knew that we were going to be alright later on. Maybe the feelings that came from not knowing is what made it all work back then. I don't see a lot of these guys that much today. Funny though, once we had a reunion and it was like we were thirty years younger and hanging out all over again. We all acted the same way. The same kind of jokes, the same chemistry, and the same connection that existed when we were eleven, existed when were forty-one. We all shook our heads in amazement that it could still be like that.

Life got so complicated since then, but the simple things lasting forever are all sorts of special. We said good-bye and hugged each other knowing it was special back then. We came away with a respect for the little kid in all of us even more because of it. We went back to our busy lives honoring a little more of what we believed back then, because it was still something we would have believed in today. It was a breath of fresh air for us to admit we still had the kid in us from thirty years earlier, thirty years earlier when all I needed was a rubber ball.

# V Timeless

I thought my life was a sequence of things that had a progression of values which accompanied them as time went on. I later realized the sequence only exists to accommodate the body and the way the brain digests information. This has little to do with accurately prioritizing all messages from all ages. Physically, we can't experience everything all at once so the only way left is sequentially. To believe there is a value given to an event at age five that is less than an event at age forty is a big mistake. Each event is as important as the other. When relative time changes the way we receive messages the truest meaning is skewed. Time is our construct, and when it frames the way we experience things, it takes away many of the gifts we would enjoy.

If there was one question that could take away beauty every time it entered your life, what would that question be? It would be, "Why didn't this happen sooner?" This question destroys everything good that can ever be experienced. When the toil is gone and the rewards come, we cushion them for fear of more toil, and then all that's left is struggle. How much pleasure do we allow ourselves to revel in before we let the idea of too much time, or not enough time, take it all away?

Many of the things that make us feel bad involve time and an expectation of what should have occurred in that time. The measurement of what took place in a given time and whether it was good enough or not. We are beings that digest things in a sequential way, although, the times of our life and the meanings of certain things are not necessarily time significant. I'm too old for this or I wasn't old enough for that. What we may experience at age five could be a lesson we are reminded of at age eighty-five. One time was no more significant than another in the message, only in the way we viewed our relative time to the message.

Each moment at each age is as important as another where sequence is more a delusion. Every experience is a message and all a way of showing us life. Destiny is what comes with integrity and awareness. Whether we are ages one, five, fifty, or fifteen it doesn't matter. It's all love and life realizing itself through the events of our life posing opposites that push us to shed judgments, and help us touch our existence. Life, death, calendars, clocks, and our second-by-second determination of what's "good enough", is an illusion. If you took everything that measured the passing of time and removed it, what would that state be?

The MOMENT

Let us dance, sing, love and laugh

Rejoice and allow for the happiness of those around us

Let your own essence of love shine through

Enjoy it without requiring it from another

Relish the laughter and let others revel in theirs

Always make people feel enough and always make yourself feel like you're enough

Cast no stones but be the strongest shield to all stones thrown

Don't elevate through the damnation of anything or anyone

You are already as elevated as possible

Nothing is bigger than you are

Be still and relish in the divinity of everything

Realize drastic occurrences that seem to be happening may be more to crystallize the opposite

Resist the temptation to believe in a conclusion without a greater feel for what allowed for the happening in the first place

Savor life and the subtle touches of people and things

Let it drench over you

You will never be younger than you are right now

Enjoy this moment

This is not a trial run for what life will be

This moment is your life

Life is in this moment and in this moment love's proving grounds come in and out of play. Experiences illustrate all the possibilities where love is tested and crystallizes it for us to further see what the source of life and love is. I use "love" and "life" synonymously, as without life there is no love, and without love there is no life. Love is more than the personalized view of love. The energy of love is one with our life and life source. What else would love's proving grounds be if not the full spectrum from hate to loving rapture? Hate robs life and love gives it. What else would a spectrum have to contain to truly show all of what love is, if not the horrors, pain, loss, and struggle?

What better way to realize it than to forget it, and then relearn it again and again with events, players, turmoil, dramas, agonies, defeats, gains and losses? Different days in different ways, a love of unbelievable magnitude is sustained by the spectrum of opposites. In variances and degrees love is reflected in life forcing its way through the filters of the human brain. Love is a force beyond even what the word "love" can describe. Love touches us very deeply within and surrounds us always.

And The Wheel Turns

The wheel turns with each opposite testing all that is, as compared to what was and from here we decide what we think is real
Looking to love someone as the exception to this wheel of life
Seeking an embrace that is beyond the wheel and its impending opposites
Hoping for something that doesn't take part in the wheel that turns
There must be that love I could get from another person or situation
And once again we embrace a prop as the wheel turns and love eventually sees hate looking at it
One exception we tried to sneak in
I am the lover that can contain a separate love
I am the husband, wife, boyfriend, girl friend, fling or other that can hold it as mine
You are the job, career, and identity that can be made the bigger love
I know a love has to be the almighty justifier for what I want to make real and exclusive of life's wheel
Can I let a separate love be my outlet for so many of life's frustrations?

Can I contain it, own it, trap it, possess it, secure it and let it act as a blanket against all else?

And the wheel clearly turns again reminding us that love is where we emanate from to begin with and not what we can trap as ours alone

It wraps around us and we can't wrap around it

So, we take it personally when it fails to be trapped

Show me the wheel of love that never sees its opposite and I will show what is already within you

I will show you a person who allows the experience of spirit, and who allows love without the need to get it from another

And the person who experiences it as shared and not derived

Where we aren't acting in division of a love that is truly shared by all

Where we are receiving with each other acting in completeness and in recognition of the greatest love to revel in and not possess

Allow its possession of you for it already is you, in you, and about you

But the body says love is outside, because that's what the body needs to claim itself as the imposter of you

Even though the unmanifested is represented in and of what's manifested, the physical representation alone never really allows the total experience our incomparable and unseen source is emanating

Love is one with the universe before we decide to name it or separate it in an attempt to possess it

It's one with the miraculous source and energy of existence itself

As if trying to contain the ocean in a glass only to see its inability to contain it fail

As if we were left holding the broken pieces as what truth was supposed to mean with the pieces of glass hurting like our broken hearts

A love that's not the exception we try to sneak in, but an uncontainable, indefinable, infinite, and all allowing love where outside need is not trying to replace what is our source, our light, and our very being

An ever present light that simply is us already

The love from which we emanate has no axis to turn on, for it is before and after all axes

All our frustrations with relationships, loving another, and all hurt surrounding it is simply the totality of love being realized

We are love realizing itself, through the frustrations of life's wheel

Allow it to be the directive toward the greater, rather than being lost in its toils

As physical love approximates the space of our source, let us not forget we are already it before and after all our trials and tribulations with one physical and emotional relationship after the next

Show me a person who realizes this and allows the experiences of this

and I will show you a person who knows what love is
And I will show you a person who feels the spirit within, around, and residing in all things and all people, and not out there, but in here—in me---and in you
And I will show you a person who is truly spiritual

WHAT IS LOVE, WHERE IS LOVE, YOU ARE LOVE, LOVE IS YOU.

Are you looking for yourself in your relationship with others? Are you looking to derive some sense of physical connection to actualize an immense intangible connection? Do you always want others to be different than what they are? Are relationships and friendships becoming hardships? Is there no comfort in embracing the intangible, or rather letting it embrace you, when afterwards you look around and you are all alone doing it? Is there nobody you can share your rarefied journey with? Does it become so lonely that you would rather be with people in disconnected tendencies than without them in connected tendencies?

People want to feel empowered with the decisions they made so if you speak in a way that dismantles their structures they grow to resent it. Going through an enlightened period doesn't mean everyone is going to applaud your revelations. You may find the opposite.

How am I finding you when you read this? If you are a little depressed about anything focus on something small and beautiful and make it bigger and bigger and bigger until it takes up all your thinking, and leaves no room for anything else. Move what you "C" and take what's reactive and turn it into what's creative. If we were the grandest of the grandest force in the cosmos as part of our very essence how long could anyone be satisfied with deciding that they are really this or they are really that? If you ever cared so much about something or someone that you lost your sense of completeness without it, it wouldn't be long before that worked against you. Not because of bad luck, but because trying to operate out of the law of physics won't work. You are already complete and one with everything so to make anything better or bigger is a raft with a hole in it.

Is there anyone who doesn't carry with them disappointment from expectations unfulfilled by another? A parent, a brother or sister, a boyfriend, girlfriend, husband, children, a wife, or even an employer may have disappointed you. Is there anyone who isn't sad just a little bit from someone who could have acted differently, should have said something they didn't, said something they shouldn't have, and maybe still won't act in a particular way? We carry with us a heavy burden of disappointment in other people. It seems when push came to shove with so many people they didn't go the extra yard, give the extra effort, or take the better, although sometimes harder and higher road, in reference to you. Empowering others may increase them empowering you but it won't exclude a lifetime of people generally disappointing you.

The reason is not so much a statement about you, or something that is your deficiency. The reason is the people you know are merely a small sampling of society. Parents, brothers, sister, friends, everyone you know is a sampling of what society has cultivated. Its family habits, traditions, religions, judgments, damnations, loss of compassions, loss of loves, and lack of empathy all tend to be representative of human traits driven by clinging fears. Fear is what we tend to default to first. It's also something we try to hide from others. Hidden fears look like affronts to people when they are shared, so most of the time people don't share their fears. We even fear the way our fears will be received if we talk about them. Leonardo da Vinci said, "Fear is that which comes first", and I believe it arrives in the middle and end too.

It can't be assumed that everyone is completely conscious when each person's unconscious mind is playing a big part. This is not something that is debatable. It is simply a fact. Each person has parts of themselves that makes them a stranger to even themselves. So, why would it surprise us when they become a stranger to us? If every person has parts of them that make them a bit of a stranger to themselves, then how could we expect anything from anyone consistently? They can't even expect their allegiance to their own conscious state consistently.

Funny though, after they hurt us we walk around as if something was wrong with us for having to endure the suffering of it. In a way, that too perpetuates what will hurt another human being because that breeds unconscious behavior in us. Perceived pain from it leaves us open to even more ingredients of it, and it shortens our fuse to extend extra human compassion when called for with others who *are* conscious. A needy person we meet will then suffer from the expectations unfulfilled from us. They too will then walk around with that same look like we had, like people owed them more than what they got. Now you're the one that owed someone more than what they got.

Once you believe something, it's as if you just placed a dot on the circumference of a circle. It's a circle of opposing energies, so once a point is chosen its approximate opposite has to be located. We are not what we determine as a defined point or even what that defined point isn't, but rather the middle of the circle, using the points as an accommodation, and certainly not using them as a self-image or definition. So if you deeply believe in the love of something or someone without awareness of such opposing energies inherent there may be a big problem waiting.

Any love we lose our self to, except what's already contained in our own essence, inherently contains opposing energy. Any plotted point of energy given away on life's wheel would have hate waiting just around the corner. It's an illusion to make anything or anyone bigger than you so the wheel will turn and it will turn harder because of the conviction without awareness that accompanied it. It's a natural tendency to want to hold on to what feels secure with a desire for something not to change in its comfort. It's an image that is created because it feels insecure not to, but there is no hiding from the wheel of opposites, and to believe any position can exist without its opposing forces present is a delusion.

It's not a little thing because no one is void of hurts that came from this habit. It will continue to come from this habit throughout life. It's as if we are looking to separate from a whole with a belief that seeks to control and determine a separate path from natural energies. When a path seeks to name and define who we are by deciding what someone else is, we are opposing the life energy that brought us here in the first place. Once you lose yourself to a concept or idea about who you are, or who someone else is, slowly but surely there will be life events that stop that mental path from continuing.

All things along the circumference allow for the nothing in the middle, or rather, the all-allowing everything in the middle. In the apparent nothingness is all of life's energy. This is where we naturally reside. In the life force of the space in the middle is where creativity and our life's force rests. Once we select a point on the circumference as an identity defined and a position decided as bigger than our life force, we are exchanging the most powerful point for an energy seeking its opposite. Once we exchange our life force for what becomes a new definition of self, we become part of the periphery of the wheel in motion and away from the mindfulness of the middle.

These things we do are an accommodation and ultimately fail as a replacement for our identity. It's the difference between being one with life's energy and separating from it. The wheel will remind us of that over, and over again. It will all seem meaningless within the parameters of an approach ignoring such a force, but once in witness of the duality of energies we exist in, we can shine. Passion for something or someone is beautiful, as long as passion for your life source and your self isn't sacrificed. Tip your hat to what you appreciate, but don't give your hat away.

All life events regardless of the time they came, or the veils, analogies, and puzzles they came in, are not isolated unto their self. The times of our lives are not just to be passed over as the "same ole thing", but each event helps us come closer to being one with who we truly are. It works to truly experience something if that something has contrast. If you were always shed with the same angle of light you would only experience what shadows and highlights were presented with that view.

A lot of what we do consciously and unconsciously is done just to see what would happen if…..If I jumped off that cliff successfully into the water, what would that feel like? At the very moment I decide to change from not jumping, to proceeding with the movement toward jumping, I would need a strong conviction. The position is empowered by the repelling of the previous position. In fact, I think this endeavor would work best if I had no recollection of the previous stance to not jump. I would need to dis-identify from the previous mentality completely, as any identification with it would stop the new endeavor from happening. Do we end up trying on the clothing of different approaches and then only end up knowing one look, while forgetting what we looked like with other clothing worn or other roles potentially playable?

As a collective energy force actualized in a type of opposing energy in body, we act as if it would serve the experience of living to have no recollection of any metaphysical essence. We seem to keep our spiritual allowance elusive, rather than ever present, and as an unconscious serving of our physical journey. We only tend to elevate what we see and little attention is given to what we can't see. This fragmented viewpoint promotes a tendency to ignore meaningful excursions and crystallize body pleasures, physical gains, money, travel, eating, and visual pleasures. In the end, a level of discord will always be experienced, because the producer of physical experience originated from a spiritual essence, and no matter how powerful the stimuli from tangible things, truth can only be traveled away from for so long before unseen forces regain their balance. Glimpses of it then appear as if it were a phantom. Those phantoms very much disrupt our identification with anything or anyone we may have erroneously been using to represent who we are.

The mind interplays both dimensions revealing that the unseen is in and of everything, and our physical pleasures or frustrations are only part of the totality in which we reside. Just as the mentality that allowed for jumping off a cliff once held the mentality that said not to, our physical existence is very much contained in a spiritual origin. No matter what we identify with physically, the spiritual part of us doesn't lose connectivity to the totality regardless of the role we play today.

In a way, our physical world realities work to crystallize their opposite. The mind is overseeing this little game of purposeful forgetting for the sake of allowing the physical experience to better be embellished. The mind is seeing the experience of spirit seeping through while a forceful energy exerts itself continually through meaning sought in physical attributes alone. Tendencies being generated from a mixture of body and spirit sit in direct contrast to what we, the movie producer, look to portray only physically.

We go around in mental circles looking for meaning while implementing an approach that has as its attributes the parameters for never finding it. The frustration keeps us trapped and it doesn't yield an opening. We are denying a part of us so it feels as if we are acting in a play we wrote, but we forgot we wrote it. It's not anything we want to share too much with others. When the mental scorecard on the games being played comes out, those immersed in the games grade us badly, and then we are not only frustrated, we are alone because of it. The mental circle is further reinforced by the all-powerful need to be accepted and connected to others, and this means valuing what they value. We can value what isn't seen but then how can we share it with another? We don't want to make it another prop to elevate or bash.

If we look at any other species, many qualities are inherent. As soon as a dog is born it seems to know things even before seeing it done by any other dogs. The same is true for cats, lions or any other living thing. We as humans are not excluded from having inherent qualities, but they are seldom acknowledged, and usually personalized. We have innate mental and physical tendencies we fall into as if we were a piece of paper in a file folder. It would benefit us to be more aware of what these natural qualities were. Evolution has certain traits lingering that were once meant to help us in our human development, but now they may be hurting us. The primitive way we handle fears, and the stronghold physical insecurities play on us, may not always be helping us. Looking at a bigger picture may serve us better.

Magnetism, high pressures, low pressures, and gravity are all the invisible effects of what moves the waves of an ocean. They are the most obvious, consistent, powerful, predictable patterns on earth. There is electricity going through our body and through the human brain. Would all these parallels exist for us to ignore them? Waves, from wind, gravity, and magnetism exist in the very nature we are one with. The forces that move them are the forces that move us. Waves of thoughts, moved by the forces of gravity pulling in associations and references to other thoughts, are affected by the electricity, magnetism, and pressures of one thought after the next. Our internal sequence of thought consistently acts in a circular pattern, and this circular pattern engulfs us. It feels like we are going around in circles in our brain when moving toward and away from our spiritual selves.

Within the energy and tug of war of this pattern we are missing the grandeur, splendor, and the magnificence of our very essence. We are getting caught up with mediums of exchange and losing the glory of existence to a fight or flight impulse; to fears, to insecurities, and to feelings of inferiority or loss. When we stand in recognition of these forces we stand in recognition of our very essence. The planets, the ocean's waves, and light are all the life force of our very existence. So we aren't every passing event as much as we are the force that allows for them. We are in harmony within a totality of energy which we are one with, and not separate from. Passion is beautiful, as long as passion for your life's source prevails over all that's temporal.

While human beings exist on a rotating planet we are part of something which has opposite forces propelling it. From this point of view we see two imposing bodies in the sky. The sun and moon are our most imposing views and they mean something more than just physical appearance. One such imposing structure goes around us and one we go around. We are on a planet rotating because of the opposing energies we are contained in. This circular motion exists in all of nature and therefore this impetus is all of what we are of as well. We are merely plugging our living experience into an already existing circular force. It's as if we are on a merry-go-round, and even after we get off of it, it still keeps going around. When we jump back on, we are joining an existing momentum. This existing momentum is always here and one with our life energy. Plug in our life, plug in the next life, it doesn't matter what wire is used to conduct the electricity, but it does matter how the power is applied. Yet, the same forces remain before and after every life.

We create elements and activities and experiences to accommodate a pre-existing force without a cognizance of the energies we are supporting. The earth's orbit exists because of an approach and avoidance, a push and a pull of gravitational forces. What we see around us is not separate from us, but rather a representation of what we are, and we are a representation of the same force that it is. There exists a diametrically opposed series of energies to support what is a circular force. We are part of these energies just as the planets are. By their very opposition they create a type of circle and by our internal opposition we replicate it. It's far less personal than we can ever imagine.

The file folder of our metaphysical state, and file folder of our physical body, are in battle. The dynamic that operates in us, which acts in concert to balance opposing forces, are thoughts and life events. Our experiences plot a diametrical energy propelled and populated by circular energies. We approach and go away from our intangible essence and then approach and go away from our tangible essence. It's as if scenes in a play are arranged representing the circles of our existence. We are perpetually offsetting, by various experiences embellishing our physical or spiritual self, opposing forces. They are more just than an analogy for the magnetic opposition that surrounds us. They are the very essence of what also contains us.

We have an ethereal essence going around us that sometimes we are in touch with and other times it's hidden from us. We have the moon going around us that is sometimes hidden, sometimes fully visible, and sometimes partially visible. The sun rises and sets in our view but we are actually going around it and turning at the same time. The analogy here is that light is intermittently shown to us, just as our spiritual essence sometimes seems less obvious than others. We are shown the varying reflection of it with other things. Events and circumstances are portraying a reflection of this. The night moon reflects the physical light, which is the sustenance of our very bodies and is an imminent physical reminder of what is always there through the reflection of it.

There's a pursuit of completion within the toils of life. However, higher wisdom and insights flow in us when we stay aware of necessary, ever present energies that propel certain toils. Rather than immersing ourselves in the toils themselves, the need to step back and see the energy they stem from, and why they exist, would better serve us. We don't exist isolated from opposing forces. How easy it is to forget that life events are merely filling the file folder required for the balancing, and offset of extremes.

When we move too much away from the stance of witnessing a direction, and instead become that direction, we have stepped out of the seer's wisdom. Strong events may then take place, as if they were forced in by a magnetic charge, to remind us of this place of higher wisdom. From there we reside in a presence that sees energies without being the energies. Most people never see the energies too long before defaulting back to the viewpoint where the brain's nine categories get appropriated to it. We run the course deciding we are them until we once again are strongly forced out of them. Most stay lost in the toils that are propelled by opposing energies until death. Seeing them is a state of enlightenment.

A thought carries an electrical charge. This electrical charge doesn't operate exclusive from the totality of all energies. The circular activity of an opposing thought or charge supports the circular motion of the energy that surrounds us. Once again, we are in and of what is sustained by opposing forces and therefore one with these opposing forces. Feeling that we are one with opposing energies can help us look at all challenges in a very different way. Everything in the world seems to be accompanied by its opposite. Even within our bodies there is life and death going on. There's death of germs and other cells while birth and generation of new cells go on as well. Death accompanies life as one grand example of the ultimate opposite. Anything, including life itself exists with its opposite. Death is an ever present and needed energy for life's sustenance.

Isaac Newton's law of gravity refers to spherical objects, such as planets, and he figured out the exact measurement that this force has. To me, reading that there was a unified measurement throughout the cosmos that computed gravitational pull of spherical objects was more than just same old accepted proven fact. Anything uniformly proven throughout the cosmos unifies what otherwise appears as separate objects. To locate this uniform force is a paradigm shift of epic proportions. It showed me that we were part of what was of the source of everything, and everything was part of an order.

This energy, which includes the gravitational force of spherical objects, propelled the question of what was spherical within and around me that I couldn't see. I wasn't acknowledging the tendencies of this brain-machine to also be affected by what needed to act in diametrically opposed patterns.

Were the thoughts and words, before every event forming the next spherical body, be for positioning what would perpetuate what was circular? The gravitational forces, of what had circular tendencies, were exhibited in actions and experiences that perpetuated this pattern. Gravitational pull of thoughts can be isolated into a very real physical law just as Newton did with the cosmos.

So, if there was a loss of self into what was deeply physical in nature, there would be a very strong energy demanding more of an intangible journey. In my case standing so close to the events of September 11th, 2001, may have propelled me further into my spiritual journey. If there was a loss of self into an intangible journey, a very strong energy forcing physical reminders would be imminent. After this deep excursion into my spiritual journey, very strong physical challenges overtook me. It seems wrong to think that losing ourselves to an image of spirituality would be an undesired direction, but an image of spirituality is not spirituality. If there was a viewership and awareness of these opposing energies, rather than a loss experienced under the domain of them, then we would be of mind and not of brain. We would be of wisdom and not of intellect. We would be one with spirituality rather than separating it and losing our self under the umbrella of an image of it. We would also be one with the spirituality behind the physical demands of life as well.

An **idea** of spirituality is one that pulls us in a direction away from higher wisdom. It confuses us because true spirituality happens out of what is not an idea of it, but of what we are one with to begin with. When we make an idea, a religion, an identity, or a separate story of it, we are no longer of true spirituality. In our attempt to define it with "ideas" we went into what the brain-machine was using to reclaim itself, and no longer stemmed from "mind", which is one with spirituality. The brain-machine wants the image, the naming, the rituals, and the need to share and compare. It fits into its categories that it has to use to sustain itself. So, the extent to which we personalize and own spiritual energy under the image of it, or beholding to the naming of it, we deter an experience that allows for being one with it. I don't think there is anything trickier in life than that concept, and even using words to point to it is a challenge, because what are words but a product of the brain? If you are not one with the ocean in which you swim, but are looking for the God of fish, you have left the truest connection to your life source and therefore are no longer one with it.

Yet, we fulfill the spherical patterns in the brain that are propelled by uncontrollable forces by leaning toward physical or spiritual concepts. It's not our fight to fight. It's more an energy to realize without unconsciously being swept away under either the physical or spiritual umbrella. The acceptance of oneness with this energy, rather than resistance to it, frees the rope from the pier where you are then one with the wind filling your sails. We unify with a higher mind seeing this duality.

Therefore there is always the wheel of opposites revealing each opposing portion of a spectrum in every facet of life. Within every experience there exists an energy containing a respective offset. Plotting each point with a value given to each stimulus and its respective offset would produce a circle. What else would it be but a wheel or a circle just as the earth is? As living draws us to our spiritual source and the human brain and its functioning draws us away from it, frustrations should rather be looked as the very reason for our existence.

Just as the earth circles the sun, and the moon circles the earth without ever reaching it, our higher mind is circling our brain. The human brain is continuously opposing our passage into our formless essence. The human brain drives us back toward the physical world, and it forces us to hold on, even when no physical demands of our body require it. This offsetting energy is necessary for our existence and is what makes up the totality of the universe. Awareness opens the door to what includes, rather than resists, natural energies. Again, it's not our fight to fight. It's our flight to soar and experience above it.

It's as if we were surrounded by brain mirrors and reduced to the firing synapses within the confines of those reflections. What we see on the outside, the earth, the moon, and the sun is a reflection of the circular patterns that not only allowed for planets and stars, but allowed for and created us. The most imposing views, the moon and the sun, are representative of a message beyond their physical appearance and beyond their accommodating physical qualities. They are possessing characteristics and qualities we have within our very nature. It's all one big physical representation for what we cannot see in and of ourselves. We are a great reflector of the shining light of life, and if that is something we have trouble feeling big enough to be, then maybe we can enjoy seeing it in the greatest tangible exhibit shown. The Moon is the most imposing and most present physical figure seen. Yet, we are looking at its light as if it is only its own when it is only a reflector. We are also looking at our light as if it is only our own, and we too are a reflector.

The moon does not shine its own light but that of another source. We shine the light that is in and of our body, but something else is the source of it. It's also present and not visible, but more pervasive than our apparent self. The true source of the light of the moon is the Sun, as the true source of our light is not our physical self but of something else more ominous. In essence, we are not of ourselves alone, but of a reflection of something possessing far more comprehensive characteristics unseen. We are a physical reflection of a non-physical energy and we are representing that very fact.

If the sun was higher wisdom and enlightenment, and the earth was our physical body, and the moon was our spiritual essence, then we would be circling our higher wisdom and enlightenment while our spiritual essence was circling us. All along higher wisdom and enlightenment was one with what gave us life and sustained life, while the reflection of that light existed intermittently through our spiritual essence which was represented by the moon. We circle the sun while being on earth and the sun is our life source in its sustaining characteristics of light and heat. It looms as our life energy. This physical source of life we can only see with our eyes half the time and experience as a total body all the time, just as we partially feel connected to our intangible life source and partially feel disconnected, while all along our body remains supported by it. We are supported by the sun even when we don't see it by the gravitational balance it provides.

We also allow changing amounts of enlightenment within ourselves. It's a circle in a circle. Our life source is in balance with the energies that keep us in orbit on our axis. As if our brain is orbited by our mind as the brain-machine attempts to make everything explained tangibly, so is the moon reflecting the light of our source in orbiting us. The Sun is the formless pull at the center of our galaxy. It is a gaseous fireball, appearing in definite form from a distance, and at the very source of what keeps us all alive.

Keeping cognizant of a force we are part of, would certainly remove some of the burden we place on ourselves. The significance of three, the earth, sun and moon, also can't help but loom large as without such a perfect harmony from the three there wouldn't be the right amount of light, temperature and water to have life here on Earth. The fact that there are three bodies held in perfect harmony by what can't be seen, the earth, sun and moon, parallels the physical, the intangible, and the wisdom of higher mind that is one with all forces. Mind, mind to intangible, and mind to physical are the three experiences represented in the three most imposing views of our existence.

Are the tangible planets, moons, and sun more valuable than the air, space, gravity, and the dimension that allowed for their existence in the first place? I can't say that they are when even the slightest change in gravity would eliminate all of it. I can't say we are more valuable than what allows for us. There shouldn't be a thought elevated higher than the field or dimension that allows for it either. Isn't it this circular energy that keeps having our brain diminish what would be enlightenment, and isn't it in the noticing of this that would allow for enlightenment?

The light divides and is shown in different colors. We see all the different colors that came from what originally appeared as clear. We decide that its divisions are each color alone and not a diffraction of one single light. Light is the combination of colors and all colors are divisions of one light. If you sought to find what made up the light, and rejected any one of the colors, you would lose the totality that is needed to make up the light. In the sub-stances the totality is missed and in the combination the colors are missed. On the surface one wouldn't think that light could diffract to red, orange, yellow, green, blue, indigo, and violet. You also wouldn't think when combining them the outcome would be clear light either. So in the parts we miss the totality and in the totality we miss the parts.

When I was in seventh grade the science teacher took one flask with one clear liquid in it, and one flask of another clear liquid, and then combined them. To my class's amazement, the third flask, with the ingredients now combined, was not clear but a light red color. We were asked to use the microscopes in the classroom to examine this further. The class was divided up with each half getting each one of the original clear ingredients. Microscopes were used along the wall of the classroom as one half of the class looked for red in one of the ingredients, and the other half looked for the color red in the other ingredient. After looking through all the available lenses with the varying magnifications, both groups admitted to not being able to find any color in the ingredients, even when using the highest magnification. We were all very confused right up until the end of the class when the teacher finally gave us the answer. He said that the result came from the combination of the two liquids, and we would never find properties in either one separately that would show any color red. He said each ingredient contained clear powders with very specific PH levels, and when they were mixed with other clear powders with certain PH levels, the combination creates the color red.

The red color could not be seen in either ingredient. It would only show up when both colorless ingredients were combined. Just as blood changes from a deep dark red to light red when mixing with oxygen, which looks like nothing, so was the case back in science class that a change resulted from something that was not so apparent.

Are we missing the crucial ingredients of every result by the way we look at things? We are using the viewpoint derived from a combination as well. The combination of a spiritual essence and a physical essence may force us into a stance that is in fact pushing us away from being in touch with our truest essence. In looking through the viewpoint which is the parts of me combined, my source can be equally elusive. I have to enable this amazing experience from the higher mind to wash over me instead of trying to understand it. It feels like every cell in my body thanks me when I do.

Results are oftentimes hidden from the independent characteristics of the ingredients. Physical dominance alone cannot command the order of our everyday experiences. Knowing and applying this opens many doors previously closed. It's disguised where an outcome originates. I could have looked under various magnifications in science class for the next fifty years and not found red in those separate ingredients. Focusing on something in terms of the appearance in a result could be very misleading. Given that same insight, how could I expect to experience my intangible essence by only valuing the thoughts of the brain?

If we are the third property of two things combined whose origins can't be seen once joined, then an "everything attitude" placed on what can only be seen, and a "nothing attitude" on what can't, would have to be very misdirected. The message seems to be that if we get too wrapped up in what isn't measurable we won't get any results that are measurable. This is the gravest mistake of mankind. Considering both the dimensions we reside in, and witnessing them from a higher wisdom, would result in the greatest possible outcomes. This would tap into our greatest strengths.

There's a lot of pain if we embrace only the props in the play of life. There is a tendency to value only what appears. The props serve the need to use the brain and body by seeing, touching, measuring, valuing, comparing and using symbols to elevate, diminish, devalue and sadly enough, separate. If I can't decide I am something definable, then I am something indefinable, and that scares me so much that I have to go back and work real hard at proving who I am in reference to what's tangible. The brain doesn't like the position which sees this outside of its thought prism. That place doesn't serve its categorical references. One approach it can work with and one approach it can't. Thus we are either the victim of its limitations, or the one which sees it. Unfortunately, while playing with the idea of only being in one dimension, we may very well have become the experience of only it.

The see-er and not the be-er of props, situations, events, happenings, occurrences, experiences, sights, pictures, images, and feelings are all what is the highest human experience. It's all part of a greater message eventually directing us back to the source of our light or life force. If there is spirituality in everything then everything means something. The biggest part of what we look for in physical reality is already what we have in our non-physical reality.

Let imagined security, lost or found in our material existence, confirm us not as merely material. Let imagined security, lost or found in the mere image of something called spiritual, confirm us not by anything or anyone deemed separately spiritual. Let what we are one with, which is in and of us, be where we emanate to see the necessary forces, and certainly not be them, to feel true enlightenment.

# VI  Edu-wasting

In schools, religious instruction, family settings, and with each other, anything rooted in mystery should be treated as if it is one with us. Instead it is being replaced with arrogance, manipulation, greed, lies, control, egoistic strivings, and power-hungry abusive leaders. Servitude to all who claim to know makes other people feel bad for even asking about anything else.   To take what is unknown about the greatness of you and let others decide about it, and act as if it is known through their way alone, is the greatest travesty and dehumanization that could ever exist.  It's not something to brush over as meaningless and acceptable when yielding is what helps the next group control you. It is the axis of manipulation.  It undermines connectivity to our greatest essence.  To change the way we look at our origins by portraying false ideas to serve, is the most horrible, belittling, and primitive thing the human species could ever do. It's not insignificant to quietly feel opposed to what's misdirecting us. It's everything we are truly all about.

It's the breeding ground for all that's wrong with education, religion, and any group that uses arrogance to control you, including your own family. It undermines democracy, humanity, compassion, love, and the development of the entire human species. There's a critical effect from brushing over what is yearning inside you.   Our questions and the answers we accept are erroneously making determinations about who we are.  What we are told doesn't jive with what we feel, and the results become a deeply felt hurt that has little to no avenue for expression.  It then resurfaces in many ways that end up being detrimental to ourselves and others.

Every strength that would have already been identified as one with you is told not to flourish because it belongs to a god, or to something or someone else.  We feel inferior to the guidelines we absorbed which have been given to us by others. They leave us feeling like we are not measuring up.  We feel this way because we internally disagree with them without an avenue validated for expression.  To compound this effect, the information itself is designed to have you serve something that also makes you feel lesser.

Age groups, genders, cultures, religions, languages, and skin colors wouldn't have separated us if we were bound in common mystery regardless.  Love, rather than fear would have been chosen each time anything portraying differences was veiling our unity. Instead the foundation for alienation has been laid down in granite at the very beginning of our life. Common mystery would have yielded different results if accepted as only that. Groups by their very nature are hard to change. People gravitating to groups give them strength, and their dominance is reinforced in society by this attendance and unquestioned support.

There's an implication that what a group is portraying is automatically an accepted truth because of the quantity of people belonging to it. It appeals to this very common need in all of us to be accepted and feel as others do. It brings "security" to apparent insecurities presented by not knowing, and not having an organized way of accepting mystery. Groups give people something to believe in and people desperately need that. Unfortunately, in groups, misdirection is perpetuated, and the group makes it harder to breathe in truths. Hiding, instead of challenging norms, becomes the easy way out. Responsibility to integrity and truth can easily be put aside once belonging is ritualized. Groups give us some things, but in that process take away much more.

Why do we have to act like we know, when in reality, we don't even have a clue. It's as if it's more acceptable to be confident about something whether there's a real basis of truth behind it or not. When groups run amuck in their teachings, consciously or unconsciously, we have almost disarmed ourselves from being in a position to do anything about it. Many of the ingredients that go into establishing groups are inherently dangerous, yet they remain protected by followers that wouldn't on an individual basis act to veil the truth alone, the way they do in a group, in a million years.

It's as if when you are part of a group you are not only shielded from blatant errors in judgment, you are shielded from the results as well. The propensity to not delve deeper into what may need further investigation is further perpetuated in groups. The need to know, even when knowing is not possible, squeezes falsehoods into mainstream thinking.

In school I felt squashed. I remember how I used to pass the hours in class wondering why the focus was on so much of the minutia and so little on what was impacting our lives. It's almost like we were killing time with nonsense until it was figured out how to really communicate about life. Isn't getting along well with others an important thing to talk about? What about techniques for better communication? I hoped they would talk to me about some of the things I might be interested in, but they didn't care. They had too many students, too much to do, and so little time to do it. They made me feel that unless we did well with what they taught, we were not only considered a bad student, but a bad person.

The things taught oftentimes didn't seem to matter anywhere else in life except in the classroom. Students literally killed themselves because they were made to feel like a failure when they didn't do well at what ended up being meaningless. So, they are deemed to be valueless at what is meaningless and they hurt themselves one way or another because of the way the education made them feel. Is this masquerade for real? Are we supposed to get up and laugh at some point or clap for how well the show is made to look real? This is the information that's been chosen as the most important things to speak about? This is education?

They keep telling me what was important when everything I saw outside of this classroom told me it wasn't important at all. I felt like we were on some kind of island where nothing else that took place in the outside world mattered. We had to serve them so they can have an identity. What is the identity of the school if they don't have so much impertinent stuff for us to have to know? I remember thinking I was sent to school to spend the best years of my childhood on something that nobody else thought mattered.

While I was attending high school two more wars broke out around the world. I wondered during that time if my children were going to be studying these very same wars. I also remember feeling that we weren't ever going to talk about how people around the world should get along better with each other. When are we going to talk about all the best ways to avoid wars? When are we going to delve into that facet of the human personality that seems to keep creating wars? When are we going to acknowledge that mankind has been finding ways to kill each other for thousands of years? If it is so much a part of our make-up, then maybe we should be more aware of what would stop more wars from happening in the future. Instead the need to mechanically remember dates, names and places without understanding how and why only destines us to ignore these signs in the future. It only places the focus on what we didn't want rather than on what we wanted.

We could seek relevancy in what we would do now given the same circumstances. Why was it more important for me to memorize the date we dropped an atomic bomb than it was for me to know what ways could have been chosen to avoid killing and maiming thousands of people? Isn't there anything else they could have talked about that would be more pertinent to what we need to bring more happiness and understanding to life? It just made me feel so distant from everything when they told me what I was supposed to consider important. Since that was information that was so respected, it really made me question the image of who I truly was.

I brought up the curriculum to people outside of school. The adults I spoke to were also at a loss about why certain things were being focused on. Yet, their taxes were paying for it and their children were being affected by it. It was just another thing we created that took on a life of its own afterwards. Just another thing that was in origin supposed to accommodate us, and instead it turned into something we were serving that was no longer helping us at all.

I was considered disruptive because I didn't blindly follow. If I challenged them, and they didn't know how to answer, to avoid them showing everyone that fact, they would punish me. Was this what was preparing us for the farce that's perpetuated in life? This is how I looked at education thirty-five years ago, and looking back on it, I still feel the same way today.

I remember when all the teachers got together and wanted to leave me back a grade. I was in 6th grade and supposed to go into seventh next. They thought I should stay in 6th, but around the same time the scholastic tests were given to determine reading and math levels. They held off their decision until then. The tests revealed I was 12.9(12th grade 9th month) in reading, and 13.4(thirteenth grade fourth month) in math. I was at college level on both and scored among the highest marks in the school. Now instead of leaving me back a grade they decided to skip me. I looked at the whole system and wondered what the heck was going on. I graduated High School when I was sixteen, and did well in College, but I only remember three classes in twenty years of schooling that were ever worth their time. Why should that be? I am far from alone with these perspectives.

Regarding religion, well, I remember as a kid when they shuffled us off to catechism after school. They had to decide what religious denomination I was, and where I went after school, so they asked me what religion I was. I didn't even know. It's not anything we ever really spoke about in my house. The time came where I had to answer one way or the other. My mother came to school and they asked my mother. She was a little taken back actually. She didn't think the need to make the decision would come so soon and seemed a little introspective about it. She wanted to speak to the teacher without me present, so she went into the classroom while I waited outside wondering what my fate would be.

I didn't know what the special fuss was all about, but when she came out the choice was made for me to go to catholic instruction once a week after school. Mom seemed uncomfortable about the whole thing. She went along with it and never let on she felt any other way. I got the feeling that part of her wished the question never had to be asked. I think she was happier that she knew where I was the extra hours after school than she was hell-bent on me being taught religion. I never had a reference to religion before this, but after this episode some of my friends questioned why it took so long for them to decide what my religion was. I didn't know why and I didn't even know enough to care.

It wasn't until years later when I told my buddy I was going over my Uncle Bernie's house for Thanksgiving Day that the dichotomy in my roots became even clearer. Even though Catholic school was chosen for me there was more to it than just that. My friend confirmed with his mom that Bernie was not a Catholic name. The question then came up whether I was Catholic or not. I went home, asked my mom, and she explained that she was born Jewish and converted when she married my dad. So in the Jewish religion I was considered Jewish, because it goes by what your mom was born as. In the Catholic religion I was considered Catholic, because it went by what my dad was born as and how I was raised.

She said she wanted to raise me Catholic because she converted and since she was now Catholic and my dad was Catholic that's what made sense. I asked her why she converted and she said all the people in her life that hurt her the most were Jewish. Yet, since she was born one way and changed she wasn't so gung-ho either way. She liked the fun Catholic holidays but was never big religious. This ridiculous logic that had me embrace any religion had me unwinding erroneous garbage thrown at me the next 40 years. The blasphemy transferred from one generation to the next was in full swing. It was further confused by one religion pinned against another rather than the question of whether either belief should be embraced.

So I had to go back to my Italian Catholic friend and tell him that I was really half and half. His mother was there and it seemed that this was a dividing element. My friend's mom looked like she didn't want him to play with me after that. It was never the same. We were practically joined at the hip and the best of buddies, but after this news was revealed my best friend was always too busy for me. This great friendship I thought we had was now over. He fought with his parents over this but his mom and dad won. We were the two smartest kids in the whole school, like two peas in a pod. I'll never forget when he told me the truth. He said it's not something he wanted but he couldn't go against his parents.

Both of us loved learning new things and both of us would hang together to do everything, but it was never to be again. So many times I came knocking on his door after that and so many times nobody answered when I knew they were home. Other times when they answered, they turned me away with various excuses. So, my best friend not only wasn't my best friend any more, but he told others who used to be my friends and they put me off now too. All my Catholic Italian friends who always thought I was 100% Catholic and Italian now knew I wasn't. The person I thought was my best friend spread the word that I was half and half. I was not treated the same by anyone after that.

First they gave me grief because I had no dad around, then they picked on me because I was now the "half breed". So, right when that song "Half Breed" came out, it was discovered that I was both Catholic and Jewish. It was silly, but I couldn't live that down for years. I didn't know what I had to do with any of it personally, but it gave people an excuse to pick on me, so they did. In that respect it was a little tough growing up in the Bronx. You had to have tough skin because when they got a hold of something they didn't let it go. Some guys would walk up to me and just start singing that song "Half Breed" in my face. It was ridiculous. The horrible judgment and alienation was passed down from our parents to hurt some more.

So, there I was going to Catholic school for Catechism. All the children lined up separated between Jewish, Catholic and Protestant. The only time we were ever divided before then was to separate gender, and in a way that should have been less a dividing element as well. It was strange looking at people on other lines wondering what now made me separate from them. I arrived at a Catholic church where they had classes upstairs. Nuns taught the classes. They taught from passages in the Bible. I knew nothing and accepted nothing. I sat there remembering how my kindergarten teacher told me years earlier that my question about why I was here in this world was one that was meant for my parents or a religious instructor. Well, my parents were of no help on the subject. One of them I seldom saw and the other changed the subject every time I asked her. Now was my big chance.

I sat there hearing the nun tell us that God was everywhere and God created everything and God always was. I heard her say God made us in his image and God, God, God, God, God. I finally raised my hand and asked a few questions. One of them questioned our origins as people and she attributed that to God. I asked the origin of God and no origin was available, so we were lead to believe that this God always existed and didn't have an origin. I then put the two pieces of information together and questioned whether our image, if made in Gods, had an origin, when his didn't. I also asked what other parts were different from this so-called "same image".

She started to get upset. I said, "If this desk has a beginning, and we can determine when it was made, then how come we can't determine when God was made? How could God always have been? Everything comes from something right?" She said, "Mr. Raymond, please step out in the hall. I would like to speak with you in private." The class gave a collective, "ooooooooooohhhhh".

I stepped out in the hallway and the nun said, "You are here because this is what being Catholic is, and the faith is that God always was." I said, "It doesn't make sense, and I don't want to believe it if it doesn't make sense." She told me to hold out my hands. She then took her ruler and started to reel back to hit them. I moved them away real quick and she demanded I leave them out in front of me straight out. I listened because I thought it was part of the threat she wanted to impose, but it wasn't just a threat because she then wacked my knuckles as hard as she could with the wooden ruler. I'll never forget how devastated I was. I imagined this kind, loving, enlightened representation of something special and I got physically abused for simply asking questions. I was crying and she said, "I want you to go back into that classroom and not say another word, and stop that crying".

After Catechism I walked home and stayed inside until my mom came home. When she came home I told her that the nun hit me and she was appalled. She said on Sunday I should go with her to church and she'll tell the Priest. She told him and he said he would make sure that it didn't happen again. My mother also went to the school and told the nun that she was not allowed to hit her son. They went back and forth and the nun insisted she had the right to do it because my questions disrupted her class. My mother went back to the priest again and the priest was very upset by it and told her that he would speak to the nun again, She didn't hit me after that, but I never asked another question after that either. I never said another word in that class or any religious class after that. I didn't believe what they were saying, but I had to put up with it and that was that.

The whole experience did a real number on me and introverted me even further. I felt so different because I didn't believe what everyone else was so readily accepting. All these older people, who were supposed to know the truth, were all so uneasy with the beliefs they accepted. They all had so much trouble answering basic questions coming from a little kid. They had to turn to deception, avoidance, redirection and even violence to express themselves.

These were the most basic questions about why we are here, how we got here, and what we we're meant to do while we are here. The questions were given with a step-by-step logic being applied. They were the most basic and the biggest at the same time. They were the simplest to ask and the most complicated to answer. They were what came naturally to ask and what came with great difficulty to answer.

It occurred to me, since I was put off for so long before when I asked such questions, that now it was very clear that nobody really knew the answers, and all along they were all just pretending. I waited all those years for a religious instructor to be the shining light of truth and I got a vicious pigheaded instructor who couldn't handle my questions without turning to violence. Instead of getting something positive from asking what I thought were good questions, which also took a lot of courage for me to ask, I was treated as if I was disruptive, invasive, and defying. My most insightful questions were received with defensive replies that ended in an attack.

My mom was overtaxed raising two children while working full-time, cleaning, and doing everything on her own. The last thing she needed was something else to burden her. Telling my parent meant being punished for causing a disruption, and most certainly having a nun representing the idea of our intangible essence by smashing the bones of my hands with a ruler was a horror that left its mark. I was glad to see my mom go to bat for me, but she still made me go when I didn't want to and that hurt. If I would have been given the assignment to study the answers on my own that would have done me a whole lot more good, but she wanted to know that I had a religion and that I was part of this thing she chose to be part of. As weak as that sounds is as weak as it is generation after generation.

My family system, the education system and the religious system laid down their foundation. Mine was a microcosm of the world and the root of so many problems. It was as if the best defense was an offense. My mother was spoken to time and time again about my questions and I was in trouble for the problems they kept causing. The nun who hit me left her mark, and asking questions or even talking at all was not something I ever wanted to do there again. In my quiet, watchful way I grew further and further away from not only the nuns teaching the messages, but from other children who so readily accepted the messages. Is this the way the most advanced species in history handles questions about life?

When a conclusion is derived regarding a subject whose origin is based in mystery, there is an overcompensation exhibited through aggressiveness. This is adapted to avoid the deep down insecurity that comes with accepting as fact, what is actually unfounded. An attack outwards allows the attention to move away from their deep down self-image of weakness, and now appears as strength. They no longer have to be connected to that insecurity because they derive security from attacking another. Students would then have to defend themselves against not only the proctor's abuse of power personally, but the abuse of power derived from attaching to a group they are representing. It affirms their position and hard coats what otherwise is a complete insecurity.

Religion, whose only basis was rooted in bringing greater closeness to our own totality, has not allowed for that. It has a controlling, fear inducing, manipulation of mystery which is put forth in punishments and is wrapped up in some kind of collective misdirection. Stories told and events passed down created a certain religious following. Things supposedly written down thousands of years ago, by the few who could write and understand, has tried taking the place of our magnificent power. The unexplained physical occurrence of this or that is what we hang our hat on to decide how our religion has its basis. It is really an illusionary anchor from insecurities experienced within from a massive intangible power.

The basis of religion as a whole is absurd. The definitions of Gods and Religions are the greatest travesties of mankind. There's a ridiculous need to measure, compare, and define everything. This need is even illustrated with the one thing that should be the least definable, least measurable, and least understood. This ultimate mystery many claim to own and define when the opposite is true. Are we so egotistical that we have to know everything, and show how we know everything to everyone else, when all we have to do is admit that we truly don't know? All we have to do as human beings is admit we are just like all other human beings who truly don't know either.

Instead we take the primitive approach in proposing who God decided to speak to, where God decided to go, and how only some people are special and everyone else is not. We have to kill in the name of knowing the mystery and elevate that position to avoid admitting that we truly don't know. We have to damn others, alienate people, and destroy in the name of what ends up being truly nothing. We create this whole story around something that is only a thought used to comfort the fearful. I am saying religion is the worst thing mankind ever invented. We have taken the mystery that was supposed to be our greatest resource for our spiritual adventure and we have turned our adventure into a crime-drama. We should be in awe of our miracle and all the miracles that surround us, yet instead we choose to seek exactitude on the level of thought when our spiritual essence inherently is the opposite of those confines.

Religion has taken our greatest strength and turned it into our greatest weakness. We have created all these different gods and we have given these gods a definite appearance. These gods then take on characteristics to suit a control of information in which they are punishing, vengeful and condemning gods. We can stay in the mystery and allow for our completeness or we can seek to define the mystery with lies and disguises.

Where did this all start and why? Was religion just a show that got a little out of hand? If a subject came up where nothing other than mystery was available, long before our knowledge advanced in science, biology, geology, physics, and astronomy, it created a great deal of unrest. Childbirth, death, disease, catastrophic weather, earthquakes and other occurrences forced the hand of people to ease the pain of not knowing and the threat of what might happen.

Back in the days before religion, those professing to know our spiritual essence would make money in the only media available, and that was public speaking. These were just the ingredients every speaker relished as an opportunity to seize the next audience. Various claims by one speaker or the next regarding our mysterious essence would appease fears of the unknown. Everyone would eventually be so uncomfortable with not having at least some answer that could make take away their fear, that getting any answer, especially one that many others agreed upon, would certainly be comforting. Paying for it made it even more credible.

So, all the miraculous things that have ever happened can now be explained under a single caption called "religion". All mysteries were, and are solved for by creating the image of a god, and stories about this image, in a very structured dogmatism. Now we can define our amazing glory rather than share in the mysterious splendor of it all. We can define all that stuff that wasn't definable. If this sounds ridiculously primitive and ignorant, it's only because it is.

When the beauty of nature and all its amazing balances are observed, we can now say that it's from a god, and we can make a whole religion around this god. When we are this separate creation, and spirituality is recognized, but only away from us, then we are removed from our own spirituality. We can then perpetuate stories of those that wrote about this god, and how their image of 'God" is proposed. We can further learn how it all neatly explains every unexplainable event in one collective package. We can be manipulated by opportunists who have been taking advantage of what is unknown for thousands of years. We may continue to be manipulated even when the very roots of religious stories are dispelled with science and discoveries. We may still blindly accept many things that proposed religion as the answer when unexplained happenings didn't have wisdom placing a bigger light on them. If it seems archaic and strange to sit in a group of people swept away in lies and song, it's only because it is.

I never understood why everyone found it so unacceptable to simply say they don't know. It struck me that this very type of circumstance has existed throughout history. We have to act like we know because it's more acceptable to be confident about something. We are most susceptible to false claims without a real foundation because they come from something else that we have already bought into. We then can group it with that same feeling or conviction. The world says anything is better than admitting that you are not knowledgeable and can't take a stand. It's much more acceptable to take a confident stand than one of quandary even when it brings everyone in the wrong direction.

Advancements in human knowledge chipped away at many falsehoods previously latched onto for security. Discoveries in math, physics, astronomy, geology and all the sciences allowed for greater understandings so we didn't have to make up something to appease fears. A way of existing with research, studying, learning, and questioning the unknown brought amazing insights about the world around us. The greatest minds that ever lived, the geniuses that discovered gravity, the big bang, time/space, and quantum physics all pointed us in the right direction. We then took these amazing insights and went back to primitive tendencies with god elevated explanations.

I see us trapped in dogmas, religions and rituals of god worshipping that ignorant people leaned on before all our insights. We are dominated as early on in life as we can remember by religions, traditions, and rituals that take our greatest strengths and turn them into a mockery of our very essence. We damn those who believe other than that and lose our spirituality to a lot of hogwash. Is this a statement of how human beings are evolving in a positive direction? Even in the belief that we are evolving rests the self-serving trappings of being awash in misrepresentations.

We stay with traditions from thousands of years ago because they are imbedded from generation to generation, and they thwart every chance at evolving. They are passed down with a strict adherence that doesn't allow for growth in sciences and wisdom to be applied. We could be more advanced in our receptiveness to metaphysics, philosophy, psychology, and the embodiment of all the strength that comes with these developments. We could be more enlightened to see from a place of wisdom.

We should have revised our approach with the greatness, insights and intelligence we gained. Instead, we took the preciousness of our intangible essence and decided it's in the dogmatism of stories we have to study. When we did this we removed it from our self. We should have discarded these primitive attachments to this idea of gods being responsible for all that is not understood. Why are we still primitive?

I feel like a thousand years from now the human species is going to be looked back on and laughed at for the way we kept religion going as long as we did. We'll be known as those small-minded idiots who couldn't believe their own magnificence without handing it off to some imaginary god. The little children will be walking away with their quantum physics books shaking their heads and laughing at how stupid we were. Should any part of the energy that brought us here not be considered as part of what is also glorious in you?

I suppose when people were so afraid of lightning, a god of lightning had to be created to alleviate them of the fear that came with that mystery. Yes, but what about earthquakes? Ok, Shazam, there's a god of earthquakes. OK, but I'm scared of the snow. Oh, OK here's the god of snow. How about wind? Well, wind is particularly unusual in that it can't be seen, but it affects other things which can be seen. Wow, that's unusual. OK, got it covered.

Then someone decided that if we make one god for everything that would take care of all fears. Any fears not yet revealed would also fall under this domain as well. Maybe the one god theory came from someone who had trouble remembering all the other gods. Not exactly a photographic memory you know.

So now we have one God, which of course accounts for not only everything mysterious out there, but it also takes us away from any mysterious essence that would be considered within us as well. So just in case you had something left uneasy, after previously naming a god for everything else, now this one can take that away too. So people could take great comfort in the one amazing god that accounted for everything. He's the one-stop-shop God. He's responsible for anything that has an intangible basis or hard to explain experience as part of its occurrence, including us.

Yep, that's right, the God of us. Now, anything you wanted to experience that wasn't tangible before, now was, and is now handled just like the mysteries of all those other things. OK, that covers that. Put your money in the hat and call it a day. This is the way the most advanced species in the history of the world handles the mystery of their unseen essence. Outside of fancier architecture in the places of worship, I really couldn't tell you how we have advanced as a species regarding the intangible mysteries of ourselves. Please forgive me if I jolted any religious people, but I am only mocking the thing that I feel has subtly mocked and belittled us. I don't have respect for what brings the greatest disrespect to all of us.

Attack and a defense are elicited with any religious approach. It's the origins of combat and war. Now we compete with each other toward our constant ideas of what is good and what is bad according to what we now decide our special God would want. If it doesn't fit in with that, we'll make it fit, don't worry. A holy war, what the hell, why not? We take all our greatest insights and put them back into this miserable formula. Another religious based war broke out as I was writing this. Instead of unifying us in mystery, it is where the theft of the common human spirit has taken place. It's not something that is easily noticed or it wouldn't have happened. It's not something that we can see with great ease, or experience with things we think we know. It is not as personal as you may think. It is a universal problem. Religion, ironically, is where the connection to our ethereality is contorted.

I had so many questions in my mind about religion, birth, the meaning of life, and I always got answers that came with a great deal of conviction and confidence. In each case when I drilled down beneath the surface of such answers I would come up to a brick wall. It always ended where my questions could no longer be answered with facts. Instead my curiosity would be squelched with adamant words that would come in chorus to make me feel less for not believing. I would be treated as one who lacked faith, a rebel, and a freak because I didn't go along with the crowd. All along throughout my education it seemed to me that everyone was claiming to know more than they really did. What's wrong with only speaking about what is known?

All along so many of them felt the same as I did when I thought I was alone. They were all such good little soldiers and I was the malcontent who didn't buy into the system. I was so convinced for so long that they were part of the very structure I hated. I looked at the whole thing as one big institution and one big monster that I had no control over. Since it was so big and since everyone looked so entrapped and supportive of it, I thought I was surely alone in my view. Yet, when I was away from school playing with other children, and I expressed an aversion to the school system, they would always agree.

I was allured so many times in life by people who when alone with me were almost just like me in experience and expression, but when they were with others they got lost in the so-called power of the group. So many times this blindsided me as I leaned against a mountain of truth only to have it become quicksand when those who commanded the crowd undermined my support. People, because they act differently in groups, have greatly disappointed me throughout my life.

Parents, education, religion, culture, and the misdirected study and perpetuation of our own history, with all its vanities, egotism and denial of human reverence prevails. We keep denying anything that represents "weakness". The idea of weakness is wrong when it is used to label those who don't know. Equating one's worth or self-opinion to that "weakness" is also greatly misdirected. Since truth oftentimes means to admit mystery, any clutching at what isn't truth may test you through analogies to reveal otherwise. We may be tested by the most impactful analogies yet.

When we deny our truest self by naming it something else, that doesn't mean the truth goes away. When we decide the messages of our experiences are not of us, it doesn't change the energies behind what's real. The truth will be revealed in other ways. To avoid what is known, and to avoid what isn't, is to deny the natural flow of energy. The results will emerge from denying what is true about religion with a force so powerful, it will feel as if we tried to stop water or electricity from flowing. Suppressions absorbed will just build up and become bigger. It doesn't go away. Through dreams and various life situations truth still seeks to actualize itself. We can't change reality by pretending the truth isn't there. Situation after situation will force our hand.

Contrary to many beliefs, there is no one, Big Kahuna God that has individually and separately been shown to anyone. A mysterious energy is in the essence of everything that has ever existed in the history of the world. It is actualized with our very existence. Religions, if anything, depict more of an analogy and not a reality. They oftentimes say God is "everywhere", but the thing that seems to be left out is that "everywhere" would have to include you and me. And "everywhere" includes "everything" as not a separate creation, but as part of us and our power. Everything is of this unseen power. Maybe we should keep looking, or better yet, maybe we should start feeling.

I am not making light of this. This is a crucial point of logic in the history of mankind. We are a physical form and we focus on what we can see. An unseen force is also part of all that we see. One problem is that what we see doesn't seem to satisfy all our needs. Even when we acknowledge what's impalpable, we default back to something physical to represent it. So it becomes a physical presence, once again, that came in body, to be all that can't truly show itself. The answer is once again neatly wrapped up in what can be seen when the being of a god, or a messenger of god imagined as "seen" becomes representative of all our collective intangible essence.

We lessen identification with our dematerialized identity by leaving the shore of our own completeness because of the innate physical need to survive and be protected. With all that amazing beauty we are all born with, is it even possible to be around adults, with their entire accompanying luggage, without having shock overcome us? Is it possible not to hurt a child with all their pureness of love and spirit? In the experiences of a baby, there are certainly obvious events we *know* hurt a child, but so many more we don't. There is a pain felt by the lack of affirmation of our spiritual magnificence as the physical world dominates us. An emptiness is felt because each individual feels that only they have a lack of congruence with their environment. In actuality everyone needs to adapt to balancing both the physical and spiritual life, but adults have forgotten what it means to be so connected to only a spiritual essence. A newborn baby, although not able to communicate their experience, is very much connected spiritually.

The little baby in each and every one of us has suffered. The conscious and unconscious identification with our parents or caretakers, and the hurt that had to follow by experiencing the unconsciousness adults have of their own arrival, had to leave a bit of hole in all human beings. So, we begin our lives with what everyone believes is a hole in only them, when in fact it is experienced by everyone. Our original pureness and spiritual magnificence shining through our eyes, now gets experienced as something other than that. We feel shorter physically, mentally, emotionally, and get thrown under the assumption that the adults have to be more connected spiritually than we are. It's simply not the case.

The hole from the hurt and disappointment seeks to be filled. The attachment grows even stronger to the world outside of us in hopes of filling that hole. That hole is deepened as insecurities with survival are prevalent. Primitive man and primitive woman always needed others to survive. We needed others when we were hungry, tired, sick, weak, vulnerable, and fearful of the unknown. These tendencies over thousands of years created a type of yielding inherent in our collective human makeup.

The second we are born we have mystery thrown upon us. We are fearful, clueless, hungry, naïve, and very, very small. In fact we stay that way for a good long time, don't we? We are in total mystery and have no choice but to trust the group we are born into. They relieve us of our fear of survival. This wonderful group called family is providing comfort, nurturing and protection. They are larger than we are physically. They also appear to offer security with their apparent knowledge of all that is going on around us.

When they do something we have no choice but to assume it has to be what's right. We are born into a situation where decisions are made for us without the knowledge of any other way. Our family provides life sustaining nourishment and love and we go along with all the messages and rules of our family. Vulnerability to our surroundings is something we all share as our first experiences of life, and with this acceptance, comes our acceptance of other things, other things that we spend the rest of our lives trying to undo.

Associations with groups therefore are as strong as our innate need to survive. This is why attachments of all kinds become as important to us as life or death. We lose our self immediately and unconsciously to a system of words and thoughts foregoing our greater selves for the new physical representation we unconsciously digest as our identity. There is a singular message worldwide regardless of culture, religion, or economic status. Association with a group, because it's at the very onset of life, is positively reinforced to the greatest extent imaginable. It saves our life to do so. What could possibly produce a greater bond than that?

Thus, as our parents and guardians stayed locked in to the doctrines put forth by their parents, so do we, and so do our children. We are not really given the choice to go back and tell our parents that we don't want to go to the school they decided on or reject the spiritual/religious choices they made for us. This wouldn't go over well. Any spiritual evolving we would have done is subtly undone through institutions. Unfortunately, when a claim is made about anything that is acting in place of a mystery, the foundation for separation exists. Anything we accept as fact, that we don't really know is true, lays a foundation of internal discomfort.

We are acting on the surface to satisfy the masses. When we are alone we realize in many ways we combined what we know with what we don't know, and changed what is happening inside of us, for what we thought was needed on the outside. This approach then gets applied to everything after that, and becomes the breeding ground for dissension throughout our lives. It creates alienation, attack, defense, judgment, discrimination and even war.

Invisible characteristics, which we are of, and which we possess, are denied and lied about. This creates an effect on us because these are the most dominant life questions there are. We then create a framework for handling anything after that which also has invisible qualities. A "security-blanket" belief pattern circumvents deeper investigation. We are clinging to falsehoods with regards to our spiritual essence. This robs us of our greatest attributes as human beings. Dissension inside creates dissension outside when we handle any mystery in a way that falsely defines it.

We didn't just gravitate this way without a reason. In its origin this approach gave us the rare commodity we are always looking for, which is "security". There is also a sense of security when there are a bunch of other people sharing the same ideas, location, meetings, and initiatives. Yet, there is the "everything" attitude placed on these very tangible places of cultures, religions, and educative processes that exist generation after generation. They keep us serving masters not representing the greatness of ourselves.

Let's face it. People are skating on very thin ice with conclusions embraced regarding the mysteries of our source. The ways these mysteries are handled become the file folder that determines the way everything close to mystery after that is handled. Conclusions are latched onto for dear life and those against them are damned and judged for that.

When an intangible event happens a physical reason is assigned to it. If one is not present, sometimes one is made up. People have made them up for thousands of years and they stick to it. We see what the groups are doing and we go along with them. People defend decisions made from the fear of what could hurt them, and anything that has mysterious characteristics is handled in a fearful, clutching, alienating pattern. A belief is decided on, and all those who act against it are shunned.

The way we handle the questions of our existence is not just some little thing. The very thing we are making second nature in the patterns accepted for approaching the mystery of our source, is the very thing that robs us of our greatest identity. When we take on a method of deciding our mystery, we lose a great deal more. Every physical object on a molecular level has a mysterious basis at its very lowest denominator. Everything has its very essence based in the same mystery. So we are actually accepting one conclusion after the next about everything that in a very fundamental way just isn't true.

What groups do to establish themselves are the same things that make them potentially very dangerous. They bring large numbers of people together. They establish certain philosophies that make every member feel bound to those philosophies. Members know it's the shared beliefs of the group that are keeping them together. It's because of this power, which deems what's valuable to the group, that all values outside the group are affected.

This feeds the tendency to serve what was created, and what the group becomes, rather than be unified with the spirit that created it in the first place. We then seem to allow for only that. Even as groups we attach to move further away from their original meaning and purpose, we still serve their misdirection. Allegiances to categories described in a group contort even all new issues not originally considered. They get squeezed into those categories because that's what's available in the group's domain.

The computer age is a good example of this. We have lost the ability to think outside of this manmade box. So many systems we created, that had their origin based in one definition of assistance, have instead become the total definition. Even when different needs arise, that weren't originally addressed in that system's design, the original nature of that design is now applied to the new needs because we are serving what the creation has become without review. We have given up our responsibility to be in search of truths. We attached ourselves with certain groups and systems that have taken that searching away. Just like we need to be part of others when we are born, we have grown dependent on systems to help us with the complete discomfort of any subject.

If you make spirituality religious then it can't be talked about in mainstream conversation. It then gets confined to the strict traditions, history, and habits of a person's religion. Since that can be very different from person to person, all that was once of oneness, becomes separate. Religion in origin was pointing to a connection to what couldn't be seen about us, and in practice created a way of sectioning off and removing that commonality. In turn religion has divided the human species. Life would be more compassionate, feeling, and connecting if the mystery of humanity remained just that. There is no other truth.

It would shine like the brightest star if the original feelings, before religion, were actually maintained. The human brain needs to categorize and label everything and that leaves us at the mercy of these mental and physical groups. Physical creations, like associations and groups, generate the same self-serving patterns that the brain-machine creates leaving no room for growth. The brain-machine also needs to compare and measure, so contorting everything to fit this operation changes how we receive things.

After watching the daily horrors that surround us, and the horrible patterns of human beings throughout history, one must eventually stop denying and resisting what is quite apparent. All value given to what's out there and the pursuit of it becomes just about who has the most or the best of "out there" value. The daily newspapers, that our child could pick up to read, displays barely dressed women as a first page or third page attraction. Throughout the newspaper sexuality and exposure are the messages instead of wisdom, insights, discoveries, inventions, or stories involving strength of will.

What's shown to the young adults who want to be smart and pick up a newspaper? Not what they should be valuing inside of them, only what they should be valuing outside of them. Lust, money, things and all the crazy things people do for them. Our blood changes color from a deep dark red to a light shade of red once it's exposed to oxygen, and apparently, if we decide we are only what the outside determines our spiritual connection sometimes changes also.

Questions were not answered properly when I was young. They were dealt with in horrible ways. The answers confused me and tried to misdirect me. It was done in groups with everyone accepting it, with threats, with forceful pressure, and with punitive actions hanging over me. In even more subtle ways, it was done in song, in laughter, with smiles, and feast, with friends and family. That too was horrible, because the truth was being hidden and lies were being celebrated.

Deep down inside I walked with knowing that a show was put on to accept lies as truth. Wrong answers were given to me early on in life that I knew were false, yet they were delivered with such force it left me feeling wrong inside for what I felt. If I continued to express "non-conformity", it just got worse and worse. Being myself, and applying my own intuition and questioning was so frowned upon, I caved in and avoided communication.

Oftentimes, members of a group work even harder to wear the group message to overcompensate for the deeper doubts that lurk beneath the surface. An empty facade has to be worn to satisfy all those who have already fallen for underlying messages. This extra force needed to keep the doubts from surfacing uses the opposite force to suppress it. The opposite appears in these groups by people who are more adamant about the messages and more damning of others that pose different views. They defend their belief as if any challenge is a challenge not only to their need to be right, but their very need to survive.

How powerful would it ever be to move farther from the truth and farther from yourself to satisfy the mistaking majority? Why hide behind a seat in a bus heading toward crushing everyone's greatest gifts? Why help destroy what is truly most precious by hiding in destructive groups?

I took this quality of not being satisfied when something didn't make sense into adult life. I applied it from the time I was young all the way up until present. When something didn't fit, I delved deeper and stayed with it while always searching for the missing pieces of the puzzle. I can't now get lost in the next group that's trying to do what the first group was doing when misdirection weighed on me. If it was incomplete back then, it's still incomplete. The messages carry no greater weight because of some alleged foundation or some majority deciding so. I didn't blow past anything that represented confusion to me then, and I won't do it now either.

In a society that easily lent itself to superstitions, imagine a woman who took a rock, threw it in the air, and made it disappear. All would hail it as a miracle. What if she did it again? They would think of her as a god. Then if a man came along and did the same thing, it would mean the first god wasn't as special any more. Maybe they would make the man feel bad about doing it to keep the female god as special. They then may make anyone who did it feel bad about it because they only wanted the one they made special for doing it be the one that is exalted. It gave them security to elevate someone to great heights so when other things appeared and were unexplainable, they could say she wanted it that way. God made it all possible and only God has the power. Everyone agreed it would be a bit disruptive if everyone exercised these powers so curtailing it, consciously or unconsciously, as a society can easily become the norm.

So when the next generation was born there wasn't any mention of it and anyone believing they could make a rock disappear was greatly frowned upon. Everybody, in order to coexist, made rules, consciously and unconsciously, not to ever use or talk about these powers. This happened generation after generation until nobody believed that they even had such powers. So they existed in denial even while they felt those feelings tugging at them. Yet, there was that one amazing God that was spoken about in stories that could be the answer for everything that posed itself as a mystery. So we defaulted to her in experiencing the most miraculous things of all. We weren't entitled to them and gave the experience away to the idea of the "God". We decided only she could have it and so she did. No rocks were ever allowed to disappear again without giving that power to the "God" who could do that. More to the point, no extrasensory perceptions are allowed to be embellished without giving the power to God.

How do people react when they are forced to believe in what is intangible without physical proof? Are they compelled to handle it the same way they handled the biggest intangible mysteries of all? Do they leave themselves open to possibilities, or do they latch onto a conclusion because it offers the greatest immediate "security"? Ironically the greatest security is in allowing for the mystery. Once mystery is allowed for, the openness and ability to gather more information is what will bring about the truest feelings. Being closer to truth has to feel more secure than accepting an illusion. Peace comes from not attacking, not defending, but allowing mystery to be just that. This would allow the ability to see all possibilities.

We are balancing a tiny steel ball of enlightenment through a maze of obstacles, obstacles that on the surface look daunting, yet self-realization is crystallized through them. When do the obstacles become so daunting that they become what is believed as the only truth? At what point does the experience ignore the inner self-realization? If this happens will I ignore it, but how about if that happens? Will I now lose myself under the obstacle of this next prop? What disguise will have so much stimuli attached to it that I will not be the viewer anymore? What button that I create consciously or unconsciously will dominate all paths? What detour will take me off the path of embellishing enlightenment? What emotion has so much armor that it can't, or won't, be penetrated?

What insidious snake will elude my awareness? What hole will that steel ball fall down where I cannot get it back to the maze for even an attempt at balancing? What experience will exhaust, what is the opposite of enlightenment, so that all that's left to feel will be enlightenment? While I am playing with the idea of moving away from what is always waiting, so why not embrace that now? Why not watch the dance that's pretending to be me rather than being only the dance?

## VII  Too Close For Comfort

When I was fifteen years old I worked myself so deeply into the confines of my brain, and got so lost under the umbrella of my thoughts that I nearly killed myself. I elevated my dad in my mind and in my heart. His scarcity early on in life, and only short visits when I got older, made him become more important to me than even me.

Everything was hard for me those days. I was out of sync at home, school, and even with so-called friends. I really didn't fit in, but I knew one thing, and that was once a week the greatest guy in the world would come to see me, and that was my dad.

Once we leave the shore of our own existence to go on the boat of another we know that boat has to sink. Once we tip our hat to another so much we forget to put it back on our head we are doomed. So, of course this journey away had to get tested.

It was my sister's high school graduation day, and there were only four tickets available for the ceremony. It was the largest graduating class they ever had, and there was a battle at my house going on about these tickets. My dad insisted on his new wife being there, and my mother insisted that she shouldn't. The four tickets were already assigned in my sister's mind to my mother, my father, me and my cousin. My cousin was there while my sister and I were growing up and was relied on when nobody else could be there. She was real special to us so she had to be invited. I offered to not attend because I really couldn't stand any more fighting going on around me in my life, but nobody wanted that either.

The fight raged on through the phone between my sister, my mother and my father. I stayed in my room and locked the door. My mother and sister spoke to my dad on the phone and I could hear from their side it wasn't going well. Like so many times while growing up, emotions had taken over and love and caring had taken a back seat. The tension raged and I could feel it coming my way. I was called to the phone because my father wanted to speak to me. I felt this power play coming my way and I didn't want to deal with it. The banging in my door ensued. Mom screamed, "Why is this door locked? Come to the phone, your dad wants to speak with you!" I reluctantly unlocked my bedroom door and came to the phone. My mother said "What's the matter with you didn't you hear me, your father is on the phone." To this day I wished I kept my door locked.

I loved my dad so much. He wanted to know how I felt about the tickets, the graduation, his wife, and how it all should be handled. I dreaded the whole thing and wished I could just run away until it was all over. I said I would rather not comment because I don't want to be in the middle of it. He forced my opinion by saying that he always taught me to have my own feelings, so I gave it. I said, "I think we are missing the point of the event. It's my sister's graduation. It's not anybody else's and we should do what makes her happy. It should be her choice and your wife wasn't there when she was growing up. It also makes Mom uncomfortable, so why have any tension on that day?" So he said, "So, you're saying that you don't think my wife should be there?" I said, "No, I like her but I don't think she should be there." He said, "In that case, I never want to see you ever again", and he hung up the phone.

I went into shock. I hung up the phone in disbelief, went back in my room, locked the door, and the pain wrenched through as I cried. It was so loud it brought neighbors to the door. It went on for hours. I was spiraling down and I couldn't stop it. All I valued was gone in an instant. I was so blindsided and so disarmed by the way he asked me that I left nothing for myself to hold on to if he rejected me. I wanted the moment back. I felt like I said something so wrong that I just couldn't forgive myself. My dad was gone because of the answer I gave. He was so rare, so special, and so cherished by me and now he was gone forever.

I decided to kill myself. My mom was in the kitchen talking to the neighbor who came over when she heard me crying. My door was locked and I was crying so loud for so long they were threatening to break it down. I figured if I cut my wrists in the right spots along with the vein on my neck I would die when the blood rushed out of my body. I had a pocket knife that I put in my pants so I could leave the apartment and do the deed. I had to open my door and communicate so I wiped the tears away and got my head ready for this mission.

I opened the door and said I was going to go for a walk. The neighbor immediately said, "I don't think that's a good idea." My mom said, "He walks all the time and it always makes him feel better." The neighbor shook her head like she still believed what she believed and said that I didn't look good so maybe I should stay home. My mom got up and intellectually felt that staying home and crying wasn't doing me any good and thought it was alright for me to leave.

That neighbor delayed my leaving for about a minute. That neighbor cared enough to put her feelings out there at the risk of her friendship. She stepped over some obvious boundaries to do it. She didn't know it at the time, but she changed my future with that minute. Much to my neighbor's chagrin, I left. I had the knife in my pocket and I knew what I had to do.

It didn't make sense to be here anymore. I really had a rough go at life as a child growing up. If the only thing I could cherish was now gone, what could matter anymore? I really saw absolutely no reason to stay alive.

I started on my walk with a complete and total focus. I thought it out while walking toward Pelham Parkway that I would sit on this rock I went to for refuge before, cut the veins on my wrists and neck and end it. This is exactly what I was going to do and the specifics were very worked out in my head. I started out up my block to Williamsbridge Road, where I was saying good-bye to life and the area I lived, and I was only about five blocks from the exact spot where I was going to end it.

The tears started up again in a stream and the reality of saying good-bye to everything was really setting in. I looked back on all the pain of living I endured for as long as I could remember. Now the tears were really flowing out. I was approaching the Pizzeria, where I had spent many a day eating by myself. I could see a crowd out front from less than a block away and I didn't want the attention from anyone who could take me off course. So, I walked to the other side of the street. I knew it wouldn't be long now. A few more blocks up and I'll hit Pelham Parkway, then I'll walk along the grass, get to the rock, and end it there.

I had my head down and I was walking while taking a peak out of the corner of my eye at the crowd across the street, and all of a sudden a man about my sister's age popped out of the bushes. He was tall and skinny with blond hair. I thought I met him once a long time ago briefly. He said his name was Ronnie and he was my sister's friend. He also remembered that we met quickly once a long time ago. He repeated that he and my sister were real good friends. He saw I was crying and asked if I was OK. He peered into my eyes and told me I looked terrible. He told me to wait while he threw out the garbage he was holding. "The pails are right here and I live right behind these bushes, sorry to scare you", he said. He explained that he knew it looked strange that his house was hidden behind bushes, but his dad didn't like unexpected visitors.

As I wiped the tears from my face he mentioned my sister told him it was rough at my house because of my mother's choice of men. He asked if I would like to come upstairs for a drink or something. I thanked him and told him, "No thank you", and proceeded to walk away staying on course. He followed me and said, "C'mon, just for a little while and then you could leave", he insisted. I declined his company again, and proceeded to walk further away. He let me walk a bit and then I crossed the street, but he ran to follow me before the light changed. He said, "No, you don't understand, I'm not letting you go without me." I was shocked and looked at him and said "Listen, you barely know me and I just would like to go for a walk." I started walking away again and again and he just wouldn't leave me alone. "No matter what you say I'm not leaving you", he insisted.

He said he didn't like the look in my eyes when he first saw me so no matter what I said after that he wasn't going to let me out of his sight. He said pleadingly "Now we have only two choices, we can go for a walk together or you could come inside for a drink." He threw me off my plan. I said, "If I walk away you're going to continue to follow me even though you barely know me?" He replied, "I suppose you can fight me but I'm bigger and stronger than you so why don't you just come upstairs for a while? If after a while, you still want to leave then you can leave, alright? C'mon." He put his arm around me and guided me back to his house. He explained how the house was not as scary inside as it was outside and I went with him upstairs. "But your dad doesn't like unexpected visitors", I remembered. "My dad doesn't like salesmen and people pushing things on him, but friends of mine are fine", he comfortingly assured.

The man saved my life. He flat out saved my life. He stayed with me for hours talking things out and then made sure I was alright when he walked me back home. He made sure I went upstairs when we arrived back at my front door and told me that he would be calling me tomorrow. He shifted my mindset and made me realize there was something outside of the tunnel vision I worked myself into. I certainly was going to kill myself. There was absolutely no doubt in my brain. It was so over, but this man saved my life because he did something very few people would have done. He went over the line and imposed his will on me. He would not take no for an answer and I gotta tell ya, there's probably only one out of a million people who would have done what he did.

I was very adamant about not wanting his company and was very focused on what I had to do. Not many would have handled my rejections without getting so angry at me that giving up would have been the only conclusion. By all accounts I should be dead. The man saved my life because he saw in one look what I was going to do and all words after that meant nothing. He honored the look and ignored the words. He honored his feelings and went against the normal things that most people would have done. That's what he did, and that's what my neighbor did when she delayed my leaving. It was the combination of those two people caring, and going over the line, that saved my life.

How close it all was to me not being here today. Annie, my neighbor slowed up my departure just long enough for me to bump into Ronnie throwing out his garbage. Seconds changed my fate. The seconds that came from a woman honoring her feelings enough to intrude her will against a mother's decision. If Annie doesn't go over the line by telling my mother what she thought, I'm dead. Most people would have backed off, but she said it three times and shook her head saying, "No, I don't agree". If Ronnie doesn't go over the line, and physically impose his will on me, I'm dead. If he gives up after the first, second, or the third insistence on my part, I'm dead.

It took two people caring for me when my family didn't, that saved my life. My mother didn't care, my sister didn't care, and my father certainly didn't care. It took two people who honored their feelings over the norms of the physical world to change the rest of my life, or rather to give me the rest of my life. Years later, I told Annie what she did and bought her a diamond bracelet in honor of her caring. She didn't realize the impact she had at the time. She died just recently while I was writing this book but I am so happy I was able to let her know how her act of kindness gave me my life.

Ronnie knew what he had done because I told him a few weeks afterwards and it was almost too much for him to handle. He gave me my life back and although that's a big thing to wear, he should always wear it with pride. He should wear it with the compassion acknowledged because I think that is the very meaning of life itself. If not for the caring Ronnie gave me, when few would have, I would not be alive today. It not just a little thing, it's the biggest thing there is. To step out of the crowd and be different because you care is the biggest thing there is. Caring is the extra step that is the very meaning of life itself.

# VIII   The American Dream

I ended up leaving home at an early age. I was sixteen when I graduated high school, and was on my own a lot after that with college and jobs. I went away to college and getting away from home was a very smart choice. I dated plenty and had a great deal of fun. I paid for my education working full-time while going to school full-time. I moved off campus, got my own apartment, and was by myself most of the time. I eventually came back home to refuel financially, go to school at night and work during the day. I read a lot, wrote, listened to music, studied for work and school, went out dancing, and learned to like my own space. I then moved away for good at age nineteen.

I eventually met a wonderful gal in Atlantic City and got married three years later. We had a great honeymoon and came back to my bachelor pad. My wife didn't want to be where I was as a bachelor, so she spent the next summer looking for a place to live. We found a beautiful condo in a great area. We took all the wedding money we saved and some work money we shared and laid down a deposit to buy our first home together. It was a great thrill and we were very happy.

After being married for five years, we had our first daughter. She was simply amazing. Everything about her was great. She was born with a brilliant awareness and she needed lots of love and attention. Four years later we had another amazing girl. Now I had two amazing daughters four years apart. I would do anything for them. I still would.

They never knew how much I gave up to get them what they wanted, but I was always happy to do it. I worked very hard and many days I only saw them sleeping. I sold life insurance for twelve years and sometimes worked a hundred hours a week. It was a good business and I worked my way up the ladder. I also got the life insurance business in me by the way I lived my life, as if each moment could be my last. It's not just an expression. I live like that every minute. I let no love go unsaid and my feelings show as if that moment could be my last.

I oftentimes didn't really have any way to get them what they wanted but I did cartwheels to come up with it anyway. I didn't make enough money for my wife to stay home throughout both my children's early years but miraculously I figured out a way to do it for nine full years. The stock market worked wonders for me for many years. I floated cash between credit cards and used the money to catch a quick gain in the stock market, and then paid off everything. Money took on a different meaning because of the way I sometimes was able to create it from nothing as if it was with smoke and mirrors. All along, I still worked a hundred hours a week to make what the market sometimes did for me in a fraction of the time.

The life blood I gave to the insurance company for twelve years suddenly ended in October of 1999. My career was destroyed during the coldness of a conference call. I was moving up with promotions, raises, and perks, and in a sentence on a conference phone call with five others, it was all gone. My wife, my amazing four year old daughter, and my beautiful newborn daughter were waiting for me at home unaware of the freight train that just ran over me. The pain of telling my wife my career was gone was a huge blow to our security. It was only a year after we lost what would have been a son during late stage pregnancy. I was overwhelmed with the storms I was facing and my wife was even more devastated.

Dad, to me is the sweetest word in the whole world. Just hearing it makes everything I hear after that acceptable. Any problem is minimized because the music of the love behind the word "Dad" is in my ears. My father had challenges, and I swore I would wait a long time before I ever had children. When I did make that decision I vowed to try my best to have as much patience as possible.

I was hit as a kid and it was so deflating and shocking that I swore I would never do that to my children, and I never did. I waited until I was thirty to get married after we were dating for three years. We didn't live together. We saw each other mainly on weekends. We were both busy with work. I worked a lot more hours than her because I was in sales and that's what it took to do well. I waited until I was thirty-five to have my first child. I honored all the vows I made with myself and I honored the vows I made to my wife.

When I made mistakes, I would say I did. I was a father that apologized to his children. I didn't take the position that since I was the adult I couldn't be wrong. I treated them as equals when discussing things. I listened intently to whatever they had to say. When they said something I really tried to feel the heart of it. I even apologized when the things we disagreed on were a little right and little wrong on each side. No dispute was more than the love that existed before and after every dispute. I never let them go to sleep mad and if they did, I woke them up and sat with them ironing it out until there was love expressed. Sometimes this took five minutes and sometimes it took hours, but whatever it took that's what I did.

I don't think you ever met a father that loved his daughters as much as I do. I was always the one in the audience with the roses for everything they ever did. Even when they were in the last row of a choir where I couldn't hear them and could barely see them they were congratulated as if they were the only ones on stage. I would do anything for them. I would walk through fire for them and they knew it. I made whatever they wanted the most important thing in the world. In my mind I was always very careful to do what a good dad would do. I had no father around most of the time while growing up, so I really didn't have a good example of what a father should be. So, I erred on the side of loving too much. I'm a man who had a lot to overcome growing up, and I was always aware of the tendencies that a grown man with my tough background would have. I always tried to be the best man I could be in spite of it.

I had it tough growing up. My mom surrounded us with the worst element of people imaginable. Street guys, loan sharks, wise guys, made men, Mafia King Pins, number's runners, and just about anyone she ever brought home had some angle for making money the illegal way. I was more like my dad. I had no tolerance for that garbage. I hated the people she introduced us to. She seemed to have some psychological issues stemming back to her mom that made her gravitate to gangsters. She didn't seem to care how much it hurt me when she brought people into my life of ill character. My sister hated it and I hated it even more. She was impervious to our pain. In her mind she needed to get what she wanted, and would do anything to get it.

Nothing ever changed. When she was twenty-six and I was four she hurt me with men she brought home. When I was nine, after we lived with one of her horrible choices for a few years, they went out, got married, returned home, had a fight and continued on. This was her second husband and he was the worst creep you could imagine. I stayed to myself and avoided interaction as much as possible. I was honest and I worked at honest jobs since I was a little boy. I wasn't going to go that direction. I was disappointed with so many things and so many people, but I had my integrity and my insights, and I knew that my approach was the right direction for me. Yet, her second husband hurt me so deeply from ages nine to fifteen I didn't recover for years. Her third husband, a number's running street punk who was about forty years old, disgraced her and my family with his lies, cheating, and the double-life he lived.

One particular Saturday my plan was to just relax at home with the family and barbecue. My mother called up and asked me what I was doing because she was going to be in the neighborhood. My wife told me to ask my mom if she wanted to join us. Mom liked the idea and asked if she could bring a friend. I said sure, and asked who it was. She told me it was Ricky, an old friend of hers. She reminded me that he was the son of the wonderful woman who used to live downstairs from us in the Bronx. I told her it was fine and we agreed on the time for around two o'clock. She asked my address and I was confused. She should have remembered how to get to my place. She then asked my zip-code, and then I was very confused. "Are you writing me or coming over?" I asked. She explained that she needed it to give to someone and she'll explain later.

After I hung up I started remembering things about this man and wished I never invited her. There was more than one son and I thought Ricky was the good one but this one I remembered was in jail for racketeering. I thought maybe I got the sons mixed up. She wouldn't still be doing this garbage in her sixties right? I was wrong. She brought over the gangster. It was the typical choice of my mom and she still never grew out of it.

The hurt kept coming and I should have kept her away. I told myself to keep an open mind but as it turns out she was meeting him at CT State Prison, and I later found out that he just finished doing twenty years 20 years for racketeering. This, in retrospect was the type of person that could very well have had the most advanced surveillance systems placed on him. He also could have been the reason I was invisibly affected afterwards, and then severely tortured as time went on. I also found out that it could have been much worse for him but he made a special deal with the authorities.

I can't believe this was the friend she brought over my house to see my beautiful family with my sweet girls. I was nice, they were nice, my wife was nice, the barbecue was great, the weather was great, my children swept everyone away with their sweetness and we had a nice time. They left and all was fine, or at least I thought all was fine. It was the beginning of an invisible hell that was not an easy thing to explain. It was many years before I considered what may have actually happened and where the pain to follow could have stemmed from. It was confused by so many things so I don't know for sure, but near that time the slow creeping torture began. It was applied more severely when it could be confused with another event in my life, but I didn't know that part yet either.

There I was a grown man, happily married with my six year old, and two year old daughters, and she still found a way to hurt me once again with her insane choices. I just wasn't expecting it to happen anymore. My mother was in her sixties and I thought it was over. I purposely didn't see her all that much while I was married. The memories and the curve balls that would show up was not something I welcomed. I wanted my children to know their grandma, but I hoped as she got older this tendency would stop. She had to grow up someday, right? She wouldn't keep hurting herself and others with these decisions, right? I thought it would be sweet if my mother could just stay away from the bad element of people she always seemed to end up with. Like so many times in my life what I wanted got confused with what actually was.

It was soon after 9/11. My workplace was a two blocks from ground zero; and my job was on hold until the building I worked in could be inhabited again. Yea, I went through that living hell. I was as close as could be without being dead. I had trouble moving as I watched it unfold, almost paralyzed from the site of the planes hitting. I was covered in ashes and walked as a zombie would in a state of overwhelm. People looked at me after I made my way uptown as if they were seeing a ghost, and in many ways they were. Part of me died that day. In some ways I could see more and in some ways I saw less. The shock I was in lasted many years without me even realizing it. I guess when people are in shock they don't know it. The problem is the people around them oftentimes aren't sensitive enough to realize it either.

It hurt my career also because a year later I was let go after two thirds of the firm was. I was one of the last that had to be let go. I had trained a lot of the people walking around the firm so it became hard to eliminate me. When they finally did, I traded the stock market for a while. My wife was very unhappy with that decision. I had been involved in the market with work or investing for thirty years and felt differently than she did. It helped me pay for things all the years she was home with the children and she was going back to work while I was staying home. She hated that too. My wife didn't understand the stock market, but as long as it worked she didn't care. When it stopped working she crucified me with all she had.

Some parts of me would like to think she was manipulated to do so. I still don't really know which one it was. Maybe I cushion my own pain, of her personally doing what she eventually did to me, by imagining something bigger happening to her. Maybe something bigger did happen, and I am screaming in a cave that no one seems to care about. I couldn't make all the trials and tribulations we had to face bigger than the love I had for my wife and children, but as it turned out, she certainly found a way to diminish our love until it was gone.

Oh what a contrast it was in being with the sweetest of the sweetest with my little girls, and still forced to be aware of all the horrid people, and all the things that came with them. I had my fill of pain growing up and I had my fill of pain as an adult. I really only had tolerance for seeing what was good. I saw the bad but chose to turn it off because I really couldn't take any more pain in my life. I couldn't even watch the news any more. I avoided all the scuttlebutt about this bad thing or that bad thing. I just couldn't go there anymore. I didn't feel better than the pain-filled people glorified by others in the media. It didn't make me feel better that it wasn't me. It made me feel worse that there was so much horror in the world.

There are so many insensitive, selfish, hurtful people with nothing in them for the next person. I wanted what was good and kind around me and I worked real hard to have that. I had to fight my own memories and my own demons. I had to watch my words and my references. Previous references had so much pain in them that being immersed in each moment more deeply was a necessary pattern to follow even when mental recollections were conjured up that connected to current events.

My little girls reminded me of what was precious. They defined it in every way. I had to watch how I reacted when they spoke because that would not always jive with how a little girl received messages. I most certainly didn't always know how my girls felt. They were very sensitive and they didn't always reveal their true feelings. When something close to them was on their mind, you had to keep guessing until their eyes lit up, and that was the signal for what should be considered. They were like a leaf falling off a tree and sensitive to the slightest breeze. They had a very interesting wavelength of sensitivity and if I came off something else that got me flustered, I certainly would have to pause a while to find that wavelength again. Being in each moment helped me reach them even more.

My first daughter was a little harder to locate than my second but I loved them both equally and unconditionally. It is the only unconditional love I have ever felt or will ever feel in my life. My little girls got me, and for as long as I live there isn't anything I wouldn't do for them. They must know that I feel that way. I never held back my love for them. There isn't anything either one of them could do that would ever take my love away. It is truly unconditional and truly rare.

The greatest feeling in the whole world was when both my daughters hugged me at the same time. I wouldn't trade those moments for anything. We had something we called a family hug where all four of us just hugged each other in a circle. Those moments we thought would always be there for us to go to no matter what.

When I was with my girls it was as if I was walking on a cloud where a shining light surrounded us. They were sweet, sensitive, and quiet like the still water of a pond. They were feeling many things and sharing some. Their non-verbal communications soared and their love was so kind and so gentle. They would bring me into the present moment and show me many gifts.

We read to our children every night until they got older and then they read by themselves a lot after that. We had birthday parties, holidays, and lots of gifts. We went to parades, carnivals, the zoo, Broadway shows, concerts, and everything a kid would want. We did everything for our children; Dance lessons, music lessons, speech lessons, and everything they needed we provided with lots of love and encouragement always. We went on vacations, weekend getaways, camping, you name it we did it. The tooth fairy, Santa Claus, sleigh riding, snowball fights, swimming lessons, beach days, we loved and loved. I did cartwheels for every one of their special days. I always tried to come up with the right gift, the right restaurant, the right thing that would touch them the deepest. I thought for hours to try to say just the right thing in every card. I always put them first. The door was held for my wife every day for twenty years. I was always the gentlemen and enjoyed doing it.

I would kiss my girls goodnight every night and I loved those moments so much. They made it last longer. I think it was to have some fun with it. They would remember all the things they forgot right when I thought they were ready for bed. My younger one would have to arrange about fifteen stuffed animals in a particular way. Someone would forget to brush their teeth and someone would remember something for school. Someone wanted to finish a few more paragraphs in their book, and someone would not be comfortable with clothing or blankets. After all the considerations, I would kiss the younger one goodnight, tuck her in, and give her a big hug and kiss.

The older one would always ask, "Why don't I go first if I came first?" I would always reply that since she was the older one it was like she was the captain of the ship who is always saluted last. I would say when I kiss you goodnight you are also the oldest one who is making sure your younger sister is OK as the captain of this little ship right here. She understood it but always asked anyway. I think she liked hearing it. I would make sure all her blankets were just right, and the blanket she had since she was born was always last as the one she cuddled with. She would look up at me with love and I would let her kiss me first and then I would kiss her. That's how she liked it. Sometimes I would hear them get up and I would go through the same thing and tuck them in again. It was love I always wished I had from my father when I was young, and now I was able to give it to my children. I don't think my wife or children ever knew what it meant to me. No words can describe it. No words deserve it.

One time, when I went to kiss my older daughter good-night, who was barely eight at the time, she told me that she was feeling jolts to her body. Her body was jumping as if she got an electric shock. I didn't really know how to respond. I asked if it was always in the same location. She said that it was jumping to different parts of her body. I feared she had what my mom had when she was little. My mom went through a few seizures after an injury to her neck and we worried if these seizures were hereditary. I mentioned the idea of a doctor and that alarmed my daughter so much that she didn't want to tell me again. She really hated doctors and would avoid them at all costs. Yet, I wondered about the jolts and what they could mean. I asked her about them afterwards and she said they stopped, but I never knew if she said that just to avoid the doctor.

So, I would watch her when she was sleeping sometimes, and saw that her body was jumping. I couldn't tell whether it was normal dream movement or something else. I questioned her later and she said it didn't happen again. I asked my mom about her seizures when she was young, but it was such a painful time for her she wasn't comfortable talking about it.

Time went on and holidays came. I was respectful of my wife's wishes and honored her religious allegiance by being at the Seder. I did it every year since we were dating. It was a two night affair. One night was spent over her parent's house and one night was over ours. I celebrated all the Jewish holidays even though I was raised Catholic. I went along even though I didn't believe any religion, but I loved her and it didn't mean more to me than that. It was important to her so I was a good sport. I made a promise to my wife when I married her that we would raise the children Jewish. I was half and half but raised Catholic and didn't much care for any of it. My mother was born Jewish and she converted so that qualified me as Jewish in the Jewish religion.

As time went by I saw the damage religion caused, but I was sitting through another Seder with both my beautiful children. My sweet girls are four years apart, and both very sensitive. We were at my in-laws the first night and my four year old sat to my left and my eight year old sat to my right. We were taking turns reading from the Passover books. The reading came to my four year old. Both our children read well at a very early age. We read to both our children since they were born and even at four my younger daughter could make out the words slowly as she read from the book.

Everyone was quite impressed with how well she was doing. She was as cute as a little girl could be reading slowly and correctly while sounding out even the words she didn't know. She read the part about how God smite the first born of the Egyptians because of the heavy bondage placed on the Jews for so long. She then looked up at me and said, "Daddy, what does smite mean?" Her eyes were so innocent, so beautiful, and her soul so filled with love and purity, that I felt my insides ripping apart. I choked on my reply and then blurted it out, "Smite means kill. Smite means kill, and I can't do this anymore", I said. I got up, left the table and sat on the couch. I took off the Yarmulke, looked back at the table and said, "You want me to teach my little daughter that there's a God and he killed people? I can't do this, I'm sorry, no, I'm not sorry, I just can't do this", I said.

My wife's mother and father were appalled. They were strict Jews and were shocked by my reaction. I think it cost me badly. My mother-in-law worked for Rockland County and her close friend was someone who had a high position in Westchester County where I lived. I don't think she wanted me to be married to her daughter any more after that. I don't think she wanted me around my own children either. Things were done to hurt me. Many things over the years were done to hurt me simply for wanting my children to feel love instead of hate.

My wife's mother called her every day after that day and it seemed my wife's whole personality changed whenever she got off the phone with her. It got to the point where I was no longer giving her the messages. Even the children wondered why she called every single day and they noticed the callousness that came over their mother after every call from their Grandmother. Maybe my wife's mother, who hated my rejection of the Seder that day, caused me great pain. Maybe my mother-in-law's county connections hurt me in unimaginable ways. My life started to change drastically from that day forward.

During this time, I was also experiencing glimpses of enlightenment, but this pushed my wife away even further. It challenged her strict religious beliefs and she didn't like it. She didn't want the children exposed to these different ideas. I felt her and her mother's wrath at my dissension from their teachings. I couldn't perpetuate the subtle hate and division to my children in the messages of the Seder, but in turn, subtle hate and division became the undercurrent of what started underpinning my marriage.

I didn't stop her from her rituals, nor did I show any disrespect. I simply didn't read during the Seder and told my children that the messages we digest are very important. I asked them to respect their mother but always make their own decisions about what their research and feelings showed them.

My mother-in-law and my wife did not want their religious beliefs challenged. When a person does not want to experience something, they get mad at the person that directs them there. There was great friction being transmitted from the both of them. The resistance to my message about how each word can affect a child was downplayed by their desire for rituals to be upheld. The tendency to shoot the messenger was used to defend their stance. I reflected back to them the insecurities they really felt with the philosophy and the "logic" their religion embraced.

Open the closets! A fish cannot determine that it has nothing to do with the water in which it swims. A person cannot disconnect from the truth of greater wisdom. They simply will bring pain upon themselves and others with this delusion. My desire to **not** have a four year old focus on killing and revenge should not have taken a backseat to rituals.

# IX  The Dad That Never Died

The phone call came into my wife from my half-brother when I wasn't home. I got home from work and my wife made sure that she was doing a good job telling me. She said, "I'm not good at this kind of stuff but I have something to tell you and it's very serious." She took me in the bedroom and asked that I sit down. She said, "It's the worst possible news so, prepare yourself." I said, "The children, something with the children?" She said, "No, I guess that would be the worst possible news. I'm just going to say it, your father died".

Her relief exceeded her empathy. She was more proud of herself for saying it than she was considerate of my pain. She had trouble with deep emotions and sympathy, and really didn't want to go there, so she didn't. My knees got weak and I sat on the bed. She asked if I wanted to be alone. She told me that she would be inside if I needed her. I said OK. I think it was more for her, than for me, to suggest I be alone. I actually needed her with me but felt her desire to move away from any pain, so I let her go inside. She seemed relieved because it was as much pain as she wanted to experience. She did the best she could. In the end it's always up to us anyway, but going with pain alone is not something you get married for. I sat alone as if I wasn't married, alone in my pain, in my loss, and in my utter devastation.

Now this was another unfortunate thing and once again I knew that somehow I would be unconsciously deprived of passion, caring, consideration or something because of it. So far, this time, she was doing very well. She did a great job telling me my dad died and it's not an easy thing to tell someone. Yet, she really didn't see me and she really didn't feel me. It was all about her avoiding pain.

I expected a mate that was with me through better and worse and instead I got a fair weather wife. I didn't know it until the times got rough. When they were good, all was good, but when they weren't she would jump ship. She even told the kids to leave me alone, but I didn't want that either. The love of my family would have helped me get through it better but instead I felt abandoned. I felt like I was shunned when hardship affected me. I was too sad to start trying to fix her tendency to avoid people with any emotional issues.

I told my wife years earlier if my father ever dies I'm not going to do well for a while because I had always hoped he would clear the air about so many things, but he never did. Our relationship could have been so different but he hurt me so much and always refused to apologize for it. In his mind a father never apologizes to a son. He was old school Italian and that just didn't happen in his world. I told her I'm going to need some emotional help for a little while when that happens. Neither one of us could have known the extent of the pain and the extent of her abandonment.

My dad and I looked the same, oftentimes thought the same, and even had the same intonation in conversation. You could walk into a room with a thousand other people and know that was my father. I wasn't going to let anyone else call the shots on what was most important to him after his departure. He told me a few things years earlier, and some were instructions about what I should do if he passed away. I knew I had to honor them.

After a short time I went in the kitchen where my wife was preparing something and asked her how she found out. She said my half-brother called. I thought it would be my sister or my mother but it was a very distant half-brother. She said his message to me was that I should wait until he called back before going down there to Kentucky where Dad had lived. I asked my wife why, but she said that was all he said. This was my father and nobody knew him better than I. I wasn't going to wait for anything. I had to take care of his final wishes.

I checked on a plane as soon as I could. I was pleasantly surprised that there was a flight to Kentucky leaving from my local airport. I got on the next flight out which was leaving in only a few hours. My half-brother left the coroner's information and that was all I needed. The most important thing was that Dad wanted to be cremated and he wanted his ashes sprinkled over a field in Kentucky. That's what my father said to me about three years prior. That was the last time I saw him and that was exactly what I was going to do. I called the coroner who was in possession of the keys to his home, and of course, in possession of my father's body. He was as kind as he could be and said he would wait up for me to arrive to get instructions from me in person.

What a very strange thing to experience. It's so surreal. It was a complete break in how I experienced reality. I had so many surreal moments over the preceding years that surreal was starting to feel more real than what real used to be. Something was happening to me that was beyond what could be seen and some of it felt beyond what was natural.

My dad was a pain ridden, frustrated, short tempered, yet, very insightful, artistic, inventive, and creative man. Even though, I understood him the best anybody really could, he was very difficult. Yet, I knew how to be with him. I would always give him total respect when we spoke and that allowed him to show how frustrated a man he truly was. When he died it hit me hard. I would have liked to have had more closure between us on some of the things that happened over the years and now there wasn't any way for that to be experienced.

I would have liked him to get to know his grandchildren but it was no longer possible. I would have liked to have seen him at peace and happy. Well, it wasn't to be. He died of a heart attack at the age of seventy and I had to take care of all his final business.

When I arrived in Kentucky, I rented a car, and drove to meet the coroner. I got lost, because I always get lost when I go to a completely new place. I have a lousy sense of direction to begin with but to stick me in the middle of a new place at night was even a greater challenge than usual. I couldn't believe the coroner waited until 11:30PM to meet with me. He told me that no matter what time I showed up, he would be there for me. The cell phone came in handy. The coroner spoke me through the final directions to his house. He had the key to my dad's home as well as keys to the car he died in. I had no place to stay except my dad's apartment. The coroner let me follow him to my dad's apartment so I wouldn't get lost again. I didn't want to pay for a hotel if I could avoid it. So, although it felt very strange, I decided to sleep at my dad's apartment. The coroner brought me there and gave me the key.

He told me he would take me to his car when my half-brother and sister arrived. He told me my dad was very well liked in this town and he would help in any way he can. I was very moved by that. He mentioned how my dad found happiness in this town he moved to and that meant a great deal to me. I thanked the coroner for meeting with me so late and for giving me the keys to his apartment.

He told me that there was obviously no closer person to my dad than I was in the whole world. He mentioned that my dad spoke about me a lot and it was always with great pride. He told me I looked like him, talked like him, and even thought like him. The coroner left and told me that I could come see him the next day to let him know how to proceed with the body. As we were departing I told him my dad's wishes were told to me three years prior, and they were for him to be cremated and to have his ashes sprinkled over a field in Kentucky. The coroner was surprised and smiled. He said, "Sprinkled over a field in Kentucky Aye? Well, then that's what you should do." He said my dad had become very religious late in life and didn't think he would want that, but agreed that I had to stick to what he told me since he never said anything else after that. The coroner said that whatever I wanted to do to honor my father, he would do.

He kept telling me how much alike I was to my father. He thought it was amazing how similar we were. He felt as though he was still speaking to him when he spoke to me. He was happy to meet me and made me feel better by repeating how I was spoken fondly of by my father. I thanked him and left off that I would get my sister and half-brother together and come over and see him. Kentucky kindnesses and warmth swept over me from this man. He treated me as if I was family.

Quite strangely, there I was left alone in my dad's apartment. It was eerie that he was there the day before. One of his cigarettes was in the ash tray half smoked, and the scent drew me to it. It smelled like it was lit just a short while ago. It could very well have been his last. Of course, it was the strongest unfiltered cigarette known to man. He smoked two and a half packs a day for fifty-five years. Sure, he tried quitting several times, but never stayed with it. All in all the man smoked all those years, and if that was the actual cause of death then it wasn't so surprising.

I forgot to eat and was real hungry so I looked in his refrigerator and saw a half-eaten chicken. I hesitated at first wondering if it was still good. I sat down and proceeded to eat it and knew that the first half was eaten by my dad, and I may be eating part of what was his very last meal. I looked around and felt his presence by the way he kept things in his home. I remembered things from my boyhood that he still had. He liked odd things, but some were quite nice and very unique. He bought and sold some of them for extra money. I was never in his apartment before. I felt closer to him than I did the last ten years, but now he was dead. I felt bad about all that time going by without ever visiting him, but he never made it easy.

After I ate, I looked around and saw some letters involving legal strife he got into with a neighbor. I also found some letters showing fees paid to a patent attorney for some patent searches and disputes accompanied by some drawings he made of his ideas. There were also photos of his apartment and the things in it. There were three identical stacks of pictures on the shelf above his clothes on top of his closet. The pictures showed things that I remembered from a long time ago that he always had. The three stacks were obviously meant for me, my sister, and my half-brother. He seemed to know he was going to die even though it was a heart attack. Was there a medical diagnosis, or did he feel that his life was being threatened in another way? It looked like someone came in and took some stuff because there were things in the pictures that weren't in his apartment any more. Many of them were things he would have never parted with.

I saw all the things he held so dearly that were left and I thought how little they all meant now. He was estranged from me, my wife, and his grandchildren; I felt confused on how things he spent time on could mean more than people. In the end, the lost touches far outweighed whatever possessions he had or whatever stresses he could have been feeling. I still had to go through all his things because the apartment had to be emptied, and his things had to be divided up or sold.

It was seventy years of "things", the pieces of a man's life. I had to go through a deceased person's possessions once before when my wife's grandmother died. It seemed the same in some ways as it seemed then. Fake depictions, trite trinkets, and things the person seemed to cherish that appeared silly when shown in a light of what might have been more cherished.

Aren't things, not of our own artistic or creative origin, that we greatly attach to, more a picture of how preciousness was replaced in a way? When our lifetime is spent serving and honoring things that others create, without ever revealing our own deepest passions and expressions, haven't we lost our chance? The preciousness in our self to express creatively, and to share that with others, may be what we rob when it's all directed to other people's accomplishments. Paintings, writings, sculptures, inventions, works of expression, creativity, and love given could be more of what should greatly represent a person. Helping others love themselves enough to want to share this part of them is also part of a life well-lived.

Isn't caring, extra consideration, the touch we give to children, or the difference we made in another person's life, the measure of a life well-lived? Maybe feelings could have been better shared with people rather than prizing far too highly the collection of things.

So, although a beautiful painting created may better represent the passions of that person than some trinket purchased, if they badly neglected the touch of others while alive, then even that beautiful painting could seem less representative of a life well-lived. Ideally, allowing our creativeness to flow, along with our love and caring for others would be something I would want representing me during and after my life.

My dad had a picture of my daughter, his granddaughter, but he never saw her and never spoke to her. What about what was precious, and being with what was precious? What about not moving from it as if there's something else more important? Is there something to be said for touching people and expressing love before it's too late? Instead it seems as if we push strong feelings away as if to guard against them from being taken away. Loving, and being one with it without fear was speaking loudly to me that day and I was deeply quieted by it.

Do we always have the awareness to bring the subtle undermining elements to the surface that would stop the love of our self and others? Can we guard against these elements with courage and realize what truly should be held dearly? I sat looking at my life like it was about to be over also. I wanted to feel what might be precious that I may have been missing. It was too late for Dad to touch what I thought should have been sacred to him. I wanted to feel more of what was sacred to me before it was too late.

His life was now symbolized by only a few rooms of stuff. All he valued as precious meant nothing to me when I thought of all the moments he chose to not be part of. Every birth and birthday, every anniversary and holiday, every recital and graduation was missed while he was wrapped up in his tinkering. What mattered more than just one more phone call where an "I'm sorry" came out, or one more hug where true love was shown? What could he have spent less time on in exchange for an embrace of both grandchildren? One moment with love expressed to his granddaughters would have meant more to me, and certainly to them, than all his unusual possessions. All his stuff being cremated along with him would have been just fine by me. I was sad, deeply sad. There was no longer the chance to fix anything. I realized I was always holding out a hope of greater closeness that never came.

Dad was a retired patents draftsman and was privy to many advanced technologies that he made drawings for. He worked for one of the biggest tech companies in the world so he saw some of the most amazing inventions ever created. I think during retirement, his dormant inventive mind got busy trying to patent something. He seemed to be greatly bothered by something when I saw him about three years before his death. It seemed the technology company he retired from still didn't much appreciate him trying to patent anything, even in his retirement.

He wasn't allowed to patent anything while he worked for the company, so when he was retired he thought he could legally try to patent things that he was stopped from doing in the past. The company took a strong stance against him because they were paying him a pension. They still didn't want him to try to patent anything and they threatened to gain rights over anything he tried to patent. Even though the law was that he could patent things when he left employment, in order to circumvent the law the company apparently took other steps. From what I could gather from the letters left behind, they weren't very nice steps.

He waited for this moment his whole life where he could patent his ideas and he proceeded to try to do so. Yet, the company he retired from still didn't like it and made it a point to tell the patent office that anything he tried to patent should be dealt with in certain ways. Since the company had so much clout with not only the patent office, but the government, their word held true and was took to task.

My dad threatened to bring the inventions elsewhere; maybe to another country. This didn't go over well either. He brought negative attention to himself from his company he retired from, from the patent office, and from the US Government. Many of the contracts the technology company garnered were government contracts and the inventions were top-secret because they were used for military purposes. I know he ruffled feathers but I wasn't sure to what extent because I had very little to do with him the last ten years of his life. I only saw him twice. He was very to himself. In fact, the phone in his apartment could only dial out and couldn't receive phone calls. He strictly controlled who he spoke to and when.

My dad made himself scarce to everyone mainly because he had grown tired of people. He was hurt so much in his life that he broke away from everyone he knew and moved far away. Nobody who knew him back home really had much to do with him. I was his son, and I had two amazing daughters. My first daughter he only saw one time and was not kind to her, and my second daughter, who was four and a half, he never saw at all.

He was a difficult person in many respects. He was consumed with what was going on in his head and he was very cryptic even with me about it. I oftentimes wouldn't figure out what he said until weeks after he said it. He talked in stories and in riddles and few had the patience for it. I had infinite patience, but still didn't understand it all the time. If I tried clarifying what he meant he would get mad that I didn't understand it the way he said it the first time. I would think about the things he said for days and sometimes when I later understood them, and referred back to them with him, he would forget he said it. If he remembered, he wouldn't acknowledge that he intended it the way I was recalling. If I didn't get the message at the time he said it, it was not easily retrievable and oftentimes lost forever as a potential exchange.

It sounds like he was mean, and sometimes he was, but there was a feeling beneath the words that were lost unless you had a heart for the man. I had a big heart for the man because I felt the challenges he had between who he was, and what life experiences frustrated him with. I wanted the image of love for my father and I decided to have it for all the good he did, and to forgive all he couldn't do. I was sad for the loss when he died, sadder than anyone ever knew. I was sad for all I had hoped he would fix with regards to his relationship with me, sad for all I had hoped to be fixed with his own happiness, and sad for my new family, which included him as the grandparent, that now could never be all I hoped for that to be.

For my dad, work was a two-edged sword throughout his life. On one end it provided a nice income, but in contrast, the job restrictions tore at the very fabric of his being. He had this amazingly inventive mind, yet he could never develop any of his own ideas because his company would own every invention that any employee would ever create. This thwarted his creative expression. He would rather do nothing than give it away.

This point wrenched the very heart of him his whole life. He watched some of his greatest ideas sit idly while others who realized these same ideas years after he did became wealthy. He never could get himself to leave that job because he always needed the money at the very same time he had these breakthroughs. He would use money on machine parts, tools, files, adjustment mechanisms and on and on and on. The problem was he was caught in a circle of needing the job that supplied the income for the things he was creating, but couldn't patent those creations because of the inherent nature of the job itself.

You never met anyone like my dad. He would say the thing that nobody ever thought of almost every time you spoke to him. It would sound outlandish at first, but as time went by you would realize he was usually right. He painted, wrote, invented, and played his harmonica a bit. As I'm writing this I feel like in some ways I grew up a lot like him. The biggest difference is probably open-mindedness. He would get into these patterns of thought where you couldn't reach him if you stood on your head. His way was the only way and sometimes he was wrong, but good luck trying to get him to admit it.

Dad had his work frustrations, and they carried over into his personality outside of work quite strongly. That was why he was so adamant when he had an idea, because so many great ideas he had in his life were stifled. It was sad because he would express his opinion on a subject as if it was a lone cry in the forest that was never heard, and he defended his right to say it with a life or death feeling. I was afraid to interrupt him. There were many long-winded explanations, going on and on, when a child's attention span would last only so long. Yet an interruption was so harshly dealt with that no impatience was ever worth it.

Many times he showed me the drawings that were dated years before great inventions actually came out. They were his drawings, his ideas, his time, his models, his attempts at a patent, and his company nearly firing him for doing so. He would have been a millionaire, and boy did I hear that regret all the time I was growing up. He had more than a dozen ideas, but all of them amounted to nothing. Each time he thought he would leave work, and each time family, bills, divorces, medical expenses, or life's demands took over. Each time the invention ended up in the garbage while someone else made millions developing the very same idea. He had to be one of the most frustrated men you ever met in your whole life but nobody ever knew why. I knew why.

Even though I barely saw him growing up, we thought the same, looked the same, and sounded the same. The funny thing is everybody who knew the both of us always thought it was impossible for me to say the things I did because my dad was saying the same thing somewhere else without me ever seeing him or talking to him. When we did see each other there were hours and hours of conversations where we would look at something, and come up with ten ideas that would make it better. I loved the guy, but it pained us both to have such a close bond because life's circumstances kept pulling at our relationship. My mother, his new wife, his new son, his job, money, my sister, medical issues and all the dramas that surrounded everyone pretty much destroyed any chance at an ongoing relationship in the end. Yet, we had our times where we were able to say things and those things meant a great deal to me. I sat in his apartment wishing there was another fate and feeling the devastation of loss.

I was tired from traveling on a moment's notice to Kentucky, and from all the emotions that came with trying to come to grips with my father's death. I looked for a bed in his apartment and couldn't find one. It really didn't make sense. I looked to see if it folded out of a wall or something. How could a man live without a bed? What did he do, sleep on the floor every night? I feel like the place was gone through already and people took some things out of it. I finally found a mattress folded up in the corner. I suppose this is what he used or something else was stolen.

I found a pillow and tried to go to sleep but I kept hearing voices. I looked around outside but didn't see anyone. I tried to sleep again and heard voices again. I couldn't locate them but I certainly could hear them. It was very strange and it was very late. The voices were talking to me about my being in his apartment.

I concluded that some thoughts of him were lingering in my mind and that it had to be because I was tired. I felt that I should try my best to get some sleep, so I did. It was a very restless night's sleep. The horrible mattress on the hard floor, the uncomfortable pillow, and the feeling that some presence was around had me twisting and turning all night. I only got about two hours sleep in.

When I awoke, I took a shower, changed my clothes and took the rental car into town where I located a diner to have breakfast. The people there were so kind and so caring. I held the door for a while when entering the diner because some people were coming. They were a good distance away where most people would have just let it close, but I patiently waited and boy did they appreciate that. The whole diner appreciated it.

There I was sitting and waiting for a menu while a waitress and some others were talking about how kind it was that I held the door. They said it loud enough for me to hear it. I was sitting by myself but they all were right there with me. They didn't know me and confirmed it amongst everyone there. People got up and asked the other if anyone knew me. They all concluded that I must be new in town.

Finally I heard a group of them talking, "Ya know, he looks like, yep, maybe it's his son. Yep, it sure does look like him. Shame what happened. What do mean, what happened? Didn't you hear Michael died of a heart attack the night before last? Are you kidding me? I didn't know, oh my God, oh my God." One man wiped the tears from his face and then toughened up. The sensitivity and caring was unbelievable.

I sat there a good while before the waitress came over, said good morning, and confirmed I wanted coffee while she poured it and gave me a menu. I knew what I wanted already and the waitress was as sweet as could be. As I finished up with my order the man who cried the tear earlier came over to my table. He looked deep in my eyes and asked real kindly, "You're Michael's son aren't you?" I was surprised and replied, "Yes, how did you know?" He said, "Well you look exactly like him ya know. May I join you? I knew your father and I would like to speak with you about a few things." I said, "Sure, that would be fine, you knew my dad?" The man sadly replied, "I sure did, we were real good friends." He then told me all the nice times they had together and how much he enjoyed the way my dad looked at life.

He asked me about where he was being buried and I told him what my dad wanted as his final wishes, and he gladly volunteered to have my dad's ashes sprinkled over his own property. He also said he would introduce me to a few of his friends. While we were talking a few of them came over to the table one at a time. We told them about the ceremony we were going to be having for my dad on his dear friend's property. They were all so praising of my father and wanted to be there. They soon got on their way but not before I got all the phone numbers and addresses. My breakfast came and I finished it while I listened to this wonderful man continue to speak so well of my dad. He told me he had his breakfast already and would be happy to talk to me about his times with my dad while I ate.

As long as I live, I'll never forget the consideration this man gave me and the way he made me feel. He made me feel closer to my estranged father just by the deeply felt way he spoke of him. I could see my dad in his eyes as he shared stories about him. He'll never know what he did for me. He excused himself for a minute so he could finish saying good-bye to a friend he was previously sitting with and told me he would be back shortly.

I finished up breakfast and the waitress came over to get the dishes and said she wasn't sure at first who I was, but now she knew. She told me my dad ate breakfast there every morning, and he was one of the nicest men she ever met. She was real sorry to see him go and real sorry for my loss. I was grateful and overwhelmed once again about how so many people cared about him. She said if there was anything she could do to help to just let her know. I told her I had clothes and furniture to get rid of and wondered if she knew people who would appreciate it. She said some less fortunate people who work right there would be real grateful for them. I said I would return with them after I went through everything. She said I was as kind and as generous as my dad. She expressed her condolences again, left the bill, and solemnly walked away to serve other customers.

I was looking to pay the bill when my father's good friend came back and sat down. He thought it would be a good idea to take me out to his property and show it to me. I paid the bill, we left together and I followed him to his farm. When we arrived he gave me some of the things that my dad left at his farm, and showed me my father's favorite place overlooking a pond. We thought that would be the best place for the ashes to be spread. I left knowing that was the plan with warmth in my heart.

What an amazing place with such warm beautiful people. I doubted there was such a place where people acted like this? My dad found a sweet place to live where people were down to earth and cared, and after Kentucky. I must say they are some of the nicest people you would ever want to met. It sure was different back home. Yes indeed, it sure was different.

I knew some business related things had to be done whether my half-brother and sister were there or not. The apartment insurance had to be terminated, the lease had to end, the water, electricity, and phone service had to be terminated. I took care of all I could without them so they wouldn't have to deal with it. I stayed busy going through everything and figured out whatever I could with the papers I got from his apartment. Banks were visited, insurance companies were communicated with about his car and his apartment, and furniture was spoken about with some of his friends who were interested.

I kept thinking he had something more, but I later found out that he had a young girlfriend he spent time with and he obviously took good care of her. That seemed to be where the extra money went. I was happy to hear that he went out with some happiness because he sure had lots of pain throughout his life. I went on to care for most of the mandatory things, but the other things had to wait for my half-brother and sister, and they were arriving the next day. I finally finished with what I could, and after getting a little lost again while driving, I found my way back to his apartment.

Alone again, and again the voices haunted me. Some were speaking about what I was doing there, while the others were acting as if they were him. It spooked me into feeling real sad again. I remember crying as the reality of his death was the only tangible thing I could blame for the strange experiences. It was already time to eat so I went back to the diner and had some supper. I saw some of the same faces who were nice to me at breakfast and they were nice all over again. I left there happier than when I arrived. I drove around until I was so tired and emotionally drained I had to get some sleep, so back to the hell of his apartment I went.

The voices and the imposing energy kept increasing and I had no idea why. I looked around for a radio or intercom system but couldn't find one. I really felt like I had come to grips with his passing pretty well. His absence over the years forced me to get used to him not being around. His departure wasn't as devastating because separation was always his choice and always my reality. It hurt a lot that he was gone, but it didn't warrant the experiences I was having.

I knew sharing these experiences with anyone wouldn't do me a whole bunch of good. They would probably just write it off to the fact that I just lost a parent, and may even think I lost my faculties as a result. I resolved myself to the fact that once I left Kentucky, many of these feelings would go away. I thought if someone was hurting me because of my father's actions, it would stop when I departed. If it was a combination of something physical and psychological, then that should also dissipate upon my departure.

All the speculations ran rampant. Maybe someone was using my dad's death to hide what they were doing and they followed me out to Kentucky to camouflage it. Maybe they were planning it before time and now they could hide it and infer it was just my insane reaction to my dad dying. Now they could say it came from somewhere else because I went there and back at the same time horrible experiences went into full swing. Maybe anything, but I sure was confused whatever it was.

I looked through his things to determine if anything was intended for me. I got the feeling that among his possessions there may have been more than what met the eye. There may have been things that held value to other people, but there didn't appear to be anything of value to me. Drawings, failed patents, sample drawings from his work, failed inventions, legal papers, and a lot of what meant absolutely nothing. It was all nothing more than samples of the work he did when he worked on other people's inventions. Yet, everything I saw was stuff that my sister and half-brother should have a share in, so I left it alone and tried to go to sleep.

It was another night of voices and pain. I kept listening against the wall thinking a neighbor was toying with me. My dad's writings indicated problems with the neighbor. There were sounds coming from there but they weren't the same as the voices in my head. What was going on?

I tried sleeping on the floor in physical and mental discomfort. Once again, it was a miserable night's sleep. I don't even think I slept at all. If I did, it was a very broken sleep. I got up and looked around during the night a few times in the apartment. I even opened the front door twice looking outside for the source of the voices. I again tried pinning my ear up against the wall thinking it might be next door, but nothing gave me any indication where the voices were coming from.

My sister and half-brother arrived the next day and both weren't so happy that anyone was there before them. There wasn't anything of real value unless there was something I didn't know about. My half-brother felt stuff was missing and because of the pictures I thought he was right. I told him someone seemed to have gotten there even before me because there was stuff in the pictures, which I pointed out that he left behind, that had stuff in them that wasn't there. He confirmed that the last time he was there those things in the pictures were there also but weren't there anymore. He also wondered where the bed was.

Surprisingly, my stepsister arrived soon after as well. I always liked her a great deal. She was my half-brothers sister from the same woman but not from my dad. My dad's second wife passed away a few years back. I remember while growing up, she always called him Dad anyway. It bothered me a little, but I overlooked it because I figured she needed a dad since her real father died. Dad lived with her so many years that it made some sense to represent things that way, but it always irked my sister to no end. She always hated her for that reason and resented Dad for allowing it.

When my stepsister arrived she made it clear that she didn't want anything, and was only there for moral support. My sister was not nice. She still carried the luggage from her calling him dad, so I knew there was some friction in the horizon, and sure enough it came. She didn't like her being there and she let her know it. I backed off because I always lost when I came in between my sister and anybody. She would hurt me if I tried helping her and she would resent me if I didn't. There was no winning. I stayed far away. I had my fill with everything else and really didn't need any more.

Dad never had much. When he did have a little extra over the years, women and children absorbed it. He had trouble getting along with his second wife as well but never divorced her. Instead, he just got up one day and left her with two children. He went all over the country looking for peace and settled on Kentucky. His wife later came down with cancer and had huge hospital bills that Dad paid. Eventually she died, and although her daughter got married and was self-sufficient, the son they had together still needed help because he was much younger and still in school. Dad's money found a place once again.

We went over some of the papers and I told them all the things that I took care of. We went to the bank and the insurance office because there were a few more things they needed to finalize. It was my sister's idea to go to the hospital to confirm the details of the death and to make sure there were no outstanding bills. When we arrived at the hospital the people at the reception desk were very private and guarded after they heard my father's name. They said all the bills were paid and I was surprised there wasn't more somehow. We thought proving who we were would yield more information, but it didn't.

They gave us answers in a way that seemed like there was more we should know, but they weren't saying it. Maybe a shooting was kept a secret to protect the reputation of the town. Maybe there was another cause of death and some negligence was involved. Even after we received the death certificate stating he died of a heart attack, we all felt like we didn't have the whole story. Maybe they were hiding something. We all started thinking something weird was going on. Maybe the real cause of death was being hidden.

Our next trip as a group was at the coroner's office. I explained about Dad's wishes, how I organized this gathering with his friends, and how his dear friend allowed us to spread the ashes on his property. I expected a warm fuzzy feeling from them. Instead, my sister and half-brother both decided that they wanted their share of the ashes and had no emotions on anything else. I couldn't believe it. My jaw dropped! I thought I was imagining things or that they were kidding. I reiterated that his final wishes were to have his ashes sprinkled over a field in Kentucky. I was appalled and I asked, "Are you saying you don't believe that it was his final wishes? Do you think I would make it up?" They both said simultaneously, "No, we believe you, we just want the ashes."

It was two people acting incredibly selfish at the same time when it was hard enough to believe even one was. To this day I can't believe they would dishonor a man's final wishes just so they could have a bunch of ashes sitting on their shelves. The coroner heard all this and surmised that we wanted the ashes divided up three ways in three separate urns. He tried his damndest not to express an emotion, but I saw his face as he turned his head and his look said a thousand unspoken words. If it were words it would have expressed how he had seen a lot of selfishness over the years in the business of death and dying but this was a topper. The coroner went along with everything and was as nice as could be.

When the coroner got me alone he said, "You certainly are very different than they are. You're like your father. Your father never would have dishonored a person's final wishes." I said, "I'm keeping everything the same but I will just throw one third of the ashes up in the air instead of all of it". He said, "You'll probably end up with the third that has his heart and soul." We both smiled and then both said at the same time "Well, not his heart but his soul." I was so moved by his words. Our eyes met so deeply, our hands shook, and we both used our other hand as well in the handshake to hold each other's hand. I wasn't alone.

My sister, half-brother, and stepsister all followed the coroner and me in separate cars to where Dad was so we all could say our farewell to him before he was cremated. I was in the coroner's car leading the way and all the while he kept mentioning how the look on my father's face was so expressive. He said my dad was upset about something. Something was pursuing him and he felt uneasy. He said his face expressed that even at death, and he looked as though he was trying to say something. His face stayed frozen in the same way it was the moment before he died. In his twenty-five years as a coroner he said he never saw anything quite as expressive on a dead person's face before. He said he also wanted to give me something later that was found on him when he died.

We went in to see the body one at a time. I went first. The coroner felt that I was the closest to him and he was probably right. The walk in to see him took what was somewhat unreal and all of a sudden made it all too real. There he was horizontal and gone forever. It wasn't a mistake. The one in a billion hold out that it wasn't him was eliminated. It was Dad alright, and he was dead. It hit me real hard. I didn't show it, but I wasn't well.

I have seen dead bodies before at funerals but they all looked a little fake because of the make-up and chemicals. Dad wasn't all dolled up because he died just a couple of days ago and since he was about to be cremated, it didn't make sense to make the body any more presentable. Dad wasn't a fake in life and he wasn't a fake in death. He had this expression that looked like he was trying to say everything with one look. His eyes were as wide as could be and his mouth was protruding out in a circle. I thought about all the things that would have been said that way but realized I may have been reading into it too much.

The coroner also felt like the face was trying to express a message. Either way, the look on his face will always be as clear as anything I could ever think about. Good-bye Dad, few understood you, but I did, and I loved you more than you ever let yourself know.

We all went back with the coroner leading because there was one more thing to take care of, Dad's car. Well, I knew it had to be a good one because Dad loved his cars. He worked on cars since he was a young man. He used to buy them, fix them up, and sell them. He would rave about the stories he had with cars growing up. He seemed to have had every great car at one time or another. He showed up to see me with some real special cars over the years while I was growing up. Besides a fine looking woman, there aren't many things he appreciated more than a fine looking automobile.

When we got to his car, it was a 1987 420 SEL Mercedes Benz. I don't think his other son, my sister, or my stepsister had a clue what kind of engine that car possessed. My sister wasn't impressed and my half-brother had a car already. When they found out the mileage was 220,000 they both were turned off. I knew a Mercedes could go a lot longer than that. I loved the car. The thing that cinched it was that it had a ten year old tape recording of my wedding in the console on a tape deck. What a strange thing that was. Why would a man keep a tape deck of a wedding from ten years ago? Why would a man tape moments of a wedding in the first place let alone keep it ten years right next to him? They both decided the car was meant for me and I was thrilled. Dad's car, what could possibly keep me closer to him than one of the things he loved the most? I had two cars back home, one my wife drove and the other I drove, but this is the one that I would drive, that was for sure.

We told the coroner we would get the papers corrected on the car and return for it. He said to call him tomorrow. The cremation should be done by then and the ashes divided into urns. We knew it would take a while with Motor Vehicles as well so we just kept busy doing everything else we had to.

The next day we all went back to get the urns and pay the bill. The coroner shared with us one more thing. Dad had a gun on him when he died, and the coroner showed it to us and asked what we wanted him to do with it. None of us wanted any part of it. We didn't know if it was involved with anything before time and none of us ever owned a gun. It was a damned good gun and was probably worth some good money but we all decided to give it to the coroner as a gift. He was pleasantly surprised and we all felt good about doing it. He had gone above and beyond with everything throughout these difficult times for us. It showed once again that Dad was a frightened man, and to this day I don't exactly know what terrified him. Maybe the source of the same voices that were haunting me, were also torturing him.

When the coroner had moments with me alone he told me again there was definitely something going on with my dad that he didn't share with anyone. He was suffering with something that really seemed to be gnawing away at him. He had some legal strife with someone in town but he thought it was more than that. He put the mystery out there, as if I needed another, which promoted even more suspicion about everything.

Over the next two days we wrapped up all his business, got rid of his furniture, cleaned up his apartment, and had the ceremony at that wonderful man's farm. The people we invited came to his house and we went to this nice bridge over a pretty lake in a field of sprawling Kentucky land. The landowner, my dad's good friend, said my father always had a great fondness for the property. He enjoyed the peace and beauty of the place. He gave me the feeling that he sure would have been happy to know that his ashes were being spread right there. He recalled how many good times they had together and how so many were spent right there. It sure felt right doing it.

My dad got religious in his later days, so they invited a priest who knew him to say a few words. We stepped onto a bridge that went over a little lake. His friend said my dad used to stand out on that same bridge and just take in the countryside. It all seemed like it was just like how he would have liked it. If a presence of the dead is possible we all seemed to feel it. The words were spoken by the priest and they were beautiful words indeed. There was a real feeling of our own mortality, and a deep feeling felt by all present that this man, my father, touched each one of the people there in a particular way that will always be remembered.

It was now time to throw my share of the ashes into the air. It was a calm day, no wind, and as peaceful and sunny as could be. I threw the ashes in the air and a gust of wind came out of nowhere and flung the ashes right back at the crowd where it landed directly on my sister and half-brother exclusively. They gagged a bit, wiped the ashes out of their eyes and were a bit mortified. They then of course got mad at me, the wind master. I acted as if I was sorry it happened. I had all to do to not burst out laughing. I thought of how Dad would have absolutely loved that moment if he could see it from beyond. That was his sense of humor all over. You want my ashes, here's my ashes you selfish bastards. I thought to myself for a second that Dad came from the sky and threw it right at their faces.

The priest suggested I walk off the bridge away from the crowd to throw the remaining ashes up in the air. I did that and someone took a picture of me doing it I still have. After all that was said and done, we all said good-bye and thanked everyone. We especially gave a big show of appreciation to the wonderful man who made it all happen. He had a dog that smiled when he told him to and the dog smiled for us one last time. He told me I'm always welcome and to give a call if I ever come to town again. My dad loved the man and in a very short time so did I. I hugged him and thanked him once again. In that hug we both remembered a very unique man and knew we were going to miss him a great deal.

As we walked back to our cars, all of us were real happy the way it went, and everyone thanked me for putting it all together. My stepsister said that it was exactly how Dad would have liked it, and he would have been real happy that we all came together to do it the way we did. Everyone agreed it brought closure in a beautiful way. So, it was over, or at least I thought it was over.

We returned to Dad's apartment to finish up everything. I returned the rented car and put all the stuff that was in that car, into the Mercedes. I then added my share of the divided up stuff and loaded that in as well. We all said good-bye and started heading out each with different destinations. My sister had to get to the airport, my stepsister had her car, my half-brother had his, and I was driving Dad's car back to New York from Kentucky.

I drove several hours and a voice pretending to be my dad started up again. I almost started to believe it. Is it possible for the dead to speak to you? Is that what I was experiencing? Part of me wanted to still have some contact. I pulled over, stopped the car, and got out. It wasn't me and I knew it, but where was it coming from? I looked at the car as if it was the source of the voices. I then looked everywhere and tore apart everything I could to try to find out where these voices were coming from. My need to still communicate with him was being played with. Maybe this attack on me, wherever it was coming from, was now being veiled by his death. I was far too levelheaded to start doubting myself or believe in ghosts. I knew I had all my faculties and had a firm grip on everything that happened but something or someone was messing with me. Thoughts and words imposed on me were not mine.

I saw some policeman stickers and the bill of sale and remembered my dad bought the car from a retired police captain. There was a CB radio box under the back seat. I didn't think it was that but I didn't know what it was. If it was that, I didn't know what to do anyway. I thought about throwing it out but first wanted to take it apart in case my father hid something in it. He oftentimes hid things and told me years earlier to look for what was hidden when he died. He made nothing easy for me in his life or in his death. The CB was solid state and needed some tools to take it apart. I had the tools back home so I left it there and took the chance that it had nothing to do with the voices in my head.

Dad's voice continued and it was only a few hours earlier that I threw his ashes in the wind. It was telling me that he was still with me and that he will always be with me when I think about him. Was someone playing tricks on me pretending to be my dad? I questioned for a minute that he was dead, but I did see the body. What did I do to warrant this torture? Why am I being tormented? I knew right then and there I had a big problem. It wasn't staying in Kentucky and it wasn't exclusively in the car. It was with me. So what was it?

I was reasonably sure it all started while I was in his apartment, but that may not have been where it technologically originated. I had so many horrible things happen to me over the years and I was wondering if the cumulative effects took their toll. It wasn't sound thinking to believe it wasn't anything but the emotional hangover from the fact that he was dead. Sound thinking did not apply. This was the onset of a living hell coming from something outside of me.

It struck me that my cousin, who had a powerful position in the New York City Police Department, may very well have used his power recklessly when he felt personal animosities. Dad and I had this contact in common, and someone like that may have had access to such an imposing surveillance, but was this that? Even though we all used to be close, my cousin moved up the ranks to Special Detective, and the pressures along the way pushed him to the brink. He became mentally unstable and sought psychiatric attention, but never left the job during that time. He and Dad previously had a very strong bond as uncle and nephew, but with the little I heard from the both of them over the years, I gathered they were most recently at odds about many things. My cousin getting carried away with his own power was not the least of their disagreements. My cousin could have had access to high tech surveillance systems, and may have been given the privilege to apply them when he deemed appropriate. He could have affected my father and now even me with a high tech surveillance system. Yet, I knew nothing of the details of such a weapon and certainly didn't know if anything he did was actually applied to Dad or me.

Although, after much thought I considered that he could have conjured up reasons to use it on each of us. My father had access to certain intellectual properties while employed, and my cousin may have justified placing it on him and me because of that. Dad's company worked on defense contracts and this type of classified information may have caused such a need. Maybe my mother's involvement with the ex-gangster could justify placing this effect on me as well. Even though I had nothing to do with either one of them, and neither reason was truly justifiable or appropriate, the application of these systems were not as strictly investigated after 9/11. People in certain positions had far too much power, and my cousin may very well be another one who abused it. Once these systems are in place, manipulation of other people in the target's perimeter becomes the distraction from its source. That is all part of its desired effectiveness. I, as the victim, was, and still am in a confused and helpless state without a place to turn. Everything became one guess after the next after that and all the hurt was in place for others to be affected as well.

After many more hours driving, I tried sleeping in the front seat of the car but felt an imposing presence. I then heard voices, and feared that I had walked into a minefield I couldn't get out of. This was my experience all the way back to New York. I got home after a two day drive of sleepless torment. I yearned for the love of my family. I met my wife at the door where she greeted me with "Why didn't you call me more?" I turned around and walked away saying, "I'm going to wait for our daughter at the bus stop." I just lost my father and I was just looking for something a little different as far as a reception goes. That's what was obvious, but what wasn't obvious was a torture going on above and beyond that, which made the lack of consoling even more overwhelming to me. I hit my emotional tolerance limit. When this would happen I would walk away or create some space. I never wanted to react or lose my temper.

I oftentimes would go the garage to watch television or smoke a cigar when friction was brewing. This time I realized my younger daughter would soon be getting off the bus and decided to meet her. I needed to feel love and this was the kind of love I needed. I waited on the curb for my little superstar at the bus stop. I didn't feel much like having to overcome the superficialities from the other parents waiting. I stayed quiet and off to the side waiting on the curb. When the bus arrived I saw my little girl was preoccupied with something as she was walking off the bus. She saw me and her preoccupation disappeared as she ran to hug me.

My precious little girl always had love and a hug for me. I almost cried from the love but I just wanted to show her happiness, and tears sometimes are misunderstood, so I fought them off. These would have been tears of joy. I just needed love so badly and my daughter was so amazing. She said she was sorry my dad died and knew he meant a lot to me. My little girl knew how to be and that made me so happy. No words could really express it. The children we raise have their own ways of doing things and we find out about them when moments arise where no advice was ever given. My daughter shined like a superstar, which is my nickname for her because she always shines so bright. When I saw my older daughter, she was also very caring. She told me she missed me while I was gone. It was the first time she was ever away from me. She didn't like it and was glad I was back.

# X   A Mind Field

The torture continued at home with voices in my head repeating every situation, repeating my private thoughts back to me, proposing different alternatives, always reminding me that I was no longer alone. They continued to pretend to be my dead father, and this hurt even more than just any voices. They mimicked his tonality. My thoughts of him were so strong they used them against me. Although I didn't know what covert-harassment was at the time, the effects kicked in very strongly when I arrived at his home in Kentucky but may have been a disguise from what originated in New York.

When I came back from Kentucky I had a great deal of trouble sleeping. An itch in my ear kept occurring while I was trying to sleep. It seemed as though there was a fly in the room but I could never find the fly. I would itch myself awake and since I couldn't find anything flying I thought I had bed bugs. I then did all the things that would eliminate bedbugs, but I never actually had that problem. It was the phantom fly, the phantom bedbugs, the phantom lice, the phantom spider. None of these things were the cause for my disturbance.

I thought I had a physical problem. The doctors told me I didn't. My wife thought I had a mental problem because so many horrible things happened to me in succession. Yet, I had horrible things happen to me before and knew I could handle them, so I knew it wasn't that. She saw no physical things that would cause my behavior to change so she attributed it to mental things. It was unseen, and I was open to trying to understand the unseen things affecting me, but she most certainly was not. In retrospect, she was building a case that had all her actions supporting what was against me. She was at the heart of what would become the worst legal attack of my life, and she, in cooperation with others were part of an unseen attack as well.

The Seder turmoil took place right before I left to handle my dad's final affairs. Sometimes the truth is so unusual it makes it easier to believe what seems to be more commonplace. It sounds crazy when you hear someone say they are hearing voices because it is also deemed a psychological symptom for a mental disorder. The reference doesn't allow for further investigation into what alternatives it could actually be if not that.

I was there for 9/11, and lost a great job because of it. Before that, I had my career destroyed in a company that I had worked very hard for and moved up in the ladder in. I was with the company over twelve years. One day my career and my dreams were shockingly removed in a brutal way on a conference call. A new CEO fired thousands of people before leaving with increased stock options.

After that my wife and I lost a child during pregnancy. It was our first attempt at a second child. My son's life was ended due to the horrible need to terminate the birth upon hearing of his illness. Knowing the baby's life was going to end while it kicked in her stomach was a pain she never recovered from. The doctor first told me the horrible news about our unborn child on a phone call and after I told my wife I was never treated the same way again. She had a deep resentment toward me for being the one to reveal the news to her. Luckily we tried again and had an amazing second child, my superstar daughter, but the hurt left a mark on my wife she never seemed to overcome.

Years went by, and while my wife was home taking care of our two beautiful girls, her overall demeanor seemed to be in a permanent post-partum state. With all the challenges we endured, life wore on her a bit. She secretly started taking anti-depressants and anti-anxiety medicines which changed her whole personality. At the same time the stock market was beating me up with corporate misrepresentations. I was trying to make money in different ways so she could continue to stay home with our children.

I lost my attempt at regaining my footing in the insurance career by having my job removed at a new company I started at after only six months. I took a step back from everything and started to look at life differently. Many things I believed that would always be there were gone forever. I was reading a lot, listening to tapes, and felt as though I was on the crest of enlightenment. Unfortunately the beauty of this unseen experience was accompanied by a torturous artificial space that was affecting me. I most certainly could tell the difference. One was beautiful and one was painful.

The girls were always on the TV, the computer, or talking on the phone so I sought some refuge in the garage. The condo didn't leave much room when both televisions were on and talking on the phone commanded the environment. The cigar certainly wouldn't be smoked in the house in any case. The quiet needed for stock market analyzing was not available inside. I also sought refuge from the busy household and my friction with my wife by going to the gym, which was only a few hundred yards away. My family seemed more and more as though they were possessed by the media, the computer and the telephone. I kept pushing for a different approach and got a lot of friction from it. I avoided friction. I had a lifetime of friction surround me and had little tolerance for it any more. I would say my peace and walk away. Sometimes one of my daughters would join me to play catch, go bike riding, go for a drive, or go to the park. I was always so happy when they stepped away from the barrage of TV's, telephones, and computers.

When my wife and I disagreed, I was always grateful for the hour it took to smoke a cigar. Sometimes I would sit on the back deck or go to the garage, but wherever I went it gave me peace while we let the fuming subside. I never wanted to fight in front of the children, but unfortunately we did far too many times. If not for this walking away habit I learned as the years went by, it would have been worse. Our marriage was starting to suffer but we were both in it for the long haul, or at least that's what we both had agreed on.

It was very hard to deal with sometimes, because even the things that were blatantly out of my control, I was put in the doghouse for. I got crucified for being at 9/11 and not calling her even though the phone lines were down. I unconsciously got blamed for the loss of our second child. She certainly wasn't there for me when I was feeling the loss of my father, and was still mad at me for not calling more than one time while I was away. It was always when I needed a little more, that I got considerably less. Abusing me was her way of toughing it out. This approach was amplified in a big way and wore on our marriage as a series of unfortunate events ripped us apart.

I started reading more and picking up all my old journals and notes compiling what might be a book someday. I even saved notes from a diary I kept when I was seventeen. I was disenchanted with work structures and thought I could make money with an invention, writing a book, investing in the stock market, or all three. This was not received well by my wife and the strange occurrences I referenced compounded the problem. She seemed to have lost complete faith in me and became obsessed with owning a house, having more, not working, and getting ahead much faster than we were. None of that included my self-discovery, or her having patience with me regarding the intangible source of my pains.

The unseen torture kept coming, and as if she was the cause herself, she had little sympathy for it. I tried to find a logical reason it was happening. Maybe I had sleep apnea, or insomnia, or maybe it was some psychological effect from a lifetime of horrible things happening to me. Maybe it was 9/11 and the after effects so many were referencing, or maybe it was an inability to handle seeing my dad dead. I came to grips with all the possibilities, but it wasn't any of them.

I knew there wasn't any justifiable reason for anything or anyone to want to go against me. I always held true to my own integrity, and even in the face of so much adversity, I had confidence to dig deeper and investigate all the possibilities rather than take on any belief that doubted my own faculties. I treated the experience as if it could happen to many others, because if it could happen to someone who always acted as well as I, then it could happen to anyone. Though it sure was funny that the more I pursued information to reveal this intangible attack on me, the worse the voices and torment became.

That very feeling of telegraphing my own thoughts, and having thoughts imposed on me about them is torture. There isn't any aspect of it that didn't deteriorate my existence. I constantly tried to figure out what it could be that was affecting me. Inhaling too many chemicals while the towers fell could have hurt me in unseen ways. I was there a long time while almost paralyzed from the view while the buildings fell. I also recalled how weeks later they let us back in the building I worked in, which was only two blocks away from the disaster, without ever cleaning the air-conditioning ducts. It was a while before they realized it. After some complaints of the air quality they brought in air filters, and when they were black at the end of each day they realized something was wrong. The air-conditioner was on the morning of September 11th and sucked in all the ashes of the dead bodies and fallen buildings. They never cleaned out the filters. We all went back in and inhaled it for weeks before anyone realized it. People were getting sick every day before anyone noticed it. The damage was done. People's lungs got hurt. Maybe this was causing something intangible years later, or maybe terrorists released something in the area, in addition to those chemicals, that affected people long after the event.

The imposing suppressive energy surrounded me as if there was a force pressing down on me. It impeded my ability to focus on thoughts. Everything I tried to do would take me a lot longer. I was always tired from sleep deprivation and always hearing voices. I kept feeling a jolting to my central nervous system so I went to see doctors to find out what was wrong with me. They told me I had the body of a twenty year old and nothing was wrong with me.

The suppressive pounding on my head continued after the doctor visits and was still severely hurting my productivity. Sometimes I felt an electromagnetic jolt which targeted my pineal gland located in my brain. This is a sleep center and the jolt released melatonin and serotonin which instantly made me want to sleep. To want to sleep, and be able to sleep, were in constant contradiction. As strong as the energy to sleep existed there followed an even stronger energy to stop it. As if there is a neurological tip-off when sleep started to occur, it was soon followed by a jolt to wake me up.

The sleep deprivation affected the both of us. I couldn't sleep so I would sometimes get up from the bed, and that would wake up my wife. My wife and I were at odds and it was getting worse and worse. The sleep deprivation created less patience and shortened tempers. The only thing we came to have in common was the love for our children, but the way we loved them greatly differed.

I was getting paid for a while from my previous employer and able to stay at home because they felt like they hired me for something that they weren't able to follow through on. I started working very hard at being fit. I went to the gym every day. This helped me fight the harassment. I decided to get as toned as I possibly could and become a personal trainer. I wasn't going to feel confident doing it unless I was toned. I went online to see what it entailed and there was a class online. I studied it on the web, went to the gym, and put it into action. I exercised, studied to be a trainer, wrote, traded stocks, and looked for work.

I also cooked, cleaned, picked up the kids from the bus stops, and brought them wherever they needed to go. I was Mr. Mom for the first time in my life and I sure loved seeing my children a lot. My wife hated it and resented me for it. She went back to work but hoped she never had to. The children and I went to piano lessons, the orthodontist, play dates and sometimes shopping. We played catch, went to the park, and really enjoyed each other's company. My two amazing daughters helped me set the table while I made great dinners with everything they wanted. I loved spending time with them.

I went so many years where work cut into my time with my daughters. I was gone a lot with work and sometimes they were asleep when I left and asleep when I got home. Many times when I did have time they were busy with school, friends, or things that they were involved with. Now this time was precious for me and I was very grateful to have it.

I live in a condominium complex and noticed I had a new neighbor that kept very much to himself. He lived only two doors down from me. He seemed like a nice, quiet, family man. We kept seeing each other because I was home so much. He stayed inside a lot, but when I saw him outside I was very friendly. I also saw his wife, but she rarely went out. His wife wore long layers of shear gowns and his daughter was very cute and very quiet. His darker skin and attire prompted my question about where they were from and he told me he was from Pakistan.

I asked him about Pakistan and what the differences were. He said it was very poor there and only a few had the kind of "wealth" that we had. I asked him what he did for a living, and he said computer work. I saw him another time and asked him how business was. He said it was busy. I thought it unusual that I seldom saw him leave the condo. I imagined he did a lot of work from home, but I still felt like that more client visits would be part of even a business like that. When I asked if he was looking for more business he surprisingly wasn't. He was filled up with the clients he had. Yet he seemed to have time when he wasn't inside working. It's expensive to live where I live and his wife didn't work, so I thought more business would be welcome, but it definitely wasn't.

When I did see him he asked if my daughter would play with his daughter. He said she was so lonely. He thought she was being discriminated against in school. I was never tolerant of that and wanted to show that I wasn't like that. There was only one darker skinned person in the whole school and she had problems as well. I previously encouraged my daughter not to discriminate against that girl and they ended up becoming good friends. I thought the same way about this situation, but in retrospect I may have been very, very wrong.

She was little younger than my daughter so my daughter didn't really want to play with her in the first place. The first few times I mentioned it she wasn't so receptive. I asked her as a favor to help the new neighbor out by making his daughter feel more welcome. I thought the little girl could have a tough go of it in my town.

I've made the mistake of being too nice in my life and sometimes people have used that to hurt me. This time my kindness involved another person and in retrospect maybe I shouldn't have been so kind. I seldom disregard my feelings and always value my daughter's feelings as well, but I was really trying hard not to discriminate or judge the man. I always preached that to my children and certainly didn't want to be hypocritical. Later, I came to doubt his credibility but still never knew if he did anything wrong. The events to follow certainly left room for questions about everything in my life and although many problems already started, I didn't know where they came from. The roots of the problem appearing to come from another location may have been purposeful. Just because these horrible experiences were more deeply felt at the onset in Kentucky, doesn't mean it came from there.

My daughter agreed and went into their home to play with their daughter, and to this day I feel like I should have been more careful. I usually am. He lived so close and his daughter was so young and so cute. She went to the same school as my younger daughter. I felt like he was alright and that there wouldn't be any harm that could come from a 6 year old and a 5 year old playing. So my superstar agreed and she seemed to have some fun when I went and got her.

Soon after that, I needed to update the Windows 95 operating system on my dinosaur of a computer. I made the mistake of buying a version that got added on top of my current version instead of deleting the old one out and installing the new one. The way I did it was cheaper, but boy was that a mistake. The computer didn't function well after that and after many hours on the phone for many days I finally asked the computer whiz neighbor if he would help me. In exchange for his help I offered a free week at the gym that I was able to get because of my affiliation there. I ended up becoming a personal trainer and employees were given that leverage to get new members there. He wanted to get in better shape and I desperately needed my computer fixed. I thought it was a perfect connection. We set up a time for him to fix my computer.

We pulled up two chairs and sat in front of my damaged computer. He was working intently with computer code in safe-mode and drilled down to the operating system glitches. He saw where there was some overlap jamming up the functionality. He thought I may have loaded it in wrong, but then thought better of it and said it wasn't my fault. He felt there were always problems with this operating system on top of the old one. He said I should have taken out the old one and installed a whole new one. He said he would fix this, but it would take a while. He was typing in code a mile a minute. He really knew what he was doing and I really didn't. I understood a little but I could never do what he was doing. I never learned programming. It's a different language to me, but the funny thing is even when someone is speaking a different language sometimes you can tell when something isn't right.

I felt like something wasn't right with the programming of my computer. He seemed to be entering an area of the operating system that didn't need to be affected and I was so close to him that when he was doing it I got this feeling like something wasn't right with my computer. It was very old and I probably just should have gotten another one, but at the same time I was hoping he was on the up and up. I didn't know why he would do anything that wasn't, but I certainly couldn't tell one way or the other. I just got this strange feeling like I should know more about what just happened.

It was only my instincts, and no words or actions on his part really indicated that I should suspect anything, but just like someone speaking ill of you in a different language, a vibe was felt like something was amiss. Maybe my operating systems will always have some problems or maybe he messed with something. In a very complicated way, what he did could have added to my pain and many other people's pain as well. I blew off my instincts and chalked it up to simply being naïve about operating systems and programming language.

I asked my daughter again about what it was like playing with his daughter and delved a little more deeply this time. She said it was a strange experience and she didn't want to do it again. I was very surprised and asked why she didn't tell me that last time. She didn't want to discriminate either so she went along with it but thought they were weird. I should have gone in with her or honored her feelings as I always have. I asked what made them weird and she said they stored things in the walls and they acted like there was something going on but she didn't know what.

I asked what else made them weird, thinking he may have just been doing a little more than just home construction. My daughter told me the little girl never talked outside of the home, but wouldn't stop talking inside the home. I clarified that "never" meant never, ever. I asked if she spoke when a teacher asked her a question and my daughter found out that this little girl wouldn't utter a word outside the home under any circumstances. This hung over me. I thought a lot about why this would be the case. She repeated that she didn't shut up the whole time she was playing with her. I now had a doubt. I started looking at them a little differently. I told her that she didn't have to play with her anymore and she was glad.

A couple of days later I saw the Pakistani neighbor and he asked about playing with his daughter again and I politely explained how my daughter felt she was too old. I changed the subject to his car where I noticed that his car registration was expired and I reminded him about the possibility of getting tickets. He thanked me and we departed. Then days later, I saw him again and told him I noticed his car inspection was about to expired too. He thanked me again and we departed.

Instead of fixing this he put his car in the garage and acted very strange about the whole thing. It was more than just the normal ticket possibility. He acted as if he had something to hide besides that. Now I really was suspecting him. The next morning I went out to the bus stop before my daughter and saw his daughter arrive. I looked at her straight in the eyes and said "Good morning", and she wouldn't utter a sound. Then my daughter came out and the same thing happened to her. When she said "Good morning", the little girl said nothing. My daughter looked at me with an innocent quandary, whereby I shrugged my shoulders in quandary back. We both didn't quite get what was going on with that little girl but something was incomplete.

I told the town police captain. I said there were suspicious people in the neighborhood and I asked that he investigate them somehow. He considered my request outlandish. Here the President was calling for more vigilance, and now when I thought I was acting in a way that exhibited vigilance I was squashed for doing so. He cared a lot more about his lunch that was delivered to him while I sat there than anything I had to say. I got nowhere with him. I was very surprised at the way I was treated. I thanked him anyway and left. I went back on two more occasions over the following six months and he was of no help. I was extremely disheartened. I always imagined in a small town like mine that there would be a more down to earth approach. I would have gotten a much better reception in the Bronx where I grew up if I went to the police station and said the same thing. A Pakistani sleeper cell was discovered nearby only a month before that. I wondered why my request to check out the possibility of another one was treated so horribly. I still don't know. I guess it just couldn't compete with spaghetti and meatballs. Either that or there was a surveillance on me already that was somehow "justified", and anything I had to say was discounted.

This was very painful for me, not only because of what lead up to that point, but I always had a very high respect for policemen because they're risking their lives for us. Not only that, but both my cousins were police officers and I grew up seeing them and hearing their stories. I remember my dad helping my cousin become an officer when I was younger. Now, here I was trying to save their life in my mind, as well as others, and I got treated like I didn't count.

In retrospect, even if I was under covert-harassment surveillance, should this observation be ignored? It didn't matter that there wasn't any reason for me to have it on me. It only mattered that any concern of mine was not going to be treated with respect. Instead of investigating it, tactics were used to damn me so I wouldn't reveal it. The fact that I was innocent as could be somehow didn't matter. I thought even if this remote possibility was true, I should have heard from him regardless, because no matter what, the whole intent is to protect the country. If something arose that helped with that, under any scenario, isn't that what should matter? Why would suspicion of a Pakistani sleeper cell be ignored under any circumstances? Instead I was treated like I was crazy no matter what I said. I never got feedback from that report and that was in October of 2005.

The intangible harassment got worse and worse. I actually feel like I was zeroed in on as a problem even more so after this. When I went back to ask the captain about it the next time he treated me worse than the first time. I gave him more things I thought were suspicious, but to no avail. He would rather not take the word of a good, solid, citizen who only did good things in the neighborhood than honor any suspicion of such magnitude. I had nowhere to turn. The work situations were unstable and sleep was a rare occurrence. My wife and I kept waking each other up as we both got more restless with our sleep. It got to the point where I could not sleep in the same room as her. I spent many nights in the living room on a blowup mattress. This gave the impression to my children, and to each other, that we did not want to be together even more. From my side that wasn't true, but I needed to sleep desperately. From her side, the outsides became her inside and I felt the distance growing between her and me.

A long time went by before I ever thought about telling her what all my experiences were. I feared how it would be received. I wanted to trust my wife. I wanted her to know I was suffering and it was from something other than our dynamic. I asked her to come over to talk to me and we sat real close on the bed. I told her I needed to tell her something. She needed to hear what was going on with me. I shared with her the torment I was going through. She listened intently. I was so relieved to share it.

She hadn't been so compassionate over the last few years but I had to tell someone so I told my wife of all the experiences I was having. I told her I was hearing voices. I felt a presence. Things were taken from my car. I heard voices through the TV, the speakers, and from different objects. I felt as if I was stalked by something or someone. My body was being jolted when I tried to sleep and it kept me awake night after night. I told her how bad it was getting and how I didn't know where it was coming from. I was hoping that the person I had planned to spend my life with would realize something was hurting me. I thought she would look to help me and try to understand what it was. I also thought I would get her love and our bond would see us through it. Instead she thought I was going nuts. She lost complete faith in me and she didn't believe that any of my experiences were physically possible.

Many things were happening that helped her lose trust in me. I lost a large sum of money in the stock market which was earmarked for our future and the children's future. I was trying to take some educated chances so she could stay home from work. It worked before, but the voices in my head made me less than focused when I needed to be and in the stock market that simply will not be forgiven. I felt that my wife didn't forgive it either. Accounting fraud also found every stock I saw as undervalued turn against me. My recent job instability, my financial miscues, and my spiritual direction away from hers made it easier for her to label me. Now this and all these unseen experiences I was having could all be wrapped up in one neat package. She claimed I was losing my faculties.

I felt her distance. She treated me as an outsider. My wife to cherish, to love, to honor, for better or worse, in sickness and in health felt I was not well, and felt I deserved to be an outcast because of it. I knew I was fine mentally but had this unseen onslaught against me, and although I did not know of its origin, I needed her to stick by me and by her vows. Her vows meant nothing other than getting through the ceremony and when push came to shove she wasn't there for me. When all things were against me she not only did not stand by me, but she created a bandwagon against me and just kept hopping on it. The pain was as if a knife was being wrenched in my gut and it never went away. I felt the compounding effect of life events, artificially imposed torture, and a wife who was betraying me when I needed her most.

She started turning our daughters against me. She spoke about me behind my back to our precious daughters when I left the room and everyone shut up when I came back in. She rallied her parents against me and got her friends to back her up. She also began talking behind my back to my friends, and since their wives were friends with my wife they already had the voice of their wives driving home the point. She started turning everyone against me saying that I was losing my faculties. They already felt like some of my intangible spiritual talk was somewhat disconnected. It was easier now for them to label me something strange than question their own beliefs. She even turned my own mother, sister, and very dear cousin Eileen against me.

I came home unexpectedly early one day, after having a job interview canceled, and found my wife home with someone I thought was my friend. He was in the music business and was home during the day quite often. They downplayed their get together as a discussion about some mutual acquaintance. The same neighbor rallied against me later. He made phone calls backing up her lies regarding my behavior and was very instrumental in days to come when all things were set in motion against me. It later stood to reason that I was the one they were speaking of as their so-called mutual acquaintance, and what they were actually doing was ultimately plotting against me.

He was very suspicious the way he mixed up drinks so frequently when we were in social situations. On one occasion I thought he put medicine in his own drink preceding such a mix-up. It was a crowded bar and my attention wasn't focused on it so I didn't put it together at the time, but what appeared to happen as I thought about it afterwards, was that he was putting things in people's drinks. It was so slick I missed it. Maybe he did that to my wife. Maybe he was the true manipulator and was doing it so subtly that nobody noticed it.

In an attempt to restore some faith in me I showed my wife some things on the internet that specifically explained some of the things that I was experiencing. I was trying to figure it all out. I didn't doubt my sanity, but she surely did. She turned on me and she wasn't going to change her mind. She became a nightmare that was adding to the pain I was trying to get help with.

The same day I walked in on her with the neighbor, I noticed our wedding picture broken on the floor when I went into the bedroom later that evening. She said she dropped it. It looked like someone would have had to pick it up and break it the way it was done. This conclusion was supported by the fact that she refused to pick it up or fix it. She left the glass and the frame with the picture on the floor for the kids to see as we both refused to pick it up. I was appalled at her disrespect and so were the children.

Now her emotional abuse was compounding the problem. I started questioning myself and my own balance. Was I losing it? I had physical torture and intangible torture from an unknown source, and now I had a deep emotional torture from my wife. I handled many hardships in my life. I knew I had a firm grip on my mental state. It's just that all these unusual things were happening to me. I knew I wasn't crazy, but I knew I was hearing voices and when people do, it's real easy to say they're crazy.

I reviewed everything over again in my head. Was my dad's death natural? Why was my dad in such mental torment? It was not only depicted in his actions but in the writings he left behind. Was some of the pain he was in the reason for some of the pain I was now in? Did he hear voices? Was he tormented by an intangible force that he couldn't prove either? Why was this being done to me? Was it an invention my dad worked on that someone thought I now had? Was it big money or big government? Maybe his previous company needed to keep tabs on him and suppress him. Was it none of these things? Was it my wife colluding with her girlfriend, or her mother and her connections? Maybe my mother's felonious friend brought covert-harassment into my world and maybe she shouldn't be trusted.

Some of the most mind invasive technology ever invented may very well have been drawn up in the patents department where my dad worked. In fact, my father was with a tech company in the sixties when some of the stuff was being developed. He was a patents draftsman so he worked with the inventors and patent attorneys to make the drawings. He knew the deepest details of inventions years before they were actually in use. He was one of the best at what he did so the most important inventions were given to him. The patent attorneys would request the best draftsman for the most important inventions.

I don't know where or why this covert-harassment torture ever began on me. I do know it seemed to originate down there in Kentucky but I don't know for sure. It may have originated from another source and going away was a good way to hide it. Was my dad just sad, and looked for something big to make up for the fact that he felt smaller than he wanted to feel. Was I looking for something big to make up for feeling smaller than I wanted to feel?

I felt my wife turn on me and I felt others swayed by her judgments. I caught her and her rich girlfriend switching my vitamins with something. They had all my vitamins out on the table and her friend was matching sizes. The fact that they were engaged in the field of neurology together with a small start-up business that was focused on children with learning-disabilities had me thinking I was being used for an experiment. I caught them in the act, and it was such a surprise that I backed away to stop myself from a violent physical reaction. I left before that was done, and I sat stunned in my garage wondering how the mother of my children and wife of almost seventeen years could collude with a friend against me. I was literally sleeping with an enemy. One of my worst enemies was a woman I was going to spend the rest of my life with. The love I had for my children totally derailed the normal way I should have reacted when I caught her. All the smart things I should have done, I didn't. I truly didn't know what action would allow me to still be with my children. All actions that would normally be taken would have ended that chance.

Once I realized my wife had turned on me, the question of how long it was going on became a very big question. Her very harmful, rich girlfriend and she could have hired a security firm that went a little too far to hurt me. It may have escalated into all out torture. She certainly had the money to pay for whatever she wanted. I think she tried hurting me and my wife throughout our marriage without my wife ever suspecting it. There was something very wrong with her. She still acted like she was in College with my wife as her roommate. She had a deep-seated complex about all men. Her dad did a number on her that left marks. She palled around with my wife in her heyday hurting men that rejected them. Maybe now her big money gave her even more power to use it against men just like when they were younger.

I knew my wife was my enemy, but was it because she was suffering from effects just like I was and thought I was to blame? Maybe thoughts that imposed themselves on her were not detached from, and she was manipulated by the thought control rather than bearing witness to it.

I started replaying every possibility over again. I remembered feeling strange after my mother brought her highly questionable friend over my house. The most likely reason is a mistake by CT. to put the surveillance on me instead of the intended paroled gangster. This could be the most viable choice. He was a lifelong gangster. He was involved in organized crime for fifty years. He was a kingpin and was associated with very big gangster clans in New York City. It's most likely my mom, who hurt me throughout her life with her associations, who hurt me once again. If I told her this she would claim no responsibility to doing anything wrong her whole life.

She probably did very little wrong with the intention of doing harm, but the men she would end up with were so bad, the guilt by association, and the pain that came with being around them, made her decisions as costly as if she did the crimes herself. She gave the prison an address the day she left with him. She gave them an address where he was going. I remember she asked what my zip code was and that question tells me she gave them my address. My address was given as if it was his address. My family and I could very well have paid the price for that act the rest of our lives.

It's the worst injustice I have ever known and it was done to me and continues to be done to me. It is a crime beyond belief and it was done in such a way that no matter what I do to get help, nobody has done anything but hurt me more in response. The pain I live with and have experienced is so unbearable I shouldn't have been able to survive. I had my heart and head pounded electronically hundreds of times. I have damage from the many times I couldn't protect myself or move away quickly enough. Sometimes I thought I was going to have a heart attack. I've been lacking REM sleep so badly for so many years that I am continually in a dangerous state of fatigue mentally and physically. This continues to this day as I write this very sentence. Nothing has changed this and nothing has helped me.

# XI  Voices

Voices, they're always with me now. I always have company. I have a thought about something, and an opinion comes in my head. Sometimes they're similar to what I might feel, but oftentimes dramatically not. It's not my self-talk. They're unwanted words, unwanted feelings. They try to make me take on a feeling or action with words imposed on me, but I resist it. They harass me letting me know I'm being watched, I've been targeted, I'm at their mercy, they can dominate me, and they try to make me feel smaller and smaller. The voices play on my emotions, worries, concerns, fears, anxieties, desires, and whatever happens to be going on. They constantly seek to defame me and depict me in a way that justifies their torture. The voices go in the bathroom with me and they give their opinion on every private thing in my life. Even when nothing is being said it's as if there's a two ton elephant in the room with me. Different shifts control the twenty-four hour day, and they do it three hundred sixty-five days a year.

I am desperate for the time when I'll be alone in my thoughts again. I'm not well from the torment of voices. I think that's the intent. They try to know what I am experiencing every second. I try to fool them by putting a different thought in my head than what I want them to know just to have the privacy of a single thought again. They believe that thought is what is happening and the voices comment about that. I give them one thought so I am allowed to experience another. I'm only disturbed on the thing that I am projecting, and not on the thing I'm feeling that I'm not projecting. It took years of pain and detaching from my thought streams to stay strong and create some defenses, otherwise I wouldn't even be alive. The pain is beyond belief and it's not anything that anyone can really connect with unless they too are a victim. I find joy in things every day that keep me alive. I don't want what's wrong to win.

It's like you're in the middle of several theatre groups and depending on which direction your thoughts are going, is what will determine what group of actors step into the holograph. It's as if there's an all day feature in a multiplex with no walls, and one movie shuts off when you feel one way and another movie turns on when you feel another.

I'm going through something very complicated but nobody has the patience, knowledge, insight or power to do anything about it. Since this confusion, I saw the information on the internet where hundreds of other people were sharing these same horrible experiences. It's a real experience, and one aspect of it comes from radio frequencies that are being used to hurt people. You can find it on the internet under the heading "Misuse of Radio Frequencies" and "Microwave Hearing Effect". This alone has hurt me so terribly, but it has gotten even more complicated than that. Yet, since it is so advanced, nobody believes it.

Voices enter my head through my auditory cortex so people next to me can't hear them. It makes for excruciating torment and I've suffered with this for more than ten years now. There are ways this could be done with pre-programmed microchips, radio frequencies, and microwave technology. It's state-of-the-art brain invasive technology. This technology can not only be used to transmit a person's thoughts, but it can also be used to control a person's thoughts. It's a neurological crime.

I was at the library and looked up the results of my symptoms as a search on the web. I treated it like a math equation and put all my experiences in as if that was the answer, and looked for every piece of information that could be an ingredient for that answer. After thousands of hours doing this I found people who suffered from many of the same torturous experiences as I. They had something called covert-harassment happen to them. What a relief it was to find other people suffering from some version of this. I dropped to the floor crying like a baby when I saw it. I knew I was sane. I knew it was really happening. The voices talking in my head, the persecution from all aspects of my life, the tangible and intangible nightmares that have never ended had an explanation. It was covert-harassment at the very least, and a piggybacking of it by other parties at most.

I stopped crying abruptly realizing I was in a public place. I was in fear of further repercussions from the emotions I displayed. People are so intolerant of emotions these days that even when a person has good cause to display an emotion people think they're crazy. I got up pretending I fell and wiped the tears from my face as if I was just rubbing my eyes. I certainly didn't need any further troubles. Only one woman noticed what happened and looked back to see if I was alright. I showed her I was fine with a little wave. A sigh of relief came over me. I printed out what I saw so I can keep reminding myself my experiences were real. I still need to look at them even today to remind myself that this unjust torture is being done to me and it is not who I am.

Covert-harassment is a high-tech surveillance system being used by our government. It's "top-secret", but you can find it on the web. They devised a very clever way to disguise it so terrorists and criminals won't try to use it. You have to look under the words "covert-harassment". There's also a web-page in it for people who are victims of covert-harassment to speak to each other. There you can find people who have been targeted.

Unfortunately, people looking for support from this website are not protected from opportunists who would gain information on their vulnerability. If others did have the capability of gaining access by zeroing in on them, the website is providing their name and general location. At the very least they are revealing people who have been battered down and who now could be even more vulnerable. At the very worst they could also be providing a way to hack into an existing surveillance field.

In origin the website was designed to help victims but they are hard pressed to speak because they realize they can be hurt even more. It seems we keep having one intention with the internet and technology that may be good, but unscrupulous people keep changing it into what's bad. Afterwards, we oftentimes are left without any way to stop it.

This is the worst problem in the history of mankind because a hacker or security breech opens the door for others to use our weapon, and in this case the crime can affect a person's thoughts. The hacker can now control the thoughts of the people entrusted to use covert-harassment to protect the US against terrorism. They may even control them to the point where they are putting it on us instead of on them. Mind-control technology, if in the wrong hands, could be the most dangerous weapon in the history of the world.

The decision makers are using their brain to decide how to use it, meanwhile the brain is affected by the manipulation of the technology itself. If an enemy hacked into our stock market they may be able to affect financial markets. If they hacked into a mind invasive technology, they would be able to affect every decision made about everything. This would also include how covert-harassment and brain-invasive technology itself is being used. So, we are set up for being trapped in a circle of logic that would be almost impossible to step out of.

The covert-harassment web page lists all the experiences a person would have if they were targeted for covert-harassment. Here are ten of them:

1) They blanket the dwelling of the target with electromagnetic energy and bombard the target's body with debilitating electronic effects

2) They impose damaging effects on the brain using electronic invasion of the brain

3) They invade the target's thoughts using remote sensing technologies

4) The person targeted mentally hears voices imposed on their auditory cortex using a technology named "The Microwave Hearing Effect", where no one else can hear the voices but them

5) Sleep deprivation torture is done through neurological intervention

6) They force untimely sleep by pounding the pineal center of the brain with electronic jolts which release serotonin and melatonin. This causes a sudden, and oftentimes harmful sleep to occur (i.e. while driving a car)

7) They attempt manslaughter by introducing poisonous gas and toxins into a target's home through the unseen field around the electrical wires called "The Grid". The supercharged grid throws off these toxins and breathing is challenged

8) They tap the target's phone and hack into their computer

9) They blacklist the target in the labor market

10) They vandalize the target's home and car

Mind-probe surveillance utilizes a global satellite system so the administrators of it always know where the target is. There are devious people who are leveraging police systems designed for one target, and when access is gained they can affect many targets. Police anti-virus and firewall systems are behind the curve on technology. Ongoing usage of such invasive systems can get completely out of hand when a few highly skilled, power-hungry hackers turn it against them.

In this way our government's Homeland Security systems have ironically assisted the enemy. They can turn the mind-probe surveillance protection into an attack on the American people. America is a wonderful country, but it might be a little too careless; because I believe we've helped foreign enemies hurt us. If any unscrupulous person wanted to learn ways to better use mind-control systems, there's a website for that. So if they gain access, to mentally torture people, we have provided online assistance so they can be better at it. There are not enough checks and balances instituting proper supervision and monitoring of such systems. It has gone so far, there is no getting it back. The freewheeling use of covert-harassment tools and surveillance-based systems has blown up in our faces.

The government has put everything on computers with the blind faith that their systems could never be hacked into. The government systems were hacked into, the stock market systems were hacked into, and every so-called impenetrable system that has ever been set up has a way of being vulnerable to a security breech. If the breech becomes less possible because of highly advanced layers of protection, it still can't escape the human factor and the greed we are always vulnerable to. We have created something with the belief that it is "hack-proof", and when it is hacked we have no place left to go.

When people get arrested today for anything, their fingerprints and all their personal information are put on computer. All our tax records are on computer. We have totally set ourselves up for being hurt without any hope of fixing it. What do you think will happen given the fact we did that? The top systems in the world have been hacked into; to believe that these surveillance systems are invincible would be a foolish mistake. We have underestimated the genius of hackers worldwide. We have overestimated the loyalty of workers who have been entrusted with highly dangerous systems.

Just because someone is being targeted by law enforcement using covert-harassment, doesn't necessarily mean that it was done without error. If a mistake is made and it is realized, the rights of American citizens should be valued. Compensation for damages, a full explanation, and systems to guard against erroneous spreading of this weapon should be implemented. If it was spread to someone else through a breech, or tampered with by another radio frequency, the victim should not be treated the same as if they were an enemy. The possibility of covering up the mistake and continually using it as some power over others should be strictly monitored.

The Global Positioning Satellite system has been hacked into, and law enforcement uses that for surveillance. In February of 2012 I called the terrorist hotline and told them I think the GPS was hacked into. They logged the complaint and two days later it was on the internet in the news. The GPS was in fact hacked into. I thought my observation deserved some attention, so I told the FBI and CIA but I got nothing back. We had the most mind-invasive and damaging technology ever invented potentially running amuck through one more access point, and a citizen who realized this horrible breech couldn't garner a single confirmation or acknowledgement from any law enforcement agency. Maybe if I served the information with spaghetti and meatballs I would have been listened to.

Covert-harassment surveillance and torture exists, and in our government's opinion it's warranted for national security. Lately, there is a great deal of debate in congress on whether or not covert-harassment should ever be used. It most certainly should not be used on innocent American citizens and many are being unjustly affected.

They target the brain of a person and affect their functioning. This is all part of "protecting" the American people, but it's compromising everything this country was built on. All our rights have taken a back seat to big government and this is not a democracy any more.

Sometimes the voices in my head act like people I know. It's done so well I wonder if it's an act, or if it's really them. How do they replicate their voices? They know enough about them from my thoughts to portray different scenarios. There must be some tonality device that assists with sounding like them, I don't know. Maybe when I think it's a particular person they can extract my memories of the way that person sounded, and when they further portray them that makes me think it's them. I believe there may be other tortured people besides me hearing it, so some of the voices I hear might be others who are suffering. The wavelength quickly changes when any members of the communication attempt to reveal ways to relieve their pain. They aren't able to have an exchange after that point.

It's a group of people creating a type of holograph. Sometimes I will see the people out and about who were previously portrayed in my auditory cortex and they don't act like they were previously tormenting me. They don't act like something weird was going on. This is all part of the torture. The gap between what's real and what's going on in my head widens. They pound me constantly with what's not real. I have a very strong base or I wouldn't be able to withstand such a thing.

There may be cases where multiple people are targeted and the victims sense other victims and try to confirm it with them. It's in those cases where it may be possible to hear another target. It may also be that when people see each other in the physical world, they find it hard to reconcile the events of the intangible world. They are afraid of being looked at a certain way. They are fearful of being thought of as unstable. Confirming it becomes that much harder because of this fear.

It might be that I'm crazy, but people who know me tell me I'm very smart and far from crazy. I risked what people thought about me to reveal this. Most won't risk one ounce of how they appear for the sake of the hard truth. It's the superficial 2010's and we, as a society, are probably more superficial than any group in the history of the world. The "Tech Tainted Tens" will be the death of us all if we don't wake up.

IF there was a technology that affected the brain, what would we use to decide it? A technology that could use our own thoughts to hurt us would be a painful way to force the realization that we may very well be far too attached to our thoughts. An attack on our thoughts would force a view outside of them, otherwise we would fall victim to their manipulation. It seems too far-fetched that this could ever come into being. It would mean the end of a certain brain-based way of living because remaining in that state would leave us like a sitting duck. Without an awareness of potential brain-control effects, that came from a technology that has gotten out of control, we could easily be the next victim. Sounds like some futuristic science fiction story? I wish it was.

It may have all started with computers replicating the human brain. It may have further been developed to have thoughts transmitted to overcome medical challenges. It might be advanced computers being used for brain-transmission interfaces. Medical advances used these instruments to help those who couldn't speak, by transmitting their thoughts to a screen that could then be viewed. Lack of mobility also allowed wheelchair bound people, who couldn't use their arms, to now be able to use thought transmission to affect the wheel's movements.

The misuse of such a technology would indeed be a frightening thing. It would be a real tragedy because so many would be hurt for so long before they realized that their thoughts may not be originating from their own intention. Many would never realize it and succumb to the thoughts imposed. In that case they would become the words in their brain acting on another's dictation. Someone else would be deciding what they should do and what they should feel next. The deep attachment most have to the brain-machine dictation would render them near helpless if they were the victim of covert-harassment gone awry.

Every button coiled up in our emotional life would have to unwind or we would be victimized for having it. Scene's portrayed access a person's point of emotional vulnerability and the talk comes in through the auditory cortex. These scenes are called mind-games. Mind-games are using one or more voice to give you the impression something happened or is about to happen. Mind-games are designed to take your fears and desires and use them to wear you down. They use personal information gained about you and others to convince you. They can be used to make a person do and say certain things that end up being detrimental. They can cause extreme pain and hurt the things they care about most.

This obviously can be extremely devastating to a person's existence. It does damage to their nervous system, it distracts them from work, school, or anything that requires focus. They can put a person to sleep while driving a car and kill them as well as others. They interrupt their thoughts with mind-games, impose a fear upon them about people they love or care about, and they can frame them into situations where they cripple their ability to make money by hurting them legally and emotionally. They can hurt their ability to gain other employment by hurting their credit and by blacklisting them in the labor market.

Poisonous gas and radiation toxins were put into my home. This was done in a very complicated way. There's a field around the electrical wires in our home which is called an "electrical grid". It can be used to govern power through the wires in such a way that electric companies could turn off your electricity remotely. This way they don't have to send someone out to do it. It can also be used to check your electrical usage, so again, manpower is saved.

The problem with all this is that it can be hacked into. The field around the wires can be supercharged to the point where they can release a toxic chemical. People can be subtly poisoned with limited ability to detect it. This was done to me. I complained to the electrical grid home office, the local electric company, the local police, and the FBI but nothing helped. They use the fact that it has a complicated origin as a way to defend against revealing it and stopping it. Some divisions of Law enforcement are unaware of such technology. They only look for hard-core, tangible, and provable facts. In other cases they have the knowledge, but go under the assumption that if you are experiencing this, you deserve it.

They had me stalked on foot and in vehicles. They vandalized my home and my cars. They tapped my phones and hacked into my computer. Covert-harassment involves imposing an EMF field of energy that suppresses energy levels. A high EMF field can cause cancer, birth defects, depression, hallucinations, and sleep disorders. We lost our second child due to birth defects. That would have been my son. Severe depression and hallucinations affected my wife. Every symptom of the harassment tortured me and my family without any hope of anyone believing me, including my own family. This dangerously high EMF can be measured with certain instruments and is present in my home.

It feels as if you are always up against a force that is pressing against your thoughts and actions. They jolt a person in their heart, their private parts, their brain, and throughout their body. All this was originally designed for suspected terrorists who come to this country to do harm. There was something called the Geneva Convention that forbid torture of our enemies. I guess an honest American citizen does not have that protection.

I suppose if I was an enemy, I would consider using any weapon designed for me, against the perpetrator of it. It doesn't sound too complicated on the surface, but in practice it's the most complicated espionage ever designed. Law enforcement is so secretive and protective about their covert-harassment tool that when there is a problem, they protect the breech as well. Maybe I am being too kind in thinking it was a security breech. Maybe it was just a horrible mistake made by our very own law enforcement officials, or worse. Maybe it was a purposeful experiment to torture a perfectly good man. Whatever the case, having nobody to turn to for help once it was done is as bad as it being done intentionally.

What does law enforcement do when these tools are hacked into? How would they handle it? Would they admit their error, their lack of protection, their vulnerability? What happens if they make a mistake and put it on the wrong person? How easy is it to fix? This is not the product of a democratic society and it is costing us dearly.

It's not something that should have been allowed in the first place.

Terrorists aren't the only ones who could use the weapon for unscrupulous purposes. If the field is vulnerable and can spread, then these weapons could help all kinds of predators. Crooks seeking financial information, identity thieves seeking passwords and security numbers, and even neurological experimenters gaining notoriety would all find it advantageous to use this illegal brain controlling edge. Any person incentivized to gain through its abuse would also be a target to manipulate. Any person includes law enforcement. We could end up going to the manipulated perpetrator for help and only end up locating them.

Ultimately, it's a hidden attack using our own people to do it. Terrorism now becomes as easy as creating avenues for our very own unscrupulous people to drive on. It's a way for an enemy to spread this using our own people as resources to use against our very own country.

The origin of the problem exists not only in our definition of when to use it, but in our decision of whether we should use it at all. Without these determinations in place the application keeps getting looser. Now if someone looks funny they may be chosen to be tortured. People in high positions are taking liberties with this power and exchanging favors with our national security at stake. Freewheeling law enforcement people were given too much freedom with this horrific weapon and they are not technologically savvy enough to know when there is a breech in security. They aren't aware of all the warning signs that would indicate an intrusion.

They put mind-probe surveillance on a person to wear them down. They make them weaker and weaker so the target can't do any harm. Yet, when innocent people try to reveal the mind-probe surveillance that's been unjustly placed on them, they are told they're crazy and put in mental institutions. The hospitals get richer, the psychiatrists get richer, the pharmaceutical industry gets richer, and the police show they did something that month. Nobody is incentivized to reveal the horrible mistake. Town court systems get richer and people needing to justify their salaries now have one more way of doing it. Revealing the truth is like fighting City Hall and perpetuating the lie is validated through our systems.

The experience feels as if you are being watched, you think someone is against you, you're hearing voices, and you're being electronically jolted. All these symptoms can be placed in a category for psychological disorders. There is no room in society for having the experiences of covert-harassment without it being deemed as something else which brings further pain upon you. What it takes to reveal it, is also being used as a way to stop revealing it. Anyone mistaken for a "justifiable" target is still deemed deserving for fear of revealing this so-called top-secret security system.

It very well could have come from an error by a person who had such control, but that won't matter. They could have been coerced in their private life to compromise the tool they are responsible for, but there may not be enough checks and balances to stop it. It could be part of an attack from a security breech, but that wouldn't matter either. There's a defamation of character colluded on that undermines any attempt to even reveal an injustice with this tool. They believe they are insuring its secrecy by smothering any communication about it. Now we are not only thwarted in our attempt to stop unscrupulous people, but we are handcuffed by our own law enforcement personnel. We are literally paying taxes to be tortured by our own government without a means of communicating otherwise. Any reference to what is treated as top-secret is defended against with a fury. You become the terrorist even if you were merely an innocent victim.

There are ways to find out about people who are under government surveillance. A person can simply go to the web, look up surveillance detectors, and pay three thousand dollars to buy one. Now they know who has surveillance them. Once detected, it can be targeted to hurt even more people. They can take advantage of the weakened state of that individual. "Justifiable covert-harassment" or not, targeting a person or spreading the covert-harassment becomes a weapon. Information gained can be used to have our friends turned against us, wives and husbands turned against each other, and even the law can be manipulated to hurt us, frame us, and do everything to wear us down. People who wouldn't get divorced in a million years now find themselves forking over their life savings to lawyers. In other situations wealthy people traveling overseas are targeted and big money is manipulated to be spread around. Greed then becomes what stops revealing anything that would take the cover off this disease.

So, we have lost control to the unintended consequences of this technology. What was supposed to be used for protection of the American people is harming us so horribly it may never be fixed. It is the most diabolical, insidious, unseen, undetectable attack in the history of the world.

Law enforcement may unknowingly be at the mercy of these systems. If the brain control feature of the tool is used against those granted the power to use it, the result may end up being the commitment of the perfect crime. Their systems may not end up being exclusively their systems. Unfortunately this may never be realized because they are so protective of covert systems, and take so much pride in doing it "right", that speaking about any vulnerability with regards to it is taboo.

Police and other law enforcement agencies tend to focus on hard core physical proof. When the origin of a crime is not easily detectable in a tangible way, new approaches needed to reveal what's intangible may not be easily implemented. Policemen and other law enforcement personnel, by their very nature, are less likely to admit error, appear weak, or admit to being blindsided by anything. In addition, any thoughts to reveal a problem may be redirected under a mind-probe surveillance field. The field allows for the visibility of thoughts where they then can be compromised. The very same technology they we're using on potential terrorists, is the same technology terrorists can use to stop officials from revealing any hack-in of it.

Law enforcement will likely be angry and defensive at anything that would depict something other than strength, but who else is fighting for such a possibility? I am saying here what law enforcement personnel are stopped from saying. They are prevented by the role they have to play, by potential manipulators using this surveillance field, and by how they would be treated to reveal a weak link. Police are one and a half million strong possessing leverage against more than two hundred times that number. If they can't show vulnerability in protecting the three hundred million plus people, then maybe they can show how they themselves are not protecting each other. Here again, this democracy is supposed to be by the people and for the people. It has become by the government, and for the government. Our chance for keeping our democracy is being undermined, and we are fighting each other, instead of fighting those who are vying for the control of human thoughts while they are torturing our citizens.

The crime is mind-control, so if successful, the perpetrators can affect what decisions are made regarding it as well. They use technology, microchips, radio frequencies, and cognitive manipulative drugs to manipulate people in high leverage positions. This is actually a mind-probe surveillance attack. Each group of people using it feels they are justified for using it. The enemy sits back and laughs at the greed, lust, envy, egos, power abuse, and weaknesses of the people who do the crime. Each group thinks it's all about them and their edge. The enemy is using our resources against us just like they have in many other attacks of the past.

Under this disguise, while at the mercy of our own systems, identity thieves use it to steal information. Under the guise of a neurological experiment, neurologists and educators misuse it to further their strength. Under the guise of law enforcement, police use it to make arrests and foresee problems before they occur. If one person wants to hurt another, it can be used to mentally, physically, and legally damage that person irreparably. Private investigators have taken liberties with surveillance tools that were not supposed to be available to them. They are being funded to use systems that were supposed to be exclusive to our government under the most extreme threats, and even that usage is under deep question. Now, irate wives, jealous husbands, opportunists, and anyone looking to control the behavior of others can use this hurtful, invasive technology because of this national security breech.

The unscrupulous behavior of all these groups of people allow an enemy of the United States to sit back and watch the American people do enormous damage to each other. Human energy, money, power, and leverage are being used to hurt our country in the most devious way ever devised. It is truly the most diabolical plot ever devised in the history of mankind. I'm writing this knowing that after two thousand attempts at revealing this over a period of more than eight years, I still can't get anyone to listen to me. I am writing this after being tortured more than ten and a half years. It took me more than two and a half years to even have an idea what was really happening.

It's a circle in a circle perpetuated by greed, power and egotism. Our systems and compartmentalization insulate it. The fear of rejection, labeling, or sounding crazy keeps the problem locked in place. Over time, the people who are on these covert-harassment teams are so mentally damaged from the work, they could be compromised without ever being aware of it.

People adamantly damned, defamed, and belittled me. They physically and mentally tortured me. The police force, judges, lawyers, the District Attorney, the Governor, and the Senator all denied me. I lost everything

I worked for in life being the victim of covert-harassment while fighting against it and trying to reveal it. All I have done is bring further pain upon myself. The intangible things I claimed made it appear that I lost my faculties. This is what allowed for very tangible legal problems, and the legal problems kept the intangible attack unquestioned.

I bought an EMF detector to measure electronic frequencies in my home. This would be a good indicator of a surveillance field or other damaging waves. The meter needle went as high as it could go. I informed all the places that I imagined it would matter to, but it no avail. I didn't know what country I was in any more. I could prove that high EMF waves caused depression, sleep loss, tension, physical ailments, even pregnancy risks but still, there was no place to turn. All these effects happened to me and my ex-wife while she lived here with me. I still live here in the same home for twenty-three years. I've held my ground, and absorbed extreme torture.

Many who have been manipulated to use this weapon can't imagine that their very complicated trick isn't the most complicated trick of all. They think they're the end, when in fact they are merely a pawn in a much bigger chess game. Many experiences I suffered with, and still endure, can be found on an internet list regarding symptoms of covert-harassment. If targeting a completely innocent person isn't a good enough cause for concern, then my other experiences, not found on that list, should bring concerns about a greater manipulation involved.

This wouldn't be the first time that leverage using our own people against us was used to assist an attack on the US. Terrorists used our post office against us with letters laced with anthrax. They used our planes against us with the 9/11 disaster, and now they are using our covert-harassment systems against us. The only problem with this one is that it is so insidious, so hidden, so intangible, and so manipulative it may never be revealed. With every attempt made to reveal it, defamation and legal framing are increased while mental and physical torture is amplified.

How could we be sure that someone isn't controlling the brain of the President of the United States? They would be protected by law enforcement looking to hide the characteristics of this high-tech weapon. They could easily be convinced that it was all about their secretive covert-harassment tool meant for some "justifiable" target.

I don't think intellectuals are easily separated from their thought stream. They relied on it to get them where they are. Colleges and higher-level learning demand the ability to recall lots of facts and dates. They also demand a great deal of intellectual reasoning. If a student went on to become a lawyer or politician there would be even more of a reliance on intellect to get them to that point. If seeing this problem required a disassociation from streams of thinking, it could be hardest for those always driven to rely on it.

One would have to be distanced from the machine-like workings of the brain to better witness any affect on it. It shouldn't be assumed that just because a person is credited with extreme intelligence they would possess wisdom to step out from under the umbrella of thoughts. Revealing brain effects coming from mind-control technology, drugs, or even dream control does not go hand in hand with intelligence.

Therefore, possessing wisdom to go beyond the brain, and any compromising of it, is not necessarily going to fall in order with position or power. Hierarchy, respect for position, pecking order, chain of command, and departmentalized systems of handling information can all be used to further insulate the problem.

People we turn to for help with this massive problem are in their position possibly because of intellectual advances, but their ability to look at this problem may or may not be there. Intellectuals are running this country. Enlightened people, and not those acting in a manner that strictly adheres to tangible brain categories, are more in the witnessing presence of their thought stream. Enlightened people may not be part of what is making surveillance system decisions. Awareness of "SEER TRAPS" may become mandatory. This extreme adherence to our thoughts without an awareness of what's always greater is being tested, and now more than ever it needs to be realized and applied.

Since the people who have the most leverage are targeted first, intellectuals running the country may have already been targeted. They may be beaten down by the voices in their heads. They may be suffering from sleep deprivation, and they may have had facets of their life damaged. They may not be objective to their thoughts, and they may have behaved in very uncharacteristic ways. They may still be making choices very much out of character. They may be too full of pride, too fearful of defamation, and too protective of their position and power to ever reveal such a "weakness".

If people of power were compromised with the manipulation of such a technology, they may not differentiate between their chosen thoughts and the ones imposed on them. The misuse of this technology would have them believing all thoughts as their own because they couldn't intellectually fathom another origin. They may be aware of mind-invasive technology in theory, but in practice, with them as a victim, sound decision making may be overridden by the technology itself.

We are being forced to develop qualities that would recognize something as insidious as "mind-control". It demands us to be aware of what our brain does, so that any control of it would be quickly realized. We need to take an objective view of our brain, thoughts, and decisions because being subjected to them is now an avenue for weaponry. "SEER TRAPS" is not to be taken lightly. Our very lives could be threatened today if we stay trapped.

# VII   Why Talk?

New Years Eve came and after two champagnes and a nice time over our friend's house our little family went home. I forgot my body wasn't handling carbonation too well those days and the bubbly got to me. I threw up, and instead of it coming out into the toilet bowl I was aiming for, nothing came out. It turns out I aspirated my vomit into my lungs, and hours later after my first lung collapsed, the second one was starting to fill up. I almost died. My wife got me to the hospital before my other lung collapsed and literally saved my life.

The next day she came into the room and instead of being grateful for my life, she was exasperated with the hardships that had befallen us. She focused on my job pursuits and all the hardships we had gone through. She looked at me as if I was to blame for all that went wrong. I was so hurt I can't even tell you. The nurse came in appalled at the conversation knowing how close I came to dying and asked everyone to leave so I can get my rest.

My wife acted callous and unfeeling there in the hospital, just as she did when I returned home from 9/11, and just as she did when I came home after handling my father's death. I later found out that she was on an anti-anxiety drug and she stayed on it far too long. It turned out to be one of the most addictive drugs available. I read later that it was even more addictive than Heroine. She wasn't feeling anything anymore in many areas. Her love and her libido were nonexistent. Before I knew she was on this medication I took it all personally. It certainly would have helped if I knew she had a problem with this highly addictive drug.

Time went on, and things got worse between us. My answer was to ride it out and try to fix things. Her answer was to get a divorce. Only six months before that she swore she would never get a divorce. I was devastated. I couldn't really absorb any more pain in my life but it came anyway. I was all filled up with a lifetime of hurt.

I couldn't show my children the fight I was fighting and my wife already expressed her disregard for my battles. The fight was not something you could see, so I went into these long speeches about what can't be seen and touched. I would speak a long time about how what you can't see and touch is more powerful sometimes than what can be seen and touched. They seemed to understand what I meant in general, but wondered why I spoke so long about something that wasn't tangible. I left an impression that something can go on which is having an effect that can't be seen. Like the wind it can be very strong, yet when attempting to communicate about it, words, and the people you speak with don't always allow for it. I taught them not to name the mystery so they would be able to experience something they couldn't see and touch. I wanted them to avoid placing things unseen in an unreachable category reserved for some dogmatic belief.

The need to take a position, when no position is absolute without further investigation, is the parallel between religion, and my intangible torture of more than ten years. No position should have been taken without thoroughly investigating the symptoms of my experience. Those acting under the assumption I was crazy, hurting me after I showed a lifetime of love, character, wisdom and integrity, is a pain that's beyond description.

My wife and I got along many years before our deepest feelings about religion were revealed. This happened once our children became a certain age where the subject had to be confronted. That's when the differences we did have were amplified many times over.

When I was able to see beyond so much pain, the intangible attack struck me as an analogy for the imbedded way people acted when handling the biggest mysteries of life. The judgmental and abbreviated habit of handling complex intangible issues always hung over me. Every question was mishandled because of a blind faith people had to religion and God. Questioning things unknown about both my unseen experiences were adamantly opposed with equal damnation.

If the only reason we are here can be dismissed and lied about because it's intangible, then everything else intangible comes with the habit of suppressing investigation with quick judgments.

I feel the plot that is being played out is in a way a depiction to us of what is subtly happening because we took the grandest essence of ourselves and made up a lie about it. The intangible power within us and around us is not something we are meant to make up lies about. It's not serving us to do so and it has come back to hurt mankind throughout history. It only causes separation, alienation and division.

It seems the only way left to realize this without complete annihilation, would be to have our physical world played with by something that was intangible as well. After we break through the disguise to reveal the culprit, we may then see how we misinterpret other intangibles in a dangerous way. Then we would realize that what's intangible needs to be viewed in a way that allows for greater awareness. We can't be the results of confining it to the pre-defined limitations of the human brain.

The artificial manipulation afflicting us by the mind-probe surveillance attack illustrates in a big way how we wrongly interpret what's intangible to accommodate our insecurities. The creation of God and all religions are impeding our enlightenment and unity as a species. In the most painful injustice imaginable, comes a gift we may not realize until it exhausts mental attachments. We are being forced to step out of brain-based focus to see the problem. No other problem from thought and brain attachment would clarify the dilemma more greatly. If we can get past our own brain-machine habits, which default to its dependent categories, we may very well see parallels to free us from ideas of Gods and religions. It could stop the horrible tendencies human beings are burdened with.

Extraordinary events forced me to give up mental and physical attachments, or have them violently ripped from me. All the invisible effects on my life were whittling away at me little by little. Things that couldn't be seen were used to hurt me in horrible ways. Intangible things were being used to damn me. It certainly wasn't the first time that a mystery was used to manipulate others. This was a forceful, physical, mental, and legal attack.

If this could happen to a person who has lived a life as caring as I have, something drastic had to be wrong. This could very well be used as not only an individual attack, but a mass attack. It was my life, or rather my life content, that in a way existed as an analogy to harshly show me all I was knocking on the door for throughout my life. Yet, it was more than just my own life this had to be affecting, and it was more than my fight I was fighting.

My experiences showed me what people do to elevate their selves and categorize another. It showed me all the systems, and what happens to people when they lose themselves in them. It seems I went after the answers with a relentless pursuit and caught the very brunt of defensiveness at every turn. I took nothing less than the truth as an answer and confronted every paradigm. In turn, I felt the wrath of all who needed to hold on to imposters. They hurt anything or anyone proposing any other belief. They hurt me deeply. I experienced what it meant to go up against deeply imbedded beliefs and the results were downright primitive.

People needed to cling to unfounded beliefs while I was delving more deeply into what so many found quite convenient to overlook. I had so many horrible things happen to me. Life seemed to be taking everything I once held as precious and one by one slowly destroyed them. The most meaningful things in my life were obliterated. Symbols, pride, family, employment, friends, people I loved, and all the things I identified with, were all chipped away at or eliminated with blow after blow. Things I thought would be forever, were gone, gone, gone.

Many things happened during these times that closed the door on love and opened the door to hate. I felt a dismantling of ideas, attachments and strivings in myself. Those around me hated me for forcing them to redefine the mental structures they were holding onto so tightly. I saw the parallel and misconception of both invisible experiences. Yet, I was in a unique space, and unless the person I communicated this to was already there, they would think me quite unusual for referencing it. I lost touch with what seemed to matter most to many people in my circle, where their focus was dominated by physical gains, and I gained a greater feel for all that was nonmaterial.

Yet, the invisible took on two meanings, as unseen hurtful forces from another became an invisible enemy. It inflicted me at the same time this dismantling of physical attachments brought me closer to this awakening. There was an intangible attack on my body and brain. The only thing these two experiences had in common were that they were both intangible. That is where their similarities began and that is where they ended.

People I thought were close to me took great comfort in damning me. The total picture of a pain ridden man persisted. Certain quick judgments are made against people looking to reveal the unseen throughout history, and it didn't stop in my case. I was seamlessly being driven down from a ceaseless physical and mental torture.

I stopped talking. I guess that sounds strange. It was kind of a throw back from when I was a boy. Too much pain put me in a place where the only thing left to do was be silent. During that time several things revealed themselves. There was this great divide between myself and many people around me. It left me wanting only to be the silent observer until I could come to a greater peace with it. I also thought that maybe the behavior of others would change if they also saw the deception of words and voices. Maybe they would see themselves better if the wisdom, sometimes found in silence, prevailed.

Friends weren't friends and family weren't family. I didn't know what to do, so I continued not to talk so I could be more in touch with the unseen. I told my family I wouldn't talk for a while, but they didn't believe me. I went the next nine days without saying a word. They thought it was insane.

I kept many things to myself because speaking would cause others pain. I didn't tell my children that I saw their mother and her friend switch my vitamins with something harmful. I didn't tell anyone. I think I was in shock from an accumulation of so much pain. The thought of losing my family enforced my silence. I loved my daughters so much I couldn't be sure what action wouldn't bring harm to our relationship. I was frozen with pain.

In my silence I experienced a spiritual explosion. I felt all the hidden agendas and lies going on with many of those around me. I felt as I did when I was a young boy, feeling so very deeply, and experiencing on a level few ever get to. Something was about to happen that was part of bad communication and I didn't want to be associated with it. I didn't want to say a word until I understood why everyone was acting so horribly. Unfortunately, they were then more convinced there was something wrong with me, or at least they had more to use as ammunition to prove it. It was deemed crazy that I chose not to speak for a while.

I heard the words spoken and felt the feelings unspoken. To me, the information gained about the people around me was what truly should have been considered crazy. To perpetuate such harmful communications rather than take pause was not what I wanted to do. I thought my silence would bring all communications to a higher level.

My awareness level grew as I allowed things to be without imposing words or thoughts. I became attuned to all the feelings around me and all the words spoken were very separate from the deeper truth I experienced in my silence. I saw deep inside what existed before words masked feelings. The only problem was that I became aware of what was so awful that it put me deeper in shock, and sent me spiraling into a very sad and lonely place. Friends and family betrayed me and I felt that very deeply. They wanted to hurt what they didn't understand. They saw someone trying to discover life. They needed to affirm what they believed was spiritual very strongly because they felt insecure doubting it. So, by negating me in strong fashion they stopped a challenge to it.

They saw a man experiencing unseen revelations. Some were very enlightening and profound. Some discoveries were of an artificial origin where technology, neurology, drugs, radio frequencies, microwave hearing effects, and other torturous things were victimizing me in a horrible way. I went through many things when I stopped talking. One thing was I noticed body language a lot more and it showed me ugly things. That kept me quiet much longer. I felt how people were lying and manipulating words even more. I kept spiraling into sadness at the thought of losing my family.

The artificially imposed intangible technological effect was so complicated that a glaze of disbelief came over people when I tried to share it with them. Now the spiritual enlightenment, that accompanied my experience, gave people around me another excuse to doubt me. They previously opposed my sharing of a more unified theory and now had tangible ammunition to negate me as a person entirely. I was going through something and I really haven't stopped. It seems being unattached religiously allowed me to conceive of other intangible things that also required a deeper investigation.

At this time my wife was so uneasy I felt she was jumping out of her skin. My silence was revealing a part of her that had no patience left. When I started speaking again she asked that I call a marriage-counselor. I rejected the idea for a while, but then she threatened to end our marriage unless I did. I agreed and she left a number for me to call. She took the children with her to go shopping with her mother at the mall in Rockland. She told me to call the marriage-counselor about two o'clock. I agreed, and was home alone working on different things until the time she told me to call.

When I called, they picked up the phone, only said hello, and I proceeded to explain who I was and the reason for my call. They asked me how long was it that I have wanted to kill myself. I was appalled and yelled back, "kill myself; I don't want to kill myself!" They replied, "Then why did you call the Suicide-Hotline?" "Suicide-Hotline, I thought I was calling a marriage-counselor", I firmly said. They reiterated that I was calling the "Suicide-Hotline" so I hung up instantly.

I was very confused. I was so stupid and so blindsided. I simply thought she gave me the wrong number. When she finally got home late that night I asked her what that wrong phone number was all about. It was written off as an error in writing it down and better information was going to be sought. She got the number from a friend so she was going to clarify it the next day. I believed her, but it certainly felt strange.

The next day my wife left for work. I was in between jobs and was working on this book in the garage when I heard a knock on the garage door. It was the police, a truck, and another police car. I was stunned. They asked if I called the Suicide-Hotline. I told them no, I called a marriage-counselor but my wife gave me the wrong number. They said other people called to complain as well so they needed to take me away. I was adamant about the fact that calling the wrong number shouldn't warrant what they were doing. I asked how they can arrest me for calling the wrong number. They claimed they weren't arresting me. They had to take me in handcuffs to be psychiatrically evaluated at the hospital. I protested but they gave me no choice. I protested the whole ride over there.

When we arrived I was brought in a room and told to wait. They wanted my health insurance information and other standard admittance information. I insisted on the fact that I shouldn't be admitted and that it was all a mistake. They said that the psychiatrist will determine that. The psychiatrist entered and proceeded to ask me questions. All were straight forward until she came to the question about whether I felt if anyone was plotting against me. I told her of the trickery that got me there so what other conclusion could be derived. She really didn't care about the background that got me there in the first place and went back to the question.

Well, if I said no, and that no one was plotting against me, then it wouldn't make sense why I called that number. So, of course I believe I was plotted against, because I was told the lie that it was a marriage-counselor. My wife obviously had plotted against me otherwise I wouldn't be there. The psychiatrist ended the questions and said she decided I am paranoid to believe such a thing so I have to stay there. Once a person believes others are plotting against them they have no choice but to deem them paranoid. She let me make a phone call to notify a family member of my situation. I now had to resort to the very same people in my family that I already had dissension with about my spiritual views. I asked them to assist me with this character judgment being made against me. I had to call my mom.

My mom came and raised hell but it didn't help. She then treated me as if there was something wrong with me because they determined it. I later found out she was manipulated to call the Suicide-Hotline as well and because she felt bad about being tricked, she would rather watch my pain than admit it. My wife called her and told her to call the same number telling her I was in trouble and that calling that number would help me. It made it look like there was another person who was concerned of my mental health. She framed my mother, but my mother neglected to ever mention it until I found out the hard way. She was obviously too embarrassed to admit that she was tricked into hurting her own son. She ignored previous warnings I gave her to avoid communicating with my wife because of the troubles we were experiencing.

I was admitted against my will and escorted by police and orderlies to a floor with bars on the windows and doors. I felt the full force of the perfect frame job by a person I thought I was spending the rest of my life with. There, I cried a river, as Christmas, my seventeenth wedding anniversary, and New Years passed. The fabric of my life was burned, defamed, defrauded, and decimated. My children were alienated from me and were lied to about me. Nonstop puddles poured out of my eyes day after day. I was afraid the nurses and orderlies would hurt me more if I showed them my pain. I cried quietly in my room under the covers as if I was sleeping and stopped when they abruptly opened the door to check on me.

All the people I called had a reason not to help me. They went with the way it looked rather than who I had always proven myself to be. Men who were my friends listened to their wives who were friends of my wife. They didn't want to go against their wives so they went against me and turned me down for any help.

I desperately used my last quarters in a pay phone on the floor of the psychiatric ward begging friends and family for legal help. All turned me down as the last quarters were spent. They wouldn't take a chance to help me. They wouldn't put forth any part of themselves to help me one iota. My ways of enlightenment toward unity, previously attempting to dismantle their religious beliefs, now didn't serve me well. They resented me for being outspoken about the unseen trip I was experiencing so when it came time to reveal anything else, seen or unseen, they weren't going to help. They condescended to me and acted in sympathetic superficiality. They acted as if they were humoring someone that had something wrong with them. I needed a head of steam correcting the horrible injustice and instead I was trapped and alone without anyone to help.

I needed a high-powered lawyer or someone who could subpoena the tape recording from when I called the Suicide-Hotline. That would reveal that I thought I was calling a marriage-counselor. The fact that my mom worked in a law firm for thirty years was of no help. I needed someone to vouch for my character in a big way and find out why my wife did what she did. I needed a forceful legal hand to straighten her out about the way you treat a husband and the father of your own children. Nobody would get involved. The pain kept coming. It was a floodgate of pain.

I kept calling people and the disappointments mounted. My own sister wouldn't come to see me. She thought all my previous revelations were very strange so she now had no trouble doubting my mental state. She was now relieved of any discomfort challenging conclusions she had made about the unseen part of herself. Metaphysical questions which challenged her belief system from me in the past now needed no further proof.

Funny how years later she embraced the same spiritual concepts as I. Then I listened to her kindly as she gave them back to me as if we never spoke about them before. How convenient it was for her not to go out of her way for me when I needed her most. It wasn't the first time. Any time I ever needed her she treated me worse than a stranger would. It was her opportunity to show once again how she was better than me. It was based in some childish need to still coddle her hurt from younger days. I thought she would be there for me as an adult but she failed me and damned me.

All those that opposed my spiritual beliefs went against me. They were able to confirm their own need to be right about previous disharmony with me by damning me with this new situation. They can now point to something and say, "See, you were wrong about everything because you're really crazy". This philosophy came from my closest family and my closest friends. The pain kept coming with every phone call reaching out from this place where mentally sick people were walking around and where I was forced to stay against my will. The gate up front and the bars on the windows made me feel like I was in jail, and all for calling a marriage-counselor. I was framed and now damned unjustly by others who were either spoken to already or took on opinions as they heard about it.

People I thought loved me my whole life failed me over and over again as I fought off the drugs they tried to give me in this insane place. I fielded pounding questions from psychiatrists three to four hours a day, week after week. Each question forced me back in time, and back into every painful situation of my life. They made relive everything I had to overcome and made me feel like there was something wrong with me for having to go through it in the first place. They looked for something to hang their hat on and they used every challenge in my life as a way to do it. They were talking to a person who was strong and who was falsely accused. Instead of leaving an opportunity to review the previous determination, they were simply looking for any means possible to support the mistake that was made. More damage was done to me with their persistent rehashing and mentally invasive habits. They were stuck in habits and patterns they used to systematically treat everyone. A label was placed on me, and a drug was designed to fit that label which they were insisting on applying.

Funny how so many sessions ensued and after hearing so much about me, my childhood, and different times of my life, I was fine and the psychiatrist's eyes were tearing. They would say you have to be distraught after those experiences. I would tell them how I handled everything because I'm a strong person and they would keep telling me that there has to be an ill effect from all these situations. They decided they would find something wrong and no matter what I said, they did.

I would tell them about how I was framed to make a phone that was used to hurt me, and they supported the health facility's decision to keep me there. I grew up with hardship and I could take a lot, but the lies and the injustices were not giving me a voice. They only heard what could be twisted to support their desire to keep me there, and everything else was discarded. The psychiatrists were self-supporting and the longer I stayed, the more they got paid. They knew they had me. When I told them the truth about my wife's betrayal, they would keep me there because they deemed it paranoid that I believed she plotted against me. If I didn't deny the call to the Suicide-Hotline, and acted like I called on purpose, then they would keep me there for that reason. No matter what I did, it was wrong.

They were not trying to get the truth. They were supporting the depiction of the lie and not taking the time to gather the facts from the exact phone conversation. Due diligence did not prevail, but new revenue did. Bring your car to a mechanic and say, "Here's my wallet, please check to see if there's anything wrong with my car." What do you think will happen? They certainly will not tell you everything is fine.

The abusive way I was dragged to the hospital and chained like an animal against my will for making a phone call, is something out of third world country. The abuse is certainly not the product of a democracy. It's the County finding revenue for themselves at the cost of the facts and justifying it through lies and frame jobs. This literally ruined my life. They don't feel like finding out all the facts and now my life is forever ruined on what was simply my word against hers. How was I not given the ability to have a tape replayed from the call? How was I not given some way to defend myself? Why was I unable to have a voice? Why was my case decided before I even spoke?

What orchestrated this on me? What favors were traded that now had my life hanging in the balance? All I did was call a marriage-counselor like any caring husband in the world would have done if his wife was insisting on it. That is all I did. How could that case lose? How could that blatant injustice then act as a domino in deciding the next eight legal frame jobs against me? Every case was decided by the defamation of my character. My wife really was plotting against me, yet no psychiatrist would go against her.

When I was brought into the hospital with such a damning appearance, handcuffed by the police, guilt would be their conclusion regardless of the facts. The policemen's assumption became the judge's assumption. I didn't stand a chance with any of it. My wife's crime was supported by everyone and it cost me dearly.

I appealed the whole thing and got my day in court. I waited for a courtroom hearing for three weeks to plead my case. I told my story and I was convinced the truth had to set me free once revealed. My wife was called on the witness stand. She conjured up a new lie I wasn't ready for, and because of the previous slanderous determination of my mental state, the judge believed it. The new lie from my wife now was claiming

I waived a knife in her face and threatened her life. I stood up and yelled, "You're lying!", and the judge said if there's one more outburst from me, I would be found in contempt of court. The law went against me because of the frame job on the phony marriage-counselor phone call going to the Suicide-Hotline. The new false threat of violence, where a knife threat was created, appeared to support the characterization of me as crazy. Both were lies, and both were upheld without due course of justice.

Appalled, shocked, betrayed, and defamed my appeal to be released was turned down, and drugs were prescribed. I now got taken away in chains and brought to a van to return to the psychiatric ward of the hospital. I was strapped down to a bed and was carried off as I screamed, "She lied, she lied". There was no justice. Everything I believed that would save me without a problem proved to only go against me. That too had an effect of shock on me. The deceptions and smoke screens were firmly in place.

The America of civil rights, of constitutional rights, and of human rights didn't exist. The right to a fair trial and being treated as if I was innocent until proven guilty didn't exist. The railroading, the framing, and the legal manipulation all played out against me.

While still being strapped down on a bed, they removed my choice of taking medication and demanded that I take it or they were going to inject it in my veins. I screamed, "Medication for what? I called a marriage-counselor. I was framed. Get a copy of the recording. This is a horrible crime. You can't do this." They warned me for the last time and I gave in so they wouldn't inject me. I took what they wanted orally. I didn't know what it was but I had no choice.

I was sent to a room, still with all four limbs strapped down, and then all the affects started. My body convulsed, my brain felt as if it was divided in two, my head was pounding and it felt like my veins were getting bigger and bigger. I couldn't think, my nose kept bleeding, and my throat was so dry I couldn't swallow. While I was the complete victim of this drug, overwhelmed and incapacitated, the straps were finally released. My body was riveting as if poison was put in my system and was trying to reject it. I couldn't breathe without a struggle, I couldn't swallow, and I couldn't go to the bathroom.

I was in fear of the drug doing permanent damage, and I was later informed that permanent damage was certainly a possibility in some cases. My previous health habits were of vitamins, exercise and healthy eating. My body was and always had been sensitive to any change, especially drugs. Even aspirin had a big effect on me. Now, I was left in my room, told not to try to leave, and sat there convulsing. I got up, went into the bathroom, looked in the mirror, and saw the vein in the middle of my head pushing its way out as it got larger. My brain felt like it was being ripped in half. I sat down holding my head with both hands, tortured by some drug I knew nothing about, for doing nothing other than calling a marriage-counselor.

There was no way out. There was more and more pain coming in many different ways, day after day, for many years to come. I can't even look back and say there was something I shouldn't have done. I was a good father, a good husband, a good worker, and a good man my whole life. There wasn't any mistakes I made and there wasn't anything I would have done differently. Yet my fate was, and is more horrible than anyone I ever spoke to in my life.

I couldn't get out of that place for a month and a half. What a horrible pain to have everything I thought would be loyally mine forever turn on me in the ugliest ways imaginable. I was in shock. I know that now. It was a very deep state of shock. The inability to absorb the betrayal after I gave love for so long was very traumatic. I held out the hope that maybe she had the same intangible brain-control attempts happen to her as me, but didn't dis-identify from them. Maybe I needed the hope that she wasn't completely responsible for this. The idea that maybe she was coerced, or hurt by brain invasive technology, kept me hoping for an ounce of loyalty when there may very well have been nothing but a hurtful attack from a deep betrayal.

The psychiatrists kept pounding me three to four hours a day telling me nobody was plotting against me. While I was in shock and drugged, they were brain washing me without realizing it. They didn't really know the truth so the damage they were doing had no conscience. It wasn't just in my mind that my wife wanted to hurt me. All the pain was too much for me to absorb, but nonetheless it was true.

Yet, if she was really being hurt I wanted to be aware of that. She was hurting me worse than any human being ever could. Maybe the truth would reveal something other than this overwhelming pain and shock.

Maybe I just had to accept it, but if she was being hurt, who would save her but me? Wasn't I supposed to be the husband that could see past all this pain and help her if some insidious villain seeped their way in through coercion and drugs? Was I a fool for even thinking that someone who did this to me deserved an ounce of extra thought? Regardless of the facts, the psychiatrists forced the drugs, and even though there was no proof of the accusations, it all went unchallenged.

Nobody cared about her anti-anxiety pill addiction. No review was made of the side effects that could come from it. Hallucinations and callousness were a documented side effect of it, but that was never considered. Her betrayal, her lies, or her plan to get what she wanted at all costs, were all acceptable in the eyes of the law. Here's a woman who should have had manslaughter charges against her for switching my vitamins, felony charges for the manipulation of the law and health care system, contempt charges for lying in a courtroom, and conspiracy charges for the whole illegal defamation, but instead had absolutely nothing done to her except the complete accommodation of her every desire.

What happened to her? Why would she need to do such a thing? Was this simply who she was and I was in denial? I had no enemy in the world that would do such a thing, except the one who represented the very opposite to me. My wife of seventeen years, a woman I was with for almost twenty years, of whom I shared thousands of beautiful moments, had two beautiful children, and thought I would have grandchildren with, now turned on me. I had never heard of any wife who betrayed a husband worse than I was betrayed. She worked with others to frame me so she could defame my character in the eyes of my children, my friends, my family, and last but not least, the law. All my pursuits to reveal this intangible attack on me were negated by the legal attack. The legal attack was further solidified by the intangible attack. There was one party or several parties working together to make sure I was suppressed.

The loyalty to the mother of my children, the vows, and the history that I just couldn't go against had her use that loyalty against me as she ruined every chance I had at surviving. I guess I'm a fool that way. I would have given my life for her and she was literally trying to kill me. I had a thousand memories of the cartwheels I did to show her my love over the years. I had a thousand more memories of all the wonderful times we had when we were single and dating. We had a wonderful marriage for many years and had our amazing children together. It was so unfathomable that there would be any reason for her to do this to me.

Now, I was horribly trapped in a mental rehabilitation facility. Yet, I had one amazing friend who came through for me. I was so pain ridden but he consistently came to see me and brought me things. He brought me fresh clothing and toiletries. He brought me quarters to make phone calls. He told me I was great and kept assuring me that my experience was a horrible injustice. He showed me so much love it would bring tears to my eyes. He hugged me. There was someone in the world who believed in me. He gave me belief in the very fabric of life when he gave love without anything in it for him.

During my detainment at the hospital I cried a lot and came to grips with the helplessness of it. One day I saw one of the male nurses who after hearing my story believed I was fine, but nonetheless couldn't do anything to change my situation. One day I saw he was reading a book and I asked him what he was reading. He told me Einstein. I told him I loved Einstein and he lent me the book. I was so grateful to him. I got deeply immersed in it and read it cover to cover. It helped me so much. I felt elevated by the wisdom I admired. Another time that same male nurse was playing the guitar, and I asked if I could borrow it. He was kind again and let me take it back to my room for a few hours. I played a few songs that reminded me of what was sweet in life. I was finding a way to survive emotionally by amplifying small gestures of kindness and by embracing my own wisdom.

I heard one of the patients playing the piano and later played some chess with him. He didn't talk, or at least not until I beat him in chess. I got to talking with him and asked if he would participate in a talent show if I could get one together. After I beat him in chess again, he agreed. I heard another patient singing and she was great. She should have been on stage already. So, I asked her if she would be in a talent show if I could organize it, and she agreed. I got the green light from the staff to do it after I told them I had several people who would participate. I did this with two others, got agreement from them, and then put on a talent show. I sang "A Summer Breeze". Everyone did well and it was a huge success. The nursing staff and all the patients loved it.

While I was there some respect grew for me for rebuilding people's confidence. Some patients confided in me about why they were there. I helped three of them a lot. One of them I got to talk, who previously refused to, and another I helped so much she was able to leave. Another patient I got clothing for and that helped her feel better about herself. The woman I seemed to cure hugged me, which got me in trouble for hugging a patient. She got disciplined for hugging me as well and went back into her shell a bit, but still was able to leave soon afterwards.

Eventually I was released and my amazing friend came and brought me home. I walked into a house that had a stranger inside, a stranger who turned on me and hurt me almost beyond repair. The stranger was my wife. I was crushed. How could she do this to me? My children were not the same with me. I blamed my wife because they were told a thousand lies while I was away and they didn't know what the truth was any more. They loved me but were afraid to show it. They were with a woman who they couldn't go against or they would only have pain from that to deal with.

I sat in my home, the same home I brought my new wife into sixteen years prior, brought my newborn first daughter eleven years prior, and my newborn second daughter seven years earlier. I remembered the miracles. I remembered when I was so sure of the day my first daughter was going to be born when no one else expected it for at least two more weeks. I remembered working hard in the insurance business where every appointment came with so much work, and each one meant money to pay bills. I remembered the miraculous day of my first daughter's birth when I cancelled five insurance appointments because I had a premonition that she was going to be born that day. I remembered how I undid my tie because I knew what my own wife didn't sense, and what the doctor didn't predict. I remembered going against the utter amazement and defiance of my wife who was flabbergasted that I walked away from all the money that would come from those appointments. I remembered getting her to the hospital twenty-four minutes before my beautiful daughter was born.

I watched the birth as she came out with a full head of hair and eyes wide open beaming at me and staying fixed for several minutes. The doctor never saw anything like it. I sat quieted by memories of all the love and all the caring where each moment was so precious to me. I remembered when my wife got her wedding ring stolen on the beach even after I suspected a man I thought I saw go through her bag. I recalled how she blew off my suspicions and said she had it when she saw her other jewelry in her bag. She assumed the ring was there too but later found it wasn't. I remembered how she wasn't quite the same and how she kept feeling for her ring with her other finger for weeks after that.

I couldn't see her in that pain another day and borrowed four thousand dollars off a credit card to buy her another ring. I went down to the diamond district and got her an even better ring than the first one. I recalled bending down on one knee that same night, right behind the chair where I sat, and proposed to her all over again as she sat on the couch so unsuspectingly. She seemed even more taken back than the first time I proposed and tears flowed as I held her tight. She loved it so much and she couldn't believe I went past my pain too to make her feel secure again. She didn't know how I came up with the money to do it and I didn't tell her either. I replaced the credit card debt with stock market gains and never had to reveal the debt incurred. I always found a way, and nothing was going to stop me from putting a ring on that empty finger another day.

I remember how my beautiful second daughter was born, and how I got her to the hospital twenty-two minutes before she was born. I remembered when my little girls learned to walk and when they learned to talk. I remembered reading to them many nights. I remembered holding them and all the sweet stories they marveled at. I remembered when they learned to read and how we read together for a while after that. I sat in the middle of the living room in the chair, the same chair I helped my younger daughter get out her first splinter, the same chair that we sat together and did homework, and watched TV, and the same chair we sat in when they had nightmares and were too afraid to go back to bed.

I remembered teaching them to ride a bike right outside the window I looked out of, and recalled teaching them to hit a ball for the very first time. I remembered how far away they were from each task when we started, and how patient I was to see them through it. I remembered all their joys at accomplishing everything. I found a love that went deeper and further than any love I ever imagined. I found something in me I never knew I could have because of such a daunting upbringing. I remembered every hug, every present, every Santa Claus I pretended to be, and every tooth fairy my wife and I acted as. I gave nothing but love.

Now I sat in a room that was so cold the tears streamed out of my face and I couldn't stop them. I sat and felt the feelings of everyone around me and the tears would just pour out without a sound. I couldn't help it.

I felt the betrayal. I placed pictures all around our home of all the precious moments we shared. I wanted to remind everyone of all the beautiful moments, and what we were truly all about. Instead I got more coldness. My wife asked, "Why are all these pictures all over the place? I'm trying to dust, can you move these somewhere?" My wife was cold, callous, unemotional, insensitive, unfeeling, with no remembrance of anything, and no respect for anything. She proceeded without a care for me, our children, or my fatherhood. I sat in a state of shock on top of shock. The pain was incredible. Each time I would tell myself not to give in to the tears but they flowed out of my face. It was as if I was in a frozen state of overwhelming pain.

I felt the family had to survive by getting past it. I was willing to move on in spite of this attack. My wife was shocked that I would even consider it. I don't think any other man would have. It wasn't normal that I didn't want a divorce after that. No man I ever heard of in my life ever endured what I did.

It was the product of coming from a broken home as a child, and it was a man who had a little boy in him that vowed against ever creating the same broken home for his children. The pain from my parents breaking up hurt me so badly no one else could ever fathom that forty-five years later it wouldn't allow for getting a divorce. She wanted a divorce, wanted to defame me, and had no limit to what she would do to hurt me.

Maybe if I got the point a lot sooner it would have changed the defamation process. She said I was trying to make her look like the bad parent by showing that only she wanted a divorce. I told her there is no bad guy or good guy here. There are two people married a long time that should work together to get through things. She didn't want to. She gave up and she was just looking for a good exit plan. The defamation was part of it. Turning my children, friends, and relatives against me was also part of it. I told her that we have two young children and they don't deserve this.

I told her our vows meant something and I'm not the one giving up on us or them. I told her no matter what, you should be representing the love from which our children came from. It's not right you make them feel like they didn't come from a relationship that had a love worth honoring. I felt honor and respect should be there even if the love was gone. The vow that had us promise, "Till death do us part", existed because there would be children, and to dishonor that, is to dishonor them. I said even if it's over, there should be a mutual respect and honor. I told her that if I could take the horrible things she did to me then she should try to work this through for the sake of the children.

I grew up in a divorced home and I swore I would never do that to my children. I felt like that people in a family are supposed to try to help each other out and not bury them. I told her that I'm in this current moment and in this current moment I'm focused on getting a job, working on writing, reading a lot, going to the gym and coming to peace. I told her that she could be whoever she wants but I don't want a divorce. She walked away seething.

Over the next couple of weeks I went to the gym, wrote, read and looked for work. I found a job in the investor relations field, and I was very happy with the convenience to my home and the two people running it. I told her that I would be making fifty-five thousand dollars a year and she belittled that in front of the children gloating about how she made seventy thousand dollars a year. I told her I was making even more than that when I was working in Manhattan, but I would now be only eight minutes away from home and spending more time at home. The commute would be almost four hours a day less and that meant more time with the children. She opted for me being away more to make more. I told her I wouldn't even be making that much more after travel expenses, and the four hours a day I was saving was worth a lot more to me. Again she disrespected me and hurt our chances of making a go at it again. This whole conversation took place at the kitchen table with both children sitting right there with us.

I got the job and was quite happy with the arrangement. She got her divorce and then she moved out. Ironically, she moved a block away in the same condo complex. I saw the children twice a week, and while I saw them my ex-wife had them keep their cell phone on sometimes to hear our conversation. They would go to the bathroom and report to her every conversation and she gave them instructions on how to behave. I was with my children, but sometimes her influence was so overwhelming nobody could enjoy themselves.

My children are spectacular human beings. They are each a work of art in every way. They are charming, smart, sensitive and insightful. I yearn for the enjoyment that is untarnished as a Dad. The days with my daughters are some of the greatest joys in my life and maybe someday the truth about everything will be revealed. Until then, let me say that I was the happiest Dad alive and am still truly blessed with a great love between my amazing daughters and myself.

One week, while I driving with my two precious daughters on our way to the shopping mall, my older daughter asked me if she could ask me a question. She said she had a debate at school and she was given the assignment to present a case for the side against whether religion should be taught in the classroom. She said she had to get up in front of the class and make arguments against the person lobbying for the side of religion being taught in the public school system. I qualified whether she meant regular school or any other school of instruction. She clarified that it was the topic on whether it should be in mainstream public school education as part of the regular curriculum. She said they were learning the art of debate and she was being graded on the way she supported her statements and the way in which debating techniques were mastered. I was excited for her.

She said that she has a fear of speaking in front of groups and she needed to have a lot of ammunition to be confident enough to do well. She remembered all the friction this topic of religion caused between her mother and me. She asked if I would give her a few facts on why I thought religion should not be taught in the classroom. She had a pen and paper ready and she wrote them down. I was honored that my young teenage daughter asked me, and I was happy to provide a few powerful facts.

I said more than eighty-percent of the hundred million people killed by wars in the last hundred years were from religious based causes. She lit up and thought that was perfect, and that was the kind of statements that would help her. She assured me that she was going to do her own research and work hard and that she wasn't looking for the easy way out. She said exactly what I wanted to hear. I always taught the both of them to trust their own work and to do their own research without trusting the words of others.

She asked if I had any more ammunition. I said that the previous statement proves religion isn't unifying people, but in origin, that is what it was meant to do. Religion in practice seems to be defeating its own purpose. She wrote that down and felt now she had enough facts to support her argument. She appeared even more confident about the debate. I felt that I had her respect for taking the path I took regarding religion.

Divorce is so hard on the visiting parent's relationship. It seems the whole meeting is timed and contrived after so many precious years spontaneously enjoyed. This made us both happy that we could connect on something of a lasting nature. She was grateful and she seemed to really like the facts I laid out because that information is hard to find. It's not exactly something that's boasted about by any religious group. I also felt like she had her doubts about the good of religion regarding her personal growth as well. Maybe questions about her mother's hurtful attack on me showed her how viciously she was trying to define and misdirect her perspective. We both seemed levelheaded on the subject and we had a nice rest of the day shopping at the mall with her sister.

After we ate lunch, bought some nice clothing, and did a little window shopping we came back to the condo where I now lived alone. It was the home where they were born and raised in so they felt even more comfortable there, than in their new home. We looked through different things they may still want and others I held onto knowing they would someday want them as well.

I dropped them off and my older daughter must have told my ex-wife about our conversation because all hell broke loose after that. My ex-wife devised a way where I wouldn't see them anymore. It started with my older daughter who stopped coming twice a week. She opted for once a week. She said she was too busy with friends and all. The younger one wouldn't miss it for the world. We had great times together. She apologized for her mother. I told her, "You could still say Mom instead of 'my mother'." She said, "No, I'll say my mother, and I apologize on behalf of my mother."

I told her that her mother was a different woman and that the anti-anxiety pills she took changed her. I told her she was never supposed to take that drug more than six months and she has taken it many years. I tried to make her feel that her mother wasn't a bad person and her actions stemmed from a bad reaction to medicine. I thought that would help my daughter to share this with her. I don't know if it did. What a horrible shame both my children had to go through this. A father couldn't ask for two sweeter children. I have a relentless unconditional love for the both of them. There isn't anything or anyone who could ever change that.

When I met with my older daughter on our next visit she told me she won the debate on whether religion should be taught in the classroom, and got an "A" in the class. She said she walked in there dressed to the nines like a lawyer and presented her case, statement by statement, and completely dismantled all of her opponent's points. She was so happy. Unfortunately, she must have told her mother this as well, because my ex-wife's efforts to prevent my visits were in full swing.

She put a restraining order on me fabricating lies about me harassing her. The District Attorney honored the restraining order without much hope of me stopping it unless I paid big bucks for a lawyer, which I didn't have. I wasn't going to take the money away from my children every week. I decided I would have nothing to do with her, but now instead of me going to get my children a block away, they would walk to my home so I could honor the restraining order. I couldn't believe the horrible things she was doing to me and the hate she was showing our children. She seemed to be very upset about what she believed to be the anti-religious sequence she thought took place between my daughter and me.

In reality, it was simply a confidence building exercise for a teenage girl coming into her own who stood in front of a class and won a debate. It wasn't about disrupting her religious principles or disrespecting what she was trying to do. I don't doubt my daughter couldn't help but gain a broader viewpoint from the experience, and I didn't set out to disrupt anything. I don't even think my ex-wife wanted religion taught in the public school system yet she found another reason to damn me. She got her back up without truly understanding the nature of the communication. She took an opportunity to hurt me and in turn hurt my daughter who was originally feeling proud of her achievement.

In retrospect, I don't know how I could have changed any of it, but it was just more hurt for everyone involved. I went along with respecting her religious rituals when I was married to her. I always gave my opinions on how they should leave room for being open-minded. They were raised Jewish, and I let all education proceed in that direction. It grew to be a big point of contention and it was proving to be once again. I wasn't going to perpetuate what I thought was so wrong with so many people's foundations, but their mother wanted it her way or the highway.

I warned my children how groups, including family, hurt people with their self-serving tendencies. In the end I was hurt by the people whom I thought would always love me. I spoke of how the education groups misdirected people, and I watched as educational tools, like the computer, separated the people I loved from me. I spoke of how religion was a dividing element and hurt people, and I was shunned and hurt by it through ugly and primitive attacks. I spoke of how the law was behind the curve with technology. I mentioned how that caused them to unjustly categorized things and shorten processes that would reveal a greater truth if things were investigated more deeply. I was then defamed, belittled, incarcerated, tortured, drugged, humiliated, and outcast by the local police, state police, lawyers, judges, and County Executives. They wouldn't go through any extra processes to come to the truth. I warned my family about technology separating families all over the world. I was then attacked with the most complex technology the world has ever seen.

In the end, being aware didn't help me avoid any of it; it just helped me understand what was happening. I needed money, power and great lawyers to help me but was without all three. I went after the truth, the integrity, and the honesty. I took on no deception and perpetuated no falsehood for the sake of any group. I challenged with confidence and questioned with logic. I took the blows and I walked through the fires. I stand tall and I would have done it all over again, because as Socrates said, "An unexamined life is not worth living". He didn't say wait until others examine theirs to examine yours so you can fit in better. I still have not given up, and if money, lawyers, and power is what it takes to be heard in this country then I will eventually find a way.

The technological problem involving brain control surveillance systems mimics the dilemma of human existence. A big mystery has presented itself and rather than go through the painstaking work it would take to investigate it properly, quick conclusions are assumed in order to alleviate the fear of not knowing. Quick conclusions are also the lazy person's way out. Sometimes a situation or experience would take many hours to fully understand, but the need for speed misdirects it. This is another example of how we have not advanced.

It's the perfect horror to show the tendency to solve mysteries with the defense of an adamant opinion, rather than with the wisdom of patient investigation. This lazy approach stops an unending series of discoveries in all areas of life. It's what hurts human compassion everywhere. It's what can no longer be hidden. It has been called to the forefront by a huge problem facing all human beings everywhere. Tendencies to reach a conclusion, and damn another because something complicated and unseen arrives, is done in many areas of life. Falling back to accepted categories in the physical world falsely acts as the catchall.

## XIII   All That's Left Is The Will

I live by myself in the same condo where my family previously lived. The pain from memories has been overwhelming. I tried to change the appearance so it would feel like a new place. Yet, after they left there was a very real pain, besides obvious emotional pain, that certainly didn't leave with my family. In addition to the relentless voices, I was pummeled electronically to the point where it was damaging my body. I crawled around like a rat hugging furniture while being hurt in my head, my heart and my crotch repeatedly looking for an escape from the invisible enemy. I thought wrapping myself up in leather would help, but it didn't.

I lost my job right near Christmas of 2009 because I could no longer get up for work after being tortured all night. My boss said my ex-wife and others called the office concerned about me. I was very surprised because nobody called me or told me. I took too many days off at the end of the year when they needed me the most. My boss was getting more and more upset. One day I had pictures of my girls on my desk and the next day they were put away in my drawer. The pain from having them gone was too much for me to handle. Sometimes I couldn't look at them without crying. It certainly looked erratic.

At home, bottles and rocks were thrown through my windows. The first one was my chance to reveal the culprit because the bottle must have hit the window with its hard bottom first. By some miracle it somehow didn't break. It landed on my leather recliner, which was open, and rolled down the leg rest without breaking on my wooden floor. I brought the bottle to the police to get prints, and again the captain treated me like garbage. Three weeks of promises on the prints only to tell me he needed two sets of prints on the bottle for it to be valid. Of course there was only one. It was a lot of nonsense. Whatever it took for the local police to do anything for me was negated. Who throws a bottle with two hands?

After I insisted something be done he told me the prints were from the nineteen year old kid who lived upstairs from me, but he couldn't do anything. The kid had a record from other crimes and his prints were on file. That caused a confrontation that lead me to physically taking on the kid upstairs while his father was present as well. I heard them both coming downstairs outside and grabbed a pipe. I thought better of using the pipe when I saw them because it could do permanent damage. I put it down near my door.  When I got in their face about the whole affair it came to blows.

It was a fight I originally was winning.  I knocked the father down and then had the son in a wrenching headlock.  There was snow on the ground and we were slipping around while fighting with all we had.  The father finally got up and wrenched his son out of a clenching headlock that I wasn't letting go of.  I think I hurt the kid, and his father trying to pull him away from me wasn't really helping him because he was bending his neck.  The son was finally released and we both got up.  I went for the father again.  The son saw the pipe near my door, and now used it on me.  He cracked my skull with it and I fell to the ground.  I got up when he was about to hit me again, but the father broke it up because the son could have killed me with it.  I asked why they were trying to hurt me and they denied it.  To this day I don't know if the police captain was just pinning us against each other or the kid threw the bottle through the window.

Days later, more things were thrown to break the glass on my home.  This time rocks were thrown to break the huge sliding glass door in the back of my condominium, while still another broke my small kitchen window.  Coincidentally, the hole made through the glass of the kitchen window was the exact shape of an upside down heart.  It had such a force that it went right threw my wall on the other side of the kitchen.  The persecution had no end.  Someone was forcing me out of my home but I refused to leave.  I didn't know whether I would be leaving the problem to another family.  Something affected my life with my family and now it was affecting my life without them.  I vowed to stay and fight until that was realized.

One night I was told in a mind game that my ex-wife and children were being tortured.  The perpetrator went into my dreams and told me this in the middle of the night.  They kept it going all through to the early morning repeatedly warning me of the danger and torture my ex-wife and children were suffering.  I thought on a million to one shot, if the voices were right, what would I be to ignore them?  So, I took the chance on violating the restraining order, and walked one block away near her block to see if there was anything suspicious going on around the home or near the road.  A state trooper showed up at that very moment and arrested me for violating the restraining order.  I was in jail two weeks.  It ruined job opportunities, credit, reputation, and any chance I would have to continue to see my children.

I wondered how the voices put me where a State Trooper would be. The covert-harassment or the manipulation of systems used by unscrupulous people were used to frame me. I was trying to reveal what someone didn't want exposed. Meanwhile, an innocent man was being tortured and law enforcement should have been on my side against it one way or another. There was no legitimate reason why I should be tortured under any circumstances so at the very least an investigation should have been conducted. Instead, complaints to everyone I thought should care was treated as if I was insane because of the previous defamation. It was either that or the defamation itself was just further disguise for what law enforcement didn't want reviewed.

For this to be happening to me, without any chance at justice, was indicative that much more than my horror was at hand here. I continued to approach it from that perspective and looked for the bigger picture by looking at international crime websites and articles on the web. It supported the potential for a surveillance attack so I alerted Homeland Security once again, but to no avail. I told every secret-service agent in the US in an E-mail as well as twenty-six governors across the US, but once again to no avail. I wrote fifty newspapers across the US and finally saw a reference to the topic of my concern in a leading newspaper, but they never acknowledged my communication.

I feel the surveillance field on me was opening up an avenue for multiple surveillances to be created. They opened a field for thought control and a type of "brain net" that could attack the human psyche. There was more than one thing going on, but each party thought their action was the only power play. I finally got the Senator to write a letter to the town supervisor and local police. The letter stated that they should extend every courtesy to me to investigate this. When I spoke to them respectively they denied everything, stonewalled me, and lied to the Senator. The Senator also held a position where he sat on the Homeland Security panel, but they still lied to him. The infliction to my body and brain amplified further. Investigation as to the integrity of the field didn't ever seem to take place. When I called the Senator's office to complain, I was again referred back to the police captain and town supervisor. Even after I told the Senator's secretary that they denied everything and were stonewalling me, I was informed that it was all they could do.

Why would something so powerful be used on me? Masterminds manipulated a detour from our democracy in a way that stopped us from relocating the road we were on.

After the violation of the restraining order (which I incurred believing I was insuring the protection of my children) the judge extended the restraining order to include my children. They treated me as if I was a danger to the very people I would literally give my life for. I never hit my children in my life and considering me a danger to them was a travesty beyond belief.

I lived a couple of hundred feet from the shopping center where everyone at the condos would go. I went to the store and on my way there I saw my daughter, told her I loved her, and they put me back in jail. When I got out of jail, I went to the post office a few hundred feet from where I live, saw my daughter, told her I loved her and they put me in jail again. I got out of jail once again, went past my garbage, walked to the market, saw my younger daughter, hugged her, told her I loved her and got thrown in solitary confinement for two months.

While in jail I kept replaying my moment with her in my mind. As I was hugging her she said, "Dad, what if you get in trouble?" I said, "If loving you is wrong, I don't want to be right." What a feeling to be sharing a hug with your daughter with the knowledge you could be thrown in jail and have all your goals and freedoms destroyed, only to do it anyway.

In reality, it was legal to come across them considering where I lived, as it should have always been deemed "incidental contact". I should have been allowed to live where I live and be able to do normal things near my home. Passing my children within an area where I live is not a punishable event. All my rights were ignored in this way, and in every way. Instead, it was deemed a violation and I was put in jail for it five times. The court decided I couldn't see, communicate with, or get a message to my children for the next five years. I lost everything in the physical world that could mean anything to me while being tortured physically, mentally and legally all along the way.

How could I ignore my beautiful little girls knowing that it could have been the last time I ever saw them? How did I know if I was going to be alive the next day? How does anyone know for that matter? I certainly did not know if I was going to live another minute because of the constant torture I was absorbing.

After moving only 637 feet away from me, my ex-wife put a restraining order on me that was for a 1000 feet, and the county honored it. They honored it after an obvious discrepancy between her so-called fear of me was followed by her need to live as close to me as possible. No respect was given to where I lived and my right to have living and walking space near my home. No consideration was given to the law which should have allowed for unplanned incidental contact. They decided incidental contact did not exist and every contact was a violation. When I left my home I was found in violation of the order every time I crossed my ex-wife's path or my children's path. I was put in jail and all visitation rights were removed for five years.

All financial responsibilities suffered as well. All job interviews scheduled were lost out on. When I got out of jail I had trouble recovering. While in jail I was still tortured physically and mentally. The electromagnetic pummeling to my central nervous system was relentless. The covert-harassment tools came at me every time I was trapped in my cell, and they did even more damage because I couldn't move away or protect myself. The cell seemed to be a good conductor for hurting me between the metal bars and the metal bed.

I wrote this in jail: What are they stopping me from doing that hasn't already been stopped? What was it that had to be stopped in the first place? Why is the physical pounding even more intense here? It must be this metal bed. The technology they use to cause damage seems to be amplified with the metal frame under this paper thin mattress. It feels like I just stuck my head in an electric socket. It might be what they call microwave technology or electromagnetic currents being manipulated for torture.

Every time I try to sleep on the floor the guard makes me get back on the bed. Why should he care that I sleep on the floor? What's the worst he could do if I don't listen? I don't want to know. I already never leave the cell. What other penalty could there be? No food? They did that once. They just didn't feed me but I complained so they made sure I get my food now. Maybe I'll be given additional time for what he would then call "bad behavior" if I don't listen to him. I better get back on the bed and take the blows or I'll be forced to stay in jail longer. They jar me awake and zap me to sleep.

Ouch, that last one really jolted my heart. There is very little in between me and a heart attack the way these jolts are coming with such force. I think the last one did damage. My head is killing me. There's the police car outside the window. I can see him past the tree. Why would he be parked near my window? Escaping isn't really a possibility, this place has ridiculous security. There's no chance at an escape so why would he be guarding against it? Did anyone ever escape from here? What other reason could he be hovering near my cell? Maybe that's paranoid but where did the jolt come from? Maybe this is where he kills time, or kills me. Was he the one that did it?

I found online that tin foil and thermal helped reduce the specific zaps to certain body parts on the outside, but where can I get that in here? Even if I got it, what would I say if they caught me with that wrapped around me? They already think I'm weird in here because I don't leave the cell. Some of those people out there really belong in here though. I'm not going to make my life worse by getting tangled up with one of those guys.

That's all I need to do is get in a dispute with them and be stuck in here longer. One guy looked to start a fight last time I went out and another was smoking dope right next to me and hiding it. Why would I mix myself up with that and get in more trouble? I am not leaving this cell no matter what they pound me with. I'll suffer with the invisible attack because the visible attack should end some day. I will stay in solitude for the duration.

I didn't write that much and some writings were taken by the guards, but that was something that got through.

I was on a metal bed so many times in jail without any protection, and zapped so powerfully I literally was flung right off the bed sometimes. I was pummeled in my head so strongly the pain was as if someone hooked me up to an electrode and zapped me full voltage. I won't ever be the same. My ability to focus is decreased, my ability to sleep is horrible, I am always in a state of being hurt, and my central nervous system is the effect of more than ten years of torture. Any time something good happens I feel like I am about to get hurt. Whenever someone compliments me I feel like crying. I feel so much pain that even a little pleasure puts in perspective the onslaught of abuse I've been through. The light of kindness or caring shows what horrors I suffer with, and looking at the hardship, rather than being one with the fight of it, becomes so clear that tears can't help but flow.

I miss my children so much that the pain from that alone has almost killed me. It's an emotional pain and I feel guilt if I try to avoid it. It turns into a bodily response when thoughts in my brain go to my heart, then to my stomach, and suffering has to be looked at or it overtakes me. "SEER TRAPS" saves me, yet I sometimes forget when it comes to my children. It has almost hurt me irreparably when I have. I realized that when it came to my children I left no rope tied to the dock if they were ever removed from me. Sinking was the result and not being the victim of those thoughts was quite possibly my greatest emotional challenge, even in the face of these incredible odds. The people responsible live with this horrible injustice and somehow keep finding ways to justify their indifference. My children and I have found the powers that they will never know.

The last time I tried to express everything in a letter to a county executive where I live, a team of people came to my home, took me away in chains and locked me up in a mental institution. There I suffered more humiliation and psychological abuse from people insisting there was something wrong with me. The letter itself was used as the only reason they were able to take me from my home against my will. The atmosphere of the institution continued to remind me of the complete helplessness I had and still have. They kept me there longer because I refused to take drugs that very well could have affected me the rest of my life. Every civil right, human right, constitutional right, and legal right was violated.

While I was inside, bills piled up and job opportunities were lost. I finally got a hearing weeks later. After the judge listened to the hospital representative's testimony, the psychiatrist, and finally my defense, he let me go. He had trouble going against the plain fact that my rights allow me to write a letter. He had trouble when I told him that it was within my constitutional rights to do so. He was an old-timer and the word "Constitution" actually meant something to him. He found in my favor and firmly instructed the hospital to release me that day. I was released later that afternoon. About a week later I was sent a hospital bill for $27,000.

All in all, I was jailed, framed, institutionalized, tortured, berated, defamed, physically tortured, and mentally tortured even while incarcerated and institutionalized. I was even put to sleep while driving my car on seven different occasions. Once I drove off the road and flew into a ditch, another time I was awakened by the lights on the road, on three other occasions the beeping of other drivers woke me up just in time. One dreadful night had lights and sirens wake me up and pull me over for speeding. My foot weighed on the pedal while I was knocked out.

My family, friends and acquaintances were wiped out from my good graces and a few friends remain. I have been able to prove certain things to some enough for them to believe me. Most can't bear the pain of hearing it even when they do allow themselves to believe me. I lost my family, friends, relatives, acquaintances, jobs, a career, cars, my legal ability to drive, my financial stability, my legal status, my credit status, my overall health, and my home while all along trying to fight this off.

The intangible attack in a way duplicated the way most people handled what's intangible in other ways. They don't believe what's not tangible and they handle it like they handle the biggest intangible mystery of all, by making up whatever is most comfortable. They take on a belief that gives them security. Their beliefs damn anything or anyone opposed to it. All actions become justifiable as long as they keep what's unsure away from them.

In attempting to communicate my experience I have had to fight against deeply imbedded religious paradigms even when religion had nothing to do with it, directly. These preordained habits for handling the unseen undermined the patience it would take to properly investigate intangible causes. Quick judgments and conclusions have been latched onto and defended. Patience is required to allow for proper investigation into my intangible mystery. Just as religion has decided that anything unseen cannot be allowed for without abbreviated closure and judgment, so has the treatment been to me when attempting to reveal my horrible victimization. Quick closure and quick judgments are the usual course.

Two unseen forces affected me with great might, one magnificent and one tragic. One experience unseen was very rarefied and enlightening and the other was a malicious attack using radio frequencies, neurological underpinnings, electromagnetic impulses, microwave hearing effects, and all the weapons of covert-harassment. While trying to reveal the artificially induced attack upon my existence, I was hurt by a disbelief people had in my spiritual ideas. Many people close to me combined the two unseen experiences expressed and wrote it off as the one determination that I was crazy.

My friends, my family, wife, law enforcement and health facilities all found a reason to damn me to the point of incarceration. While in jail, I was still pounded with electromagnetic jolts and torturous voices in my auditory cortex. This made me wonder why it would continue if I was already out of their way. It also made me realize that it was being done for bigger reasons than just the mistake on me. The field of surveillance seemed to be kept alive and populated with this activity against me. It existed for reasons beyond the need to torture me and me alone. Something was happening beyond what was gained or lost by affecting the actions of only me.

The belief that there had to be covert-harassment, or a form of it in place, so that a pilferage or hacking of it could spread, seemed even more likely when I was mercilessly tortured in jail. Why would I warrant so much attention if I was not only never doing anything wrong outside of jail, but certainly not doing anything wrong inside? This confirmed my theory that there was an attack of sorts taking place. Otherwise there was no sense in targeting me, especially when it was long realized how harmless I was and how harmless I still am. They zeroed in on my every thought and action only to dismiss every finding from it that revealed it as a mistake. There just has to be something bigger going on for all the time and resources that are being used just to focus on me.

Fear subtly drives us and when fear presents itself we find a way to alleviate it. People need to feel secure. They would rather hurt a good person, than feel insecure about what that person was presenting. The framing, legal manipulation, and political manipulation took over my life. I don't know why I am in this situation. There are so many possibilities that go through my mind but mind-probe surveillance with torture is a tool of our government. It has certainly come with many disguises and distractions. I suppose it always would because that is all part of its use. They deflect attention by continually getting you to believe that it's other things. Along the way they hurt everyone and everything. I used to love my country. I guess I still do, but I despise the way it's being run. It's certainly not a democracy any more. I don't quite know what it is.

It was more than four years ago that I got fired and I've been so hurt by everything that getting another job hasn't come despite tireless efforts. It seems that between my bad credit, my discontinued work history, my legal framing, and most probably a blacklisting in the labor market, I am soon to be living on the street. I may have one of the more interesting stories amongst the homeless people out there. You may see me. I'll be the guy that isn't crazy but mumbling about some unseen attack.

If we wanted to create physical realities that would force us to realize an over-attachment to our thoughts, what would those realities look like? I suppose killing each other to defend one thought after the next would be extreme. Throughout history even that extreme didn't reveal the strict adhesion human beings have to thoughts. This is the reason we have never been able to escape our primitive behavior in many ways. We pick up the newspaper and see the same things happening today that happened thousands of years ago. We read further and see these atrocities happened throughout the history of mankind. They happened sixty years ago, six hundred years ago, and six thousand years ago. They have never stopped happening and we can find that they have also happened sixty-seconds ago. We have seldom had prevailing peace for any long duration in any society.

What events would even more greatly force us to see an over-attachment to our thoughts? What would depict the need to stem from a higher place than the stream of thinking in the human brain? How could it be done in such a way that we couldn't help but detach from our thoughts? What would it take to show the human species that it has a problem with the way it's evolving? What if we as a species were evolving to the state where we were too attached to our thoughts, and as a result, were moving too far away from our truest essence beyond them? If the most difficult trap to escape existed as one trapping inside another, how would that circle in a circle be penetrated?

There are holy wars today. Mass killings are taking place. Gas has been used on societies by its hierarchy, and invasive tactics are being used that violate every human right. We are still primitive in the way we haven't been able to live in harmony. There is such an obvious attachment to our thoughts that human compassion, love, empathy, and humanity are all second to our next thought. What does it matter how advanced we are in science, physics and space travel when each day we destroy each other? In a way we are physically representing the battle between our spiritual and physical existence, and representing our inability to be the wisdom beyond it.

Well, unfortunately, whether we like it or not, realities have been forced upon us in the ugliest ways imaginable. As if a provable parallel of the worst possible proportion had to reveal itself to me, pain beyond pain forced me to see what was seamless to others. All the forces were against me. All communications with everyone simply were not working out anymore. I was experiencing enlightenment and pain at the same time. The enlightenment may have helped me get glimpses of where the pain was coming from.

It was too hard to believe that people I loved were conspiring to hurt me. Other people around me thought I was losing my faculties because I acted enlightened. I was actually gaining something, but it created a distance. The distance was coming from two things, but the problem was neither one could be seen. I thought the people I knew trusted me a great deal more than they actually did. Too much talk of references unseen created a fear in those who loved me and an angle for those who didn't.

If it happened with hack-ins, computer spying, mind-control, and other crimes that are hard to detect, would *you* be able to accept the need to investigate the possibility of that without immediate proof? How about cognitive-manipulative pharmaceuticals and drugs that make you forget like Rohypnol, Ketamine (roofies), and other club-drugs? Would their infiltration into a community be something you would consider when they aren't easily noticed? Even commonly used anti-anxiety pills and anti-depressants act as cognitive-manipulative vehicles under a mind-probe surveillance field. What if all these things were going on and they were being used to hurt us? Would we develop ways to reveal and question what was so hard to detect? We have not.

There are ways to make many opportunistic people use an aspect of the overall attack with the belief that it gives them some kind of edge. What if their "clever", yet illegal activity, stopped them from ever revealing the bigger reality once it was realized? What if they feared that their involvement, which had other unscrupulous origins, would attach legal harm to them? What if that fear kept them from ever revealing any part of the total crime? There are many ways this could be veiled in our society. An enemy would not come to this country and say, "Here I am, I am the enemy, and I'm going to use a mind-probe surveillance attack against you", would they? Instead, tricking many people into using the technology would be the best way to leverage power. Private investigators may take liberties with such an illegal access if they could profit enough from its use. Ultimately, what if espionage found a way to be called something else?

What if all logic out of this circular thought pattern was excluded, and all that was included was part of the very control that was using its very features? What if this was a mind-probe surveillance attack? What if it was so complicated that even when someone realized it, they were so attached to their thoughts, they weren't able to see beyond them? This is a circle in a circle and the only way out is to be able to detach yourself from your thought stream.

An over-attachment to thoughts has all but destroyed us as a species through war and atrocities. Now, being lost in our brain and our thoughts are part of the very technology using that human quality as a weapon. Could we see the manipulation when it's pointed out to us? Can we see it even if the weapon contains what can stop that very awareness? Would we realize it if that weapon fell into the wrong hands or would we be under its spell? Could the manipulation imposed by using the features of this horrible weapon awaken the human race out of their brain-attached patterns?

The most intelligent leaders have fallen prey to their own egotism. They have been swept under the umbrella of aberrant thoughts. Many millions have fallen victim to this pattern. A covert operation with all the bells and whistles of the most advanced, most penetrating, most brain-manipulative technology ever devised has been turned around and leveraged against us. Law enforcement may think they are jolting a suspected terrorist when in fact they are jolting innocent American citizens. Everyday hard working people, pregnant women, new born babies, children, and medically challenged people are being pounded by something that has no way to be communicated about without further injustice. People we have placed in a position of power to use this technology really don't have complete knowledge of the signs when a security breech arises.

It gets even more complicated because the very thing that we would use to figure it all out is the very thing that's targeted. It's a field like the internet, only it's between brains rather than between computers. Of course it's assisted through technology, but in the end we are in a state of telegraphing our thoughts. We are vulnerable to becoming the puppet of another through their exertion in a brain controllable field. An overhang of suppression can also be used to blanket many people at once and affect the efficiency of people in masses. Sleep deprivation, and all its debilitating features, can be effectuated to hurt great numbers of people all at once as well.

The original design was for us to be aware of terrorists telegraphing their thoughts so that law enforcement would be aware before a major attack or tragedy happened. We were so blindsided by 9/11 that we erred on the side of hurting our own people. Since then, surveillance detection systems allowed those on the other side of the law to locate people under surveillance, and utilize it for their own malicious purposes. We are in terrible trouble, and although the expression of my specific horrors may be somewhat unique, my tragedy overall is not unique. No person is given the ability to freely express an illegal attack on them when it comes to this covert-harassment field. This is an enemy's dream come true. We have paved the way for an attack, and even if a person finds a way to negate everything I said, they can never negate the vulnerability to this given the parameters we have provided with the use of this weaponry.

For me, there was torture everyone could see, but the torture they couldn't see underpinned the whole horrible tragedy. Where it originated, I am only guessing. Some guesses seem more likely than others, but there have been people and events that were piled on to the original crime which complicated the facts. There may be more than one culprit here since hiding under its umbrella was made so easy. There's the first illegal surveillance imposed which had a fraudulent base, and there are those that detected it and used it for their purposes. They were probably manipulated by the primary cause, which is espionage. In the end, innocent people were tortured and continue to be hurt without any help available.

Funny thing when I'm in shock or when I'm devastated I appear to people as if I am in too much pain to even be spoken to, yet I am dying for them to speak to me. I'm dying for a hug, compassion, love or any sign that I could be cared for even when I'm not smiling. Although, quite often, when you cry, you cry alone. Some only dance when others are dancing, some only clap when others are clapping and most aren't putting forth the extra compassion it takes when someone is suffering.

I was ultimately arrested eleven times, jailed five times, put in a mental institution twice, and all without a single thing to ever justify any of it. I've been stalked, invaded, robbed, vandalized, harassed, humiliated, demeaned, defamed, emotionally tortured, and physically tortured twenty-four hours a day for more than ten years. I'm sleep deprived, poisoned, neurologically hurt, and devastated financially. If I see my daughters while walking to the store, utter a word to them, or even send them an E-mail telling them I love them, I would be put in jail for six years.

I am not a scientist, neurologist, engineer, electrician, or radio frequency genius but I read for thousands of hours until I figured out what this was. Unfortunately, nobody else will even listen to the provable summary of my work that explains what is happening to me. Maybe when it happens to them they'll care a little more. Writing this was the only way to get anyone to actually become fully aware of my whole story. The reader can select how much pain they can tolerate and when. This was my only avenue of expression left. Most can't even endure absorbing this as a potential attack, let alone believe it's currently a very real attack going on right now.

Our brain doesn't always allow all information to enter. Things too painful are oftentimes ignored for self-preservation. We may slowly allow them to seep in later when we are more able to handle them. I venture to guess at the time of this writing, many still have not come to grips with the potential exposure to this very real threat. Those that have become aware may not know what to do about it. There are also tangible and intangible systems in place to keep it going even if attempts are put forth to stop it. Awareness of this, and sharing it with others who have endured it, has to be the right path.

I don't know why this happened to me, but the fact that it could happen to me with nowhere to turn is a strong enough statement all by itself. You would think anyone experiencing this should be helped out a great deal, especially if they have no "legitimate" reason for being tortured. If a Senator who sits on the Homeland Security panel is questioning its usage and I am not alleviated of its effect, it stands to reason there should be a next step. This is what happened and there was no follow-up.

This is the most advanced, damaging, invasive, mind-control and body control effect in the history of the world. Shouldn't law enforcement, and all the powers that be, act to protect an innocent, hard-working family man who is complaining about being the effect of it? Shouldn't a person who sees beyond its effect to reveal such a manipulation be helped? Shouldn't we as a society consider this person to be a hero rather than someone we torture? Should we be so paranoid about our vulnerable technology that we act in defense of it more than we act in defense of what it was meant to protect in the first place?

Instead, many people are taking advantage of what they can get away with because someone else already paved the way. It's as if illegal surveillance was a blackout and people were running rampant looting during it. I don't think opportunists, hopping on what our undemocratic surveillance systems provided, should be ignored.

Why would they assume the person is crazy who tries to reveal an error when they know very well that these effects could be possible? These weapons could have gotten into the wrong hands and that possibility has to be accounted for. Wouldn't a law enforcement person have to always be aware of whether covert-harassment was "justified", and then match it up with the Department of Defense and their targeted threat to see if it jived? How could we act as if it is so ironclad and secure when the technology itself has been proven vulnerable before?

The people who are given the power for doing this may very well be psychologically crawling in a deep dark hole hurting people within the shell of this technological veil. There may also be thieves trying to steal personal information. They may have been tricked into doing this for what is really a larger more devious cause. Obviously, there's a technology that could read people's minds, but when the effect of it becomes a person's experience, it's imperative to have things in place to allow for review. The assumption that it is always this so-called "justified covert-harassment" is an insane assumption, and one that is crippling our country in unseen ways.

Anything that would guard against this type of crime is completely remiss, so they continue to get away with it. Yet, how powerful are the forces that keep it in place? Sometimes the voices imposed on me through this microwave hearing effect depict how the police, private investigators, and hurtful crooks are part of it. In the end I have to blame the legal system. Even if they weren't responsible for implementing it, they most certainly should be responsible for stopping it. I can't help but further suspect them because of the unfair tactics used to railroad me through the legal system.

Sometimes the voices are men and sometimes they are women. More often than not, it's a group of people, and the group changes depending on the subject matter. The subject matter is what I happen to be thinking about before they impose a thought. Sometimes they act like police and sometimes like crooks. Sometimes they act like terrorists and sometimes they act like young people. Sometimes they act like my children, whom

I'm not able to see now, and they torment me with the knowledge that I can't see them.

Everything that has happened made me weak financially, so legally fighting back becomes almost impossible. I'm then graded on the way I look, the money I don't have, the job I don't have, and the legal problems forced upon me. A great lawyer may have saved me some grief. The inevitable financial fallout stopped me from getting one. The physical and mental pain is so unbearable it's very hard to live every day. The voices have no feelings about my pain. They are relentless. I keep telling myself I am more relentless. I believe there is a light of hope, but when believing keeps being only my own echo, my will gets tested. I am not sure how much more testing I can take. "SEER TRAPS" awareness keeps me alive.

Some of the closest people to me were trying to hurt me. They saw my silence as a personal threat to them. Others saw it as an opportunity to defame my character. Some hurt me so I wouldn't think about the horrible things they were doing. The very things I started suspecting them of were of nobody else's concern. It was distracted away by the focus that now went into what I was depicted as.

I am a father without my children to see and it rips through me like a freight train every second. I am a father who cries a thousand tears every time I see a father with a daughter. I have to look away. I give myself what allows for the second rather than the content of that second. I am a divorced man who swore he never would be. I am a man who realized that no promise we ever make to our self could be solely within our ability to keep if it involves another human being.

Yet, even in my children's absence I am a dad. I feel their vibration. They think of me and I think of them. Powers from enlightenment have given me closeness to them not otherwise allowed for. I feel their enlightenment and their powers. The special days that we have all to do not to think of each other, contain an additional hurt. The birthdays, Father's day, graduation days, and every event that I would have done cartwheels to make them happy, now come and go without any tangible means of expressing my love. Psychic abilities have been called upon for the only way to communicate and they have appeared, but don't tell anyone or they may think it's crazy. That is of course unless enlightenment was allowed for through the awareness from "SEER TRAPS" or other beautiful paths. Many abilities have become available in the unseen dimension, and I am grateful for the roads that forced me to see them.

The mind-games continue to hurt me twenty-four hours a day. I could tell you who is on shift and who left. I can tell you ahead of time what mind-games they will play. I could read their minds now and I know this is an attack, because if it were only covert-harassment, then I shouldn't be able to affect them, but I know I can. My heart goes out to all those who have suffered from this. In hopes of this getting more publicized maybe we'll have a stronger voice someday.

Our evolution has to include the habit and system for being able to view our thoughts without words trapping us back in them. "SEER TRAPS" awareness does this. It took me a lifetime to figure that out as I ran in the circles words kept me enclosed in. I hope it's remembered.

If you become a victim of this harassment, you can go beyond the thought control and see you are not your thoughts, and therefore certainly not any imposed thoughts from others. I could be five, I could be fifty, but questions rooted in what's intangible are simply not handled well. They weren't handled well when I was a kid and they were handled even worse as I got older.

What was invisible almost destroyed me, but something quite different, which was also invisible, saved me. I may have lost every tangible measure of success, but I gained every intangible one, and I gained a splendor nobody could ever take away. Incredible pain forced me to realize certain truths and these truths I have shared with you, the amazing reader. Thank you.

THE END

End Note:

The time will pass, the truth will be revealed, and the wounds will prove to be the cost of truth. The preciousness further appreciated nobody can take away. I love you. I love you so much. The world is truly beautiful and I know you will make it more so. This is an example of love's proving grounds and love's opposites prove it more. The world of beauty is crystallized by its opposite.

37763950R00126

Made in the USA
Charleston, SC
19 January 2015